W9-ACB-110

Owen Swiny

Performers in ye Opera for 1 year
including ye Vacation from ye Middle of June to the
Middle of September (ye year begining & ending
att Christmas

Mrs Margarita —	400 = 00 = 00	
Mrs Tofts —	400 = 00 = 00	
Mrs Lindsey —	90 = 00 = 00	1370 = 00 = 00
The Bartnell —	200 = 00 = 00	
Maria Gallia —	200 = 00 = 00	
Mrs Cross for Jones other Women	80 = 00 = 00	

by ye 13 June — Sigr Valentini — 430 = 00 = 00
or 300 by tyme of his agrem't — Sigr Catanino — 400 = 00 = 00 } 1030 = 00 = 00
Mr Ramondon — 50 = 00 = 00
& if he learns a thro Base by ye End of ye yeare to have 10 more Mr Lawrence — 50 = 00 = 00
Mr Leveridge — 100 = 00 = 00

Mr Fleymans —	70 = 00 = 00	
Mr Dieper —	70 = 00 = 00	280 = 00 = 00
Mr Paputch —	70 = 00 = 00	
Mr Sagione —	70 = 00 = 00	
a Theorbo —		

Turn Over

The Vice Chamberlain's office copy of Vanbrugh's financial commitments to opera personnel for 1708 (document 49). — *Harvard Theatre Collection*

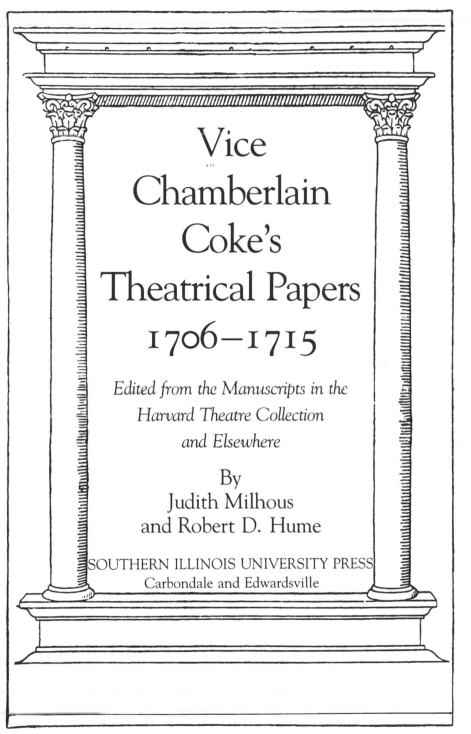

Vice Chamberlain Coke's Theatrical Papers 1706–1715

*Edited from the Manuscripts in the
Harvard Theatre Collection
and Elsewhere*

By
Judith Milhous
and Robert D. Hume

SOUTHERN ILLINOIS UNIVERSITY PRESS
Carbondale and Edwardsville

Printed in the United States of America
Edited by Stephen W. Smith
Designed by Bob Nance, Design for Publishing
Production supervised by Richard Neal

Publication of this work was made possible in part through
a grant from the National Endowment for the Humanities.

Library of Congress Cataloging in Publication Data
Main entry under title:

Vice Chamberlain Coke's theatrical papers, 1706–1715.

Bibliography: p.
Includes index.
 1. Theater—England—London—History—18th century—
Sources. 2. Opera—England—London—History and
criticism—Sources. I. Coke, Thomas, 1674–1727.
II. Milhous, Judith. III. Hume, Robert D.
PN2596.L6V5   792'.09421'2   81-5616
ISBN 0-8093-1024-4   AACR2

For Edward A. Langhans

Contents

Preface

Vice Chamberlain Coke's theatrical papers have been known to theatre historians for more than one hundred and fifty years, but heretofore they have remained largely unused. In nature and importance they are certainly comparable to *The Dramatic Records of Sir Henry Herbert*, edited by J. Q. Adams in 1917, or the Public Record Office documents unearthed and printed by Allardyce Nicoll in the 1920s. The Coke papers are an immense addition to our knowledge of the exciting period of London theatre history in which Vanbrugh opened the Haymarket theatre, Italian opera came to England, and the Triumvirate management of Wilks, Cibber, and Booth took over at Drury Lane. The financial woes of the opera and the vicious infighting among theatrical entrepreneurs precipitated almost kaleidoscopic changes in the years between the opening of the Haymarket in 1705 and the establishment of a stable situation in 1715. The Coke papers give us, for the first time, the detailed information needed to make sense of this confusing and little-studied period.

The relative neglect of the theatrical papers once belonging to Vice Chamberlain Thomas Coke (1674–1727) is attributable to several factors. The collection was sold and resold in the nineteenth century, and it was partially dispersed at auction—most of what was salable for autograph value was split off in 1876. Various early scholars made use of the papers (notably Julian Marshall, Robert W. Lowe, and W. H. Cummings), but after 1876 what remained together were largely foul papers. The eighty-two documents which came to the Harvard Theatre Collection in 1928 are exceedingly hard to use, especially by themselves. They are in no order whatever, and many of them are unsigned and undated. The other seventy-one items—mostly letters— are widely scattered. We have found Coke papers at the Folger, the Pforzheimer, the Huntington, the Pierpont Morgan, the University of Texas, Yale, Westminster Public Library (London), and in the collection of Mary Hyde. Eight turned up in other collections at Harvard—acquired separately over the years. Most of the use made of the Coke papers by scholars has been by way of British Library Add. MS 38,607—a partial transcription made by James Winston, who owned the collection in its entirety between 1834 and his death in 1843. Another partial transcription (NYPL Drexel MS 1986) has been available in the New York Public Library since 1888, but has gone almost entirely unnoticed and unused. These transcriptions are a godsend: they give us texts for thirty documents not otherwise locatable. Winston's transcriptions are substantively quite accurate, but they are not easy to use. They come in random order, and Winston made almost no attempt to date them. Consequently they have been used for particular items of information rather than exploited in any systematic way.

The Coke papers, taken in toto, are a treasure trove of miscellaneous information about the operation of the theatres in the early eighteenth century. The documents include rough drafts of orders by the Lord Chamberlain regulating the theatre; complaints against managers by actors, singers, and dancers; costume and sundries bills; performers' contracts; orchestra rosters; salary lists; tradesmen's bills; financial estimates for the opera; lists of daily receipts; complaints in fractured French by angry Italian castrati about breach of contract; and the only daily box-office reports for opera that we possess for any time in London before the 1730s. Two major clusters of documents are of special interest. They concern, respectively, Vanbrugh's disastrous plunge into Italian opera at the Haymarket in the spring of 1708, and the ferocious row during 1713–15 which saw Booth replace Doggett in the Triumvirate.

To make the Coke papers fully comprehensible requires systematic work on dating, identification, and attribution (especially from handwriting). Our aim in this edition has been to make the papers as easy to use as possible for the drama scholars, the theatre historians, and the musicologists for whom they contain valuable information. Only eight of the known documents have entirely eluded us—and one of those is probably a ghost, while another was printed in the 1876 sale catalogue, quite possibly in full. Following the model of *The London Stage* we have put the papers in chronological order on a season-by-season basis with a headnote provided for each season. This edition thus constitutes a kind of documentary history of the London theatre, 1706–15. We have added a few "interdocuments" from other sources where the material seemed highly relevant. We have also provided references to published scholarship and to other manuscript sources (particularly PRO LC 7/3) in the hope of giving the reader easy access to other relevant material. Each document has a "Comment" in which we have tried to explain what its significance is and how we arrived at a dating if the dating is ours. Taken piecemeal in raw form the Coke papers are a wretched jumble. Deciphered, dated, and set in order, they give us an immensely clearer understanding of what has always been a particularly confusing period in the history of opera and theatre in London.

Documents 1, 2, 3, 4, 6, 8, 10, 11, 12, 13, 14, 15, 17, 18, 20, 21, 22, 24, 25, 27, 28, 29, 30, 31, 35, 39, 40, 41, 42, 43, 44, 45, 48, 49, 50, 51, 52, 55, 56, 57, 58, 59, 60, 61, 65, 66, 67, 68, 69, 72, 73, 76, 77, 78, 82, 83, 85, 89, 91, 94, 95, 96, 97, 98, 99, 100, 104, 105, 106, 107, 108, 109, 110, 111, 114, 115, 116, 117, 118, 119, 121, 122, 123, 141, 146, 148, 150, 151, and 152 are published by permission of the Houghton Library, Harvard University.

Document 5, and the interdocuments of 14 August 1706, 31 December 1707, 12 April 1711, 17 April 1712, 13 February 1713, 12 November 1713, February (?) 1714, 3 November 1714, and ca. February 1715 are Crown copyright records in the Public Record Office, and are published by permission of the Controller of Her Majesty's Stationery Office.

The interdocument of 5 October 1706 is published by permission of the Osborn Collection, Yale University Library.

Documents 7, 101, 102, and 103 are published by permission of the Folger Shakespeare Library.

Documents 9, 19, 23, 26, 34, 46, 53, 64, 71, 80, 81, 88, 90, 112, 113, 124, 131, 133, 134, 136, 137, 138, 139, 140, 142, 147, and the interdocuments of 13 September 1709 and 19 November 1709 are published by permission of The British Library.

Documents 16, 32, 33, 36, 74, 84, 87, 92, and 143 are published by permission of the Archives Department, Westminster City Libraries.

Documents 47 and 62 are published with the permission of The Carl and Lily Pforzheimer Foundation, Inc.

Documents 63 and 135 are published by permission of The Pierpont Morgan Library.

Document 70 is published by permission of The Huntington Library, San Marino, California.

Documents 79 and 132 are published by permission of Professor William W. Appleton.

Documents 86 and 126 are published from manuscripts in The Hyde Collection, Somerville, New Jersey, by permission of Mary Hyde.

Document 93 is published from the manuscript in the Humanities Research Center, The University of Texas at Austin, by permission of the University of Texas.

Document 120 is published from the manuscript in the Simon Gratz Collection, Historical Society of Pennsylvania.

Documents 128 and 129 are published by permission of the owner, a private collector.

Documents 144 and 145 are published by permission of the Music Division, The New York Public Library, Astor, Lenox and Tilden Foundations.

For major assistance and criticism we are grateful to Edward A. Langhans, Curtis A. Price, and Arthur H. Scouten. For help with particular problems we would like to thank Lawrence Bachorik, Lenora Coral, Philip H. Highfill, Jr., D. F. Cook, Carolyn Kephart, J. Merrill Knapp, David Lasocki, Jeanne Meekins, and Philip Stadter. For help with foreign-language documents we want to express our appreciation to Lowell Lindgren, Linda Pepper, Annick Scouten-Rouet, and Alfred Triolo. We received exemplary assistance from librarians in institutions too numerous to mention, but we owe a special debt of gratitude to Dr. Jeanne T. Newlin, Curator of the Harvard Theatre Collection, and to her Curatorial Associate, Martha T. Mahard. As always, our greatest debt is to Kit Hume.

January 1981   JUDITH MILHOUS
                                                       ROBERT D. HUME

Abbreviations

Barker, *Mr Cibber*	Richard Hindry Barker, *Mr Cibber of Drury Lane* (New York: Columbia Univ. Press, 1939).
Biographical Dictionary	Philip H. Highfill, Jr., Kalman A. Burnim, and Edward A. Langhans, *A Biographical Dictionary of Actors, Actresses, Musicians, Dancers, Managers, and Other Stage Personnel in London, 1660–1800*, 16 vols. in progress (Carbondale: Southern Illinois Univ. Press, 1973–).
Broadley	A. M. Broadley, comp., "Annals of the Haymarket" (King's Theatre Volume), Westminster Public Library, London. (Scrapbook containing eleven original Coke documents.)
Chamberlayne, *Angliae Notitia*	Edward Chamberlayne, *Angliae Notitia: or the Present State of England*, 22nd ed., rev. John Chamberlayne (London: Printed for S. Smith et al., 1707).
Cibber, *Apology*	Colley Cibber, *An Apology for the Life of Mr. Colley Cibber*, ed. Robert W. Lowe, 2 vols. (1889; rpt. New York: AMS, 1966).
Clark, *Early Irish Stage*	William Smith Clark, *The Early Irish Stage* (Oxford: Clarendon Press, 1955).
Congreve, *Letters & Documents*	*William Congreve: Letters & Documents*, ed. John C. Hodges (New York: Harcourt, Brace & World, 1964).
Cook, *Thomas Doggett*	Theodore Andrea Cook, *Thomas Doggett Deceased* (London: Constable, 1908).
Deutsch, *Handel*	Otto Erich Deutsch, *Handel: A Documentary Biography* (1955; rpt. New York: Da Capo, 1974).
Downes, *Vanbrugh*	Kerry Downes, *Vanbrugh* (London: Zwemmer, 1977).

Drexel MS   "Coke, 'English operas,' 1725," New York Public Library (NYPL) Drexel MS 1986. (Scrapbook containing anonymous nineteenth-century transcriptions of Coke documents.)

Fiske, *English Theatre Music*   Roger Fiske, *English Theatre Music in the Eighteenth Century* (London: Oxford Univ. Press, 1973).

Fitzgerald, *A New History*   Percy Fitzgerald, *A New History of the English Stage*, 2 vols. (London: Tinsley, 1882).

Hotson, *Commonwealth and Restoration Stage*   Leslie Hotson, *The Commonwealth and Restoration Stage* (1928; rpt. New York: Russell and Russell, 1962).

HTC Coke   "Vice Chamberlain Coke's Theatrical Papers," Harvard Theatre Collection fMS Thr 348.

LC 7/3   Untitled two-volume scrapbook (restored) of theatrical documents from the Lord Chamberlain's Office in the Public Record Office (PRO), shelfmark LC 7/3.

Loftis, *Steele at Drury Lane*   John Loftis, *Steele at Drury Lane* (1952; rpt. Westport, Conn.: Greenwood, 1973).

The London Stage   *The London Stage, 1660–1800*. Part 1 (1660–1700), ed. William Van Lennep, Emmett L. Avery, and Arthur H. Scouten. Part 2 (1700–1729), ed. Emmett L. Avery (Carbondale: Southern Illinois Univ. Press, 1965, 1960).

Luttrell, *Brief Historical Relation*   Narcissus Luttrell, *A Brief Historical Relation of State Affairs*, 6 vols. (Oxford: University Press, 1857).

Marlborough-Godolphin Correspondence   *The Marlborough-Godolphin Correspondence*, ed. Henry L. Snyder, 3 vols. (Oxford: Clarendon Press, 1975).

Milhous, *Thomas Betterton*   Judith Milhous, *Thomas Betterton and the Management of Lincoln's Inn Fields, 1695–1708* (Carbondale: Southern Illinois Univ. Press, 1979).

Milhous, "Vanbrugh's Haymarket Theatre Project"   Judith Milhous, "New Light on Vanbrugh's Haymarket Theatre Project," *Theatre Survey*, 17 (1976), 143–61.

Nicoll, *History*   Allardyce Nicoll, *A History of English Drama, 1660–1900*, rev. ed., 6 vols. (Cambridge: Cambridge Univ. Press, 1952–59).

Price, "The Critical Decade"	Curtis A. Price, "The Critical Decade for English Music Drama, 1700–1710," *Harvard Library Bulletin*, 26 (1978), 38–76.
PRO	Public Record Office (London). "LC" documents (e.g., LC 5/154) are in the Lord Chamberlain's department; "C" documents (e.g., C10/261/51) are Chancery legal records.
Rosenberg, "New Light on Vanbrugh"	Albert Rosenberg, "New Light on Vanbrugh," *Philological Quarterly*, 45 (1966), 603–13.
Sands, "Mrs. Tofts"	Mollie Sands, "Mrs. Tofts, 1685?–1756," *Theatre Notebook*, 20 (1966), 100–113.
Vanbrugh, *Works*	*The Complete Works of Sir John Vanbrugh*, ed. Bonamy Dobrée and Geoffrey Webb, 4 vols. (Bloomsbury: Nonesuch, 1927–28).
Winston	British Library Add. MS 38,607. (Nineteenth-century transcriptions of Coke documents by James Winston.)

Introduction

The Theatrical Situation in London, 1695–1715

To understand the political infighting and kaleidoscopic management reshufflings reflected in the Coke papers one needs some background information.[1] The original King's and Duke's companies, established by patent grant in 1660, had combined as the United Company in 1682 during hard times. The company ran smoothly for more than a decade and might have gone on indefinitely had not Alexander Davenant secretly sold his shares to the wily and ruthless Christopher Rich. When the insolvent Davenant fled to the Canary Islands in December 1693 Rich took control of the theatre. Believing himself secure in the possession of a permanent monopoly, Rich moved to humiliate and replace expensive senior actors like Betterton and Mrs Barry with younger and cheaper ones. Within a year, the senior actors were in open rebellion against Rich's tyrannical methods.[2] To Rich's great indignation and dismay, he discovered that the actors had friends at Court, and were able to wangle themselves a license to set up a rival company.

Rich was left in control of both the Drury Lane and the Dorset Garden theatres; the rebel actors had to make do with Lincoln's Inn Fields—a cramped old theatre abandoned by the Duke's Company in 1671 and not used since 1674, except as a tennis court. The two companies competed fiercely for several years, until some fresh hard times set in (exacerbated by the Jeremy Collier crisis) and they settled into an uneasy *modus vivendi* about 1702. By this time Rich had lost his hold on Dorset Garden, which was in poor repair. The possibility of a new union was discussed several times in

---

1. The fullest account of the London theatre in this period is Milhous, *Thomas Betterton*.
2. "The Petition of the Players" (November 1694?) and "The Reply of the Patentees" (10 December 1694) are printed in full from the MSS in the PRO by Milhous, *Thomas Betterton*, appendixes A and B.

1701 and 1702, but the rebel actors would not submit to Rich's control, and Rich would grant them no autonomy. Reflecting on this situation the young architect and playwright John Vanbrugh had a bright idea: why not build a new theatre, one equipped for fancy operas (as Dorset Garden had been, but Drury Lane was not)? As of 1703 Vanbrugh seems to have hoped to unite both acting companies under his control,[3] but he could be confident that in any case the Lincoln's Inn Fields actors would welcome the chance to move into an elegant new theatre—as indeed they did in 1705.[4]

When Vanbrugh finally managed to open the Haymarket in April 1705 he found himself in the midst of a hard fight. Rich had not the faintest intention of yielding the field to Vanbrugh, and he flatly rejected all proposals for union in the summer of 1705. During the season of 1705–6 both companies mounted plays and operas, Rich with rather more success than Vanbrugh. And in the summer of 1706 Vanbrugh once again tried to engineer a union, using every ounce of his considerable political influence. What resulted was a most peculiar compromise: Rich traded some of his best actors to Vanbrugh in return for exclusive rights to present operas and other musical entertainments, though he continued to present plays as well. But what Vanbrugh really wanted was an opera monopoly, and after a season and a half of politicking he finally managed to get it.

The Union of 1708, as it is usually called, was ordered by Lord Chamberlain Kent at Vanbrugh's behest. In essence, it recombined the two acting companies at Drury Lane under Rich and gave Vanbrugh his opera monopoly at the Haymarket. Vanbrugh quickly discovered that he had cleverly arranged his own downfall: opera proved ruinously expensive to produce; income was far below his optimistic estimates; and during the spring of 1708 he lost a great deal of money. Appalled, Vanbrugh bailed out in May of 1708. Leasing his license, his theatre, and its "stock" to Owen Swiney, Vanbrugh returned to architecture, poorer but wiser. His legacy to the London theatre was a rather echoey building, an awkward genre split, and a potentially explosive situation at Drury Lane, where the actors were not enjoying Christopher Rich's extortionate management methods.

The division created by the Union of 1708 lasted exactly a season and a half, though the mischief Vanbrugh had made was to have effects for many years. During 1708–9 the actors seem to have decided that Rich really was intolerable, and with the connivance of the Lord Chamberlain's office they

3. See Judith Milhous, "The Date and Import of the Financial Plan for a United Theatre Company in P.R.O. LC 7/3," *Maske und Kothurn*, 21 (1975), 81–88.
4. On the building of the Haymarket see Milhous, "Vanbrugh's Haymarket Theatre Project," and more generally, Daniel Nalbach, *The King's Theatre, 1704–1867* (London: Society for Theatre Research, 1972).

began to sign secret contracts to work for Swiney at the Haymarket. On 6
June 1709 the Lord Chamberlain issued an order silencing Drury Lane and
putting Rich out of business. The season of 1709–10 started with plays and
operas both at the Haymarket, and neither actors nor musicians happy about
it. In November 1709 the opportunistic William Collier acquired a license to
operate Drury Lane, and seized the theatre, restoring theatrical competition.
His company self-destructed the following June, however, in a celebrated riot
vividly described by Aaron Hill in document 86 below. At this point Collier
consulted with Swiney and a new deal was worked out for 1710–11. The
principal acting company amalgamated with Collier's, and moved back to
Drury Lane, where it was to be run by Owen Swiney in cooperation with
Wilks, Cibber, and Doggett. Collier, meanwhile, took over Swiney's opera
company at the Haymarket. Swiney then had a falling-out with the actors,
and late in the 1711–12 season he and Collier swapped places. Early in the
season of 1712–13 Swiney went broke and had to decamp hastily to the Continent. During 1713–14 the cagey and well-connected Barton Booth, following his triumph as Cato, persuaded the Lord Chamberlain to insist that he be
made a partner in the "triumvirate" management of Wilks, Doggett, and Cibber. This occasioned a walkout by Doggett, followed by three years of violent
acrimony and legal proceedings. In the midst of this interminable ruckus—
liberally represented in the documents below—the death of Queen Anne in
August 1714 gave the actor-managers a chance to force out the Tory Collier,
which they did, inviting Richard Steele (a staunch Whig) to join them in his
stead. One may fairly call this series of managerial upheavals bewildering. We
count eight major rearrangements in as many years. The following table may
help sort out this tangle of events.

| | Managerial Changes in the London Theatre, 1705–1715 | | |
Date	Drury Lane	Haymarket	Lincoln's Inn Fields
1705–6	Rich; plays and operas	Vanbrugh;* plays and operas	not in use
1706–7	Rich; plays and operas	Vanbrugh (Swiney as deputy); plays with no music	not in use
1707–8†	Rich; plays only; all actors returned to Drury Lane	Vanbrugh; operas only	not in use
1708–9	Rich; plays only; theatre silenced 6 June	Swiney; operas only	not in use
1709–10	dark until Novem- ber; Collier (Hill as	Swiney, with Wilks, Cibber, and Dog-	not in use

	deputy); plays only; closed by riot in June	gett; operas and plays	
1710–11	Swiney, with Wilks, Cibber and Doggett; plays only	Collier (with Hill); operas only	not in use
1711–12[‡]	Swiney, with Wilks, Cibber, and Doggett; plays only	Collier (and Hill); operas only	not in use
1712–13	Wilks, Cibber, Doggett (and Collier); plays only	Swiney (until 14 January); then Heidegger(?); operas only	not in use
1713–14	Wilks, Cibber, Doggett (and Collier); Doggett walked out after the 11 November license added Booth; plays only	Heidegger(?); operas only	being rebuilt by Christopher Rich
1714–15	Wilks, Cibber, Booth; Steele replaces Collier; plays only	Heidegger (?); operas only	John Rich; plays only[§]

[*] Congreve was his partner until December, when he dropped out after losing more money than he could afford.

[†] The agreement of 1706–7 was terminated by the Order of Union, 31 December 1707.

[‡] Swiney and Collier traded places 17 April 1712.

[§] Lincoln's Inn Fields reopened 18 December 1714 with authority from George I.

What we really see in the years covered by the Coke papers is a radical alteration in theatrical affairs brought about by Vanbrugh's misguided scheming, followed by several years of chaotic regroupings, and finally by the reestablishment of something rather like the old status quo. The two crucial factors in these years are the tyranny of Christopher Rich and the introduction of Italian opera as a major competitive factor. The silencing of 1709 disposed of Rich; opera was left to itself as a separate entity; and the opening of Lincoln's Inn Fields in 1714 under Christopher Rich's son John re-created the competition between rival theatre companies which had been the usual state of affairs since 1660. The very stormy years between the opening of the Haymarket and the reestablishment of more normal competitive circumstances in 1714–15 are something of an aberration in the history of the London theatre. The details of Vanbrugh's disastrous plunge into opera have never been fully known; the following management changes have seemed confusing to the point of incomprehensibility. Happily, the Coke papers fill in a great many of the blanks in our knowledge.

Opera on the London Stage

Prior to 1705, "opera" in London normally referred to what Roger North calls "semiopera"—a spoken play into which extensive masques or other musical entertainments were interpolated.[5] The "1674" *Tempest* is the best-known example. Some other major productions are the Shadwell *Psyche* (1675), and Purcell's *The Prophetess* (with Betterton), *King Arthur* (with Dryden), and *The Fairy-Queen* (with Settle?) in the early 1690s.[6] Betterton was the great champion of operatic spectaculars, and by all accounts he exploited the scenic capacities of the fancy Dorset Garden theatre to the full with them. When Betterton and his fellow stars decamped to Lincoln's Inn Fields in 1695 they lost the physical theatre facilities needed to mount such shows. Rich continued to do full-scale operas; the rebel actors could reply with no better than a series of masques which emphasized singing rather than staging. "English" opera did, however, continue to flourish in the years around 1700.[7]

At what point Vanbrugh decided that the time was ripe for the introduction of Italian—or "all-sung"—opera we do not know. To anyone who had traveled on the continent, the idea must have been pretty obvious. Whether the new form would succeed in the commercial theatre was another matter.[8] The *Diverting-Post* of 28 October 1704 tells us that Vanbrugh proposed to open his theatre with "two Opera's translated from the Italian by good Hands." One, Clayton's *Arsinoe*, was promptly stolen by Rich and staged at

5. See *Roger North on Music*, ed. John Wilson (London: Novello, 1959), pp. 306–7, 353.
6. On English semiopera see Edward J. Dent, *Foundations of English Opera* (Cambridge: Cambridge Univ. Press, 1928); Richard Luckett, "Exotick but rational entertainments: the English dramatic operas," in *English Drama: Forms and Development*, ed. Marie Axton and Raymond Williams (Cambridge: Cambridge Univ. Press, 1977), pp. 123–41; and Judith Milhous, "The Multimedia Spectacular on the Restoration Stage," forthcoming in *English Theatre and the Arts, 1660–1800*, ed. Shirley Strum Kenny.
7. For a detailed account of this neglected subject, see Robert D. Hume, "Opera in London, 1695–1706," forthcoming in *English Theatre and the Arts*.
8. On the first Italian operas in England see Milhous, *Thomas Betterton*, chapter 7; Price, "The Critical Decade"; and Roger Fiske, *English Theatre Music*, chapter 1. For an interesting contemporary view see "A Critical Discourse on Opera's and Musick in England," appended to François Raguenet's *A Comparison Between the French and Italian Musick and Opera's* (London: Lewis and Morphew, 1709). According to Charles Gildon, *The Life of Mr. Thomas Betterton* (London: Gosling, 1710), p. 166, it was written by "Seignior H—— or some Creature of his"—i.e., by Nicola Haym.

Drury Lane in January 1705 with considerable success. The other, Daniel Purcell's *Orlando Furioso*, was never completed. The popularity of *Arsinoe* left Vanbrugh desperately anxious to grace the belated opening of the Haymarket with another such opera, and he arranged for a production of Greber's *Gli Amori d'Ergasto*, probably sung in Italian. The result was a fiasco. Downes tells us: "And upon the 9*th*, of *April* 1705. Captain *Vantbrugg* open'd his new Theatre in the *Hay-Market*, with a Foreign Opera, Perform'd by a new set of Singers, Arriv'd from *Italy*; (the worst that e're came from thence) for it lasted but 5 Days, and they being lik'd but indifferently by the Gentry; they in a little time marcht back to their own Country."[9] At this point one could hardly have predicted that opera in Italian would soon drive English opera into oblivion.

During the season of 1705–6 Vanbrugh had good success with a semiopera (Granville's *The British Enchanters*), while an Italianate opera (*The Temple of Love*) and a unique experiment (Durfey's *Wonders in the Sun*) failed. Rich countered with Bononcini's *Camilla*, a considerable success which remained popular for many years.[10] During the season of 1706–7 Vanbrugh was debarred from producing musical works of any sort, while Rich tried the Addison-Clayton *Rosamond* (a great disappointment, let down by its music), and another translated Italian opera, *Thomyris*. When Vanbrugh seized an opera monopoly the following season the terms of the genre split obliged him to stick to Italianate opera. Without an acting company the Haymarket had no way to mount semiopera; without singers or permission to perform music there was no way for Drury Lane to counter with long-popular English operas. Thus was semiopera driven from the stage—not by changing audience taste but by the Lord Chamberlain's edict.

The move from Italianate (all-sung) opera to opera sung in Italian by imported stars is a separate phenomenon. It came about not because the London audience understood Italian, or because they did not care to understand what they were hearing, but out of a craze for guest stars. Italian opera was written with castrati in mind, and Rich very naturally hit on the expedient of importing one as a special attraction. In March of 1707 he brought Valentini to London—a second-rank singer in Italy, but a glamorous novelty in London. For the following season he signed not only Valentini but Giuseppe Cassani, who turned out to be an expensive mistake. Cassani's contract (specified in document 42) calls for a salary of £300, £137 for travel and lodg-

9. John Downes, *Roscius Anglicanus* (London: H. Playford, 1708), p. 48.
10. On *Camilla* see Lowell Lindgren, "A Bibliographic Scrutiny of Dramatic Works Set by Giovanni and His Brother Antonio Maria Bononcini," Diss. Harvard Univ. 1972. For an accessible short form of Lindgren's study, see his "I Trionfi di Camilla," *Studi Musicali*, 6 (1977), 89–159.

ing, plus an unspecified "present." He sang exactly twice, and was received with vociferous disapprobation—to the consternation of Vanbrugh, who was stuck with the terms of Rich's agreement. Cassani's failure notwithstanding, managers felt that they had to bring in foreigners. This led initially to mixed-language performances—Valentini in Italian, the rest of the cast in English—and by natural progression to performance in Italian. The first opera (save *Ergasto*) sung entirely in Italian was Mancini's *Idaspe* in March 1710. Handel's *Rinaldo*, done in Italian the following February, was a success which naturally encouraged the trend. As Fiske observes, "Handel did not cause the fever for Italian opera, but he ensured its continuance."

The salaries demanded and often obtained by singers were frighteningly high. At the time Vanbrugh planned his company, £150 was the top salary in the London theatre, and the average salary for name actors was under £100.[11] Some grossly inflated short-term salaries had been paid to visiting French dancers (Balon and Mme Subligny) at the height of the competition between Lincoln's Inn Fields and Drury Lane, and singers had contributed to salary inflation around 1705—but the foreigners represented a huge increase, and a potentially dangerous one.

Opera was exceedingly expensive to produce (more than double the cost of straight plays per day), and because it could not hope to draw a decent house more than two nights a week, it needed much fuller houses than did plays. This encouraged the importation of expensive star attractions, which in turn drove costs up. Swiney signed Nicolini—a genuine star—for 1708–9, and in the spring of 1709 proposed a three-year contract (document 74). The proposal calls for a base salary of 800 guineas per annum, plus a benefit, and an extra £150 for helping fit up a new opera. Nicolini undoubtedly helped fill the theatre, but this huge salary encouraged other performers to raise their sights, and the Haymarket budget grew steadily less sound.

At no point in these years was the opera company financially viable. A large number of the documents printed here are testimony to the essential shakiness of the operation. Vanbrugh bailed out in a hurry. Swiney was quite ready to let Collier take the opera in 1710–11, and Collier was soon unable to pay his bills. Swiney stayed solvent less than a season when he returned to the Haymarket in 1712. Ever-shifting opera companies limped on through 1716–17, after which there is a hiatus until April 1720, when the Royal Academy of Music again mounted Italian opera in London.[12] The munificently funded Royal Academy bankrupted itself within ten years, and Han-

11. See "An Establishment for ye Company," PRO LC 7/3, fols. 161–64.
12. On the organization and financing of this venture see J. Merrill Knapp, "Handel, the Royal Academy of Music, and Its First Opera Season in London (1720)," *The Musical Quarterly*, 45 (1959), 145–67.

del, its principal prop, was unable to keep his own company afloat in the next decade.[13]

Looking back to first causes, we may ask why Vanbrugh was so determined to set up a separate company. Several factors probably affected his thinking. He really wanted a single, monopolistic company doing both operas and plays; balked, he compromised. Italian opera was an exciting novelty in London. Rich had made a very good thing out of *Arsinoe* and *Camilla*. Writing to the Earl of Manchester on 27 July 1708 Vanbrugh said bitterly that "My Ld Chamb: Upon a Supposition that there wou'd be Immence gain, Oblig'd us to Extravagant Allowances"—but a year earlier Vanbrugh seems to have been suffering from the same delusion.

During the late seventeenth century, "opera" had been a special treat. New productions were rare and expensive gambles—and all save Dryden's *Albion and Albanius* (1685) succeeded well enough to stay in the repertory. No one would have imagined that a company could support itself just by performing two operas a week for half the year—and had Vanbrugh not arranged the order for a genre split it is highly unlikely that anyone would have tried to set up an opera company on this basis. One virtue of semiopera was that it gave employment to the regular actors, and did not demand so large a musical establishment. A radically split company, such as occupied the Haymarket in 1709–10, had its own problems, as the documents below illustrate. Actors resented losing two prime nights each week; singers felt that actors had excessive influence in the management. But had opera remained a subsidiary attraction for acting companies, performed in English, it would probably have been a happier and healthier part of the eighteenth-century theatre. After 1714 royal patronage helped keep Italian opera going, however shakily at times. But it is hard to imagine that a unified company would have countenanced expensive foreign stars and performance in a foreign language. Continued support for such an opera house is historically the exception rather than the norm.

Thomas Coke and the Vice Chamberlain's Office

Who was Thomas Coke, and why did he have the theatrical papers in this volume in his possession? Little as we know about the man, we can at least give unequivocal answers to these basic questions.

The introduction to *The Manuscripts of the Earl Cowper* gives us a basic sketch of the life.

13. See Judith Milhous and Robert D. Hume, "Box Office Reports for Five Operas Mounted by Handel in London, 1732–1734," *Harvard Library Bulletin*, 26 (1978), 245–66.

The elder son [of Lt. Col. John Coke, 1653–90], Thomas Coke, was born in 1674. In 1688–9 he resided for some months in the family of a French Protestant minister at Rotterdam. He was afterwards at New College, Oxford, and on leaving the University in 1696, he visited the Low Countries, and stayed at the Loo in Guelderland with a friend in the household of King William III.

In the Parliaments of August 1698, December 1701, August 1702, June 1705, and July 1708, Thomas Coke was returned for the County of Derby, and in those of November 1710 and November 1713 for the Borough of Grampound. In the Parliament of August 1702 he was chosen one of the Committee for examining the Public Accounts; and in 1704 he became one of the Tellers of the Exchequer. At the end of 1706 Thomas Coke became a Privy Councillor, and was appointed Vice-Chamberlain of the Household, an office which he held until his death on 17th May 1727.

In 1704, having under an Act of Parliament converted into fee simple his interest in the Rectory house and estate of Melbourne in Derbyshire, previously held by his ancestors from 1628 as lessees of the Bishops of Carlisle, he commenced the formation of the well-known gardens of Melbourne Hall, which still remain a monument of his taste and judgment.

Vice-Chamberlain Coke married first in June 1698 the Lady Mary Stanhope (elder daughter of Philip 2nd Earl of Chesterfield) who died in January 1703–4, leaving two daughters; and, secondly, in October 1709, Mary, daughter of William Hale esquire of Kings Walden, Herts, a Maid of Honour to Queen Anne, who died in January 1723–4, leaving one son, George Lewis Coke, and one daughter, Charlotte Coke. The latter, on the death of her brother unmarried in 1750, succeeded to his Melbourne and other estates. Charlotte Coke had married in 1740 Matthew Lamb, who was created a Baronet in 1755. Their son, Sir Peniston Lamb, became Baron and Viscount Melbourne in the Peerage of Ireland, and afterwards in 1815 Viscount Melbourne in the Peerage of the United Kingdom. He was succeeded by his sons William 2nd Viscount Melbourne (the Prime Minister), and Frederick 3rd and last Viscount Melbourne. At the death of the latter the Melbourne estate passed to his only sister, Emily, married to the 5th Earl Cowper, and secondly to the last Viscount Palmerston (the Prime Minister), and at her Ladyship's death, in 1869, it passed to her grandson, the 7th Earl Cowper, with whose permission the present publication of Papers preserved at Melbourne Hall has been made.

The repository of these Papers is an ancient hexagonal stone building, formerly the "Dove house" of the Rectors of Melbourne (the Bishops of Carlisle) which was skilfully converted into a "Muniment Room" in 1708 by Vice-Chamberlain Coke.[14]

14. *The Manuscripts of the Earl Cowper, K.G., Preserved at Melbourne Hall, Derbyshire*, Vol. III, HMC, Twelfth Report, Appendix, Part 3 (London: Her Majesty's Stationery Office, 1889), pp. v–vi.

This bald summary would hardly lead one to suspect that this longtime Court functionary was a highly cultured man and a great collector.

A newspaper clipping from 1728[15] preserves an announcement for the sale of his possessions after his death.

> This is to Acquaint the CURIOUS,
> That on Monday the 12th of February, will begin to be sold by Auction, at Mr. Cooper's in the Great Piazza, Covent-Garden.
> The Houshold Goods, &c. of the Rt. Hon. *Thomas Coke*, Esq; deceased, Vice Chamberlain to his late Majesty; consisting of Jewels, several thousand Ounces of useful Plate, a considerable Quantity of fine old *China* and *Japan* Ware, Linnen, an easy Coach and Berlin Chariot, two fine inlaid Venetian Marble Tables, with several other valuable curiosities.
> And on Monday the 19th will begin the Sale of his celebrated collection of Pictures, by the most eminent Italian and other Masters. His valuable Library of Books will follow the Pictures, and at 5 in the Evening of the same Days, will be sold his collection of Prints and Drawings by all the greatest Italian Masters, in their utmost perfection. This whole collection may be viewed 6 Days before the Sale; beginning each Day exactly at 12 o'clock. Catalogues will then be delivered gratis at the place of Sale, and at Mr. *Calcott's* in St. Martin's Lane.

The sale catalogue itself (a copy of which is preserved in the British Library) is a rather astonishing document.[16] In sixty pages it lists 127 paintings (including works attributed to Holbein, Lilly [Lely], and Michaelangelo), 15 "Limnings and Enamels," 1,068 books to be auctioned over nine days, 443 prints, 40 drawings, and 171 volumes of "bound books of prints." The books enumerated—unfortunately not descending to such ephemera as play quartos—are striking testimony to the range of Coke's interests: history, "voyages," astronomy, architecture, painting, lexicography, classics, mathematics, French and Italian books of various sorts, numismatics, modern travel, and antiquarian subjects. Divinity is scantily represented; literature was obviously a great interest. Coke was strong on major early writers—Chaucer, Shakespeare, Marlowe, Donne. He had all the major Restoration figures—Dryden, Davenant, Killigrew, Denham, Waller, Shadwell, Etherege, Rochester, Sedley, Otway, Behn, Rymer, and others. He had turn of the century people—Congreve, St. Evremond, Addison, Roscommon, Cibber, and others. He had bought Pope and Swift, and stayed up to date, having bought

---

15. Now pasted in the front matter of NYPL Drexel MS 1986.
16. *A Catalogue of the Collection of Pictures, Drawings, Prints, And Valuable Library of Books, Of the Right Honourable Thomas Coke, Deceas'd, Vice-Chamberlain to his late Majesty, and one of His most Honourable Privy-Council* (London, 1728)—to begin Monday 19 February 1727/8.

Gulliver's Travels in the year before his death. No manuscripts, however, are listed in the sale catalogue.

In the late 1690s Coke seems to have been one of the young men about town who followed the theatre with some attention. There is a letter of 19 November 1696 from Robert Jennens to Coke, acquainting him with the success of *The Anatomist* at Lincoln's Inn Fields and reporting the dire straits in which Rich's young Drury Lane company found itself. He evidently attended Congreve's *The Mourning Bride* early in its first run, and promptly wrote an account to a friend. Despite this evidence of real interest in the theatre Coke was one of the fashionable set who drifted in and out of the theatres during performances in company with the infuriating James Brydges, who always tells us who he saw, but almost never what play was on.[17]

Luttrell records on 3 December 1706 that "Mr. Coke of Darbyshire, one of the tellers of the exchequer, has exchanged his place with Mr. Peregrine Bertie, for that of vicechamberlain to the queen."[18] Why Vanbrugh's friend—later briefly his partner at the Haymarket—wanted to make this trade we can only guess. Possibly he did not want to remain forever tied down to the routine of the royal household—and he had held the job some twelve years. In British Library Harl. MS 2262, no. 301, we find

A Warrant to the Exchequr, Out of any of her Maties Treasure (applicable to the uses of her Civil Governmt) to pay unto Thomas Coke Esqr Vice Chamberlain of her Maties Household, or to his Assignes the yearly Summe of Six hundred pounds which her Matie is pleased to allow unto him, over and above the other antient profitts belonging to that place. (Signed by Godolphin; sealed 8 January 1706/7).

This is only a quarter of Coke's remuneration for a considerable job.

The Royal Household was run by the Lord Chamberlain. All aspects of a large and costly operation were looked after by his office. Palaces were staffed and run; entertainments organized; visiting dignitaries received and housed; the monarch's schedule seen to—and so forth. And one small, essentially accidental part of the Lord Chamberlain's duties was supervising London's theatres.[19] The reason is simple enough: actors had been royal servants, entitled to a livery grant and the protected status conferred on the monarch's servants. (This is why tradesmen had to get the Lord Chamberlain's permis-

---

17. *The London Stage*, Part 1, pp. 470, 476, 526. See Lucyle Hook, "James Brydges Drops in at the Theater," *Huntington Library Quarterly*, 8 (1945), 306–11.

18. Luttrell, *Brief Historical Relation*, VI, 113.

19. For Cibber's account of the Lord Chamberlain's control of the theatres see *Apology*, II, 17–23. The full extent of the Lord Chamberlain's duties is outlined in Chamberlayne's *Angliae Notitia*, and in John M. Beattie's *The English Court in the Reign of George I* (Cambridge: Cambridge Univ. Press, 1967).

sion before suing actors for nonpayment of bills in the late seventeenth century.) By the reign of Queen Anne the actors' claim to the title "Her Majesty's Servants" was mostly a matter of form and convention, but the job of overseeing the theatres remained the Lord Chamberlain's. Anyone who has done some reading in the books of the Lord Chamberlain's office preserved in the Public Record Office knows how minor and peripheral a role theatrical matters played in the office's hectic day-to-day business.

As we understand the operation of the office in the period at issue, there were three key people involved: the Lord Chamberlain himself, his Vice Chamberlain, and his secretary. From 1704 to 1710 Henry Grey, Earl (later Duke) of Kent, served as Lord Chamberlain. He was succeeded by Charles Talbot, Duke of Shrewsbury, who was followed by the Duke of Bolton in 1715. Newcastle took over in 1717 and precipitated the celebrated battle with Richard Steele over patent rights versus the authority of the Lord Chamberlain. From 1706 to the time of his death Coke served as Vice Chamberlain. The sorts of daily business which came his way—petitioners, political intrigues, protocol of meals, problems of furnishing the whole of Whitehall—are all well-illustrated in the correspondence at Melbourne Hall excerpted by the Historical Manuscripts Commission. Coke's involvement in Court ceremonial is evident in the following letter from the Duchess of Somerset.

I have acquainted the Queen with your request, and she commands me to tell you that you have her leave to stay in town till the beginning of next week, and to put yourself and family in mourning: but as there is no Lord Chamberlain here, it will be necessary for you to leave it off the birthday, because you must appear to give those orders on that occasion, which cannot be properly done by anybody else.[20]

For many years the Lord Chamberlain's secretary was Sir John Stanley. He and Coke worked closely together, and they seem to have been good friends, to judge from the informal, chatty, sometimes teasing letters between them. (See, for example, document 76.)

When the Lord Chamberlain's office issued a formal order—as it did several times each day—a copy was written into a bound letterbook for the office record, and the separately written "original" was dispatched to the recipient. Papers coming in were dealt with and then destroyed or filed. PRO LC 7/3, for example, is basically a compendium of miscellaneous theatre-related papers which came to the Lord Chamberlain's office.

A Lord Chamberlain is a busy man, and probably most of them paid as

---

20. HMC, *Twelfth Report*, Appendix, Part 3, p. 181.

little attention to theatrical matters as they could manage. Vanbrugh wrote to the Earl of Manchester on 11 May 1708, "I have been severall times wth him [Swiney] lately in Consultation wth the Vice Chamberlain Coke, (who being a great Lover of Musique And promoter of Operas; My Ld Chamb: leaves that Matter almost entirely to him." [21] This is, in brief, why Thomas Coke was in a position to accumulate theatre-related documents. Some things he simply dealt with himself, holding onto the relevant papers. In other instances he must have consulted the Lord Chamberlain, or simply passed the papers on to him for action or directions. From the cover annotations on many of the Coke papers we can deduce that they were filed in his office. In some cases Coke evidently passed the originals on to the Lord Chamberlain, but wanted a copy for his own records. In these instances someone—the "Hand A" so frequent in the papers, probably Coke himself—copied them out and kept the copies filed in the Vice Chamberlain's office. Document 5, for example, an anonymous justification for denying Rich the right to produce plays from about September 1706, exists in PRO LC 7/3 in Vanbrugh's hand, and also in two nineteenth-century transcriptions made from the Coke papers. We deduce that Coke passed Vanbrugh's original on to Kent after copying it, and that his copy (now lost) served as copytext for the nineteenth-century transcribers. A very large proportion of the original "Coke papers" recovered, however, are holographs delivered to Coke, essentially all of them bear the office's filing annotation.

Matters of major import required the Lord Chamberlain's approval, and at times Coke seems to have drafted orders for the Lord Chamberlain to issue. Occasionally, as in the matter of the Union of 1708, the Lord Chamberlain would take an active part in the negotiations. But routine problems and complaints seem to have gone straight to the Vice Chamberlain: the theatre people probably understood very well that they were not to bother higher authority without good reason.

The Provenance of the Coke Papers

The provenance of the Coke papers is decidedly complicated, and for clarity we have divided our discussion into ten phases.

Phase 1: 1706 to 1727. At some point a substantial number of Coke's papers from the Vice Chamberlain's office became separated from the rest of his office records. Perhaps he was keeping them in his private quarters. At any rate, they became mixed with personal papers. When they were shifted to

---

21. Vanbrugh, *Works*, IV, 20–21.

Melbourne, why, and by whom we do not know. The nontheatrical papers are of all sorts.[22] They include letters from Sir John Stanley and George Granville, Baron Lansdowne, among other correspondents represented in the present collection. At this point the theatrical papers were simply part of a large and heterogeneous group which got moved—for whatever reason—to Melbourne.

Phase 2: early nineteenth century. The Hon. George Lamb (1784–1834) put together the separate collection of theatrical papers. That Lamb did the sorting out is our conjecture—but the collection first comes to light in his possession, and as the fourth son of Peniston, first Viscount Melbourne, he had the requisite access to the family's papers. George Lamb, Coke's great-grandson, was trained as a lawyer, but he had a strong literary and dramatic bent. The *DNB* reports that he was a good amateur actor; that he had a two-act comic opera produced at Covent Garden in 1807, and adapted *Timon of Athens* for production in 1816; and that he was a member of the Drury Lane "committee of management" in 1815. We should hardly be surprised that he became a close friend of James Winston (1773–1843), manager of Drury Lane in the 1820s. Our hypothesis is that Lamb recognized the antiquarian significance of his great-grandfather's papers in the family seat, sifted out what interested him, and showed them to Winston (and very probably to others). He may have had some thought of publishing them, or using them as material toward a history of opera or theatre. Some transcriptions of particular documents exist in Lamb's hand, which may be a sign of such interest.[23]

Phase 3: the creation of the New York Public Library transcriptions. At an unknown date the collection was borrowed or used by the anonymous author of "Historical Remarks Respecting the Introduction of Operas in England" (4 pages, 1816?). This gentleman transcribed many of the documents; added clippings and relevant issues of the *Tatler*, the *Daily Courant*, and other periodicals; and included a few letters not transcribed by Winston and not otherwise now locatable. The resulting compilation passed at some point into the hands of the well-known collector and music historian E. F. Rimbault (1816–76). It was sold after his death (Sotheby, 31 July–7 August 1877, item 2241), and in 1888 it wound up in a private library in New York City which ultimately became a part of the New York Public Library, where it is now Drexel MS 1986. The handwriting is not Rimbault's, to judge from the samples of his hand available in the New York Public Library. A study of variant readings demonstrates conclusively that these transcriptions do not derive from Winston's, and that Winston's do not derive from this manuscript,

---

22. The HMC volume already cited (note 14) gives a good idea of the collection.
23. For example, transcriptions of documents 120 and 124 by Lamb are now in the Folger Library, Y.c. 197 (1) and (2).

though naturally some cruxes gave both copyists difficulty. The anonymous transcriber could theoretically have had access to the collection any time up to the 1870s, but the four printed pages of the "Historical Remarks" annotated "written by me . . . 1816" suggest an earlier rather than a later date.

Phase 4: used and later owned by James Winston. The complete collection was evidently in the possession of James Winston between 1834 and his death in 1843. More than ten years previously, however, he had borrowed the papers from Lamb and made transcriptions of a large number of them. These copies constitute part of what is now British Library Add. MS 38,607, a collection of Winston's historical notes on theatrical matters. He headed the Coke section with a somewhat garbled explanatory note: "Copies & Extracts from Letters & papers lent to me by the Honble George Lamb, on Sunday Feb 23, 1823 belonging formerly to [blank] who married into the Melbourne family & at whose death all his property & papers came into the possession of the Honble G Lambs Grandfather." At some point between 1823 and 1834 the collection passed from Lamb to Winston. The 1876 sale catalogue says that "This remarkable and magnificent collection of Documents and Autograph letters was presented to the well-known Collector, J. Winston, by his friend the Rt. Hon. George Lamb, M.P., who died in 1834." The collection was, at any rate, in Winston's possession at the time of his death. In the Puttick and Simpson sale of Winston's library, 13–15 December 1849, lot 477 is "King's Theatre.—Vice-Chamberlain Coke's Papers, relative to the Italian Opera in the Haymarket, 1706–15, 2 vols. 4to." The catalogue lists most of the people whose names possessed autograph value, adds hints of some letters' subjects, and concludes, "There are various schemes, remonstrances, and papers on the disputes respecting salary, charges for dresses, daily pay to the Musicians, and other blissful enjoyments of Theatrical management." The whole collection went to "Johnson" for £12 10s.

Phase 5: the auction of 1876. The collection next reappears to sight in the Puttick and Simpson sale of Monday 21 August 1876. This sale comprised a miscellany: *Catalogue of a large and varied Collection of Music . . . Valuable Autographs and Manuscripts, Vice-Chamberlain Coke's Unique and Remarkable Collection of Original Documents Relative to the Opera in England Between 1706 and 1715 . . . Also Musical Instruments*, and so forth. Items 168 through 215 are Coke papers. Item 168 itself is described as "Vice-Chamberlain Coke's Theatrical Papers, from 1706 to 1715, 4to. 2 volumes. An unique and splendid series of papers, petitions, amounts of salaries, etc. relative to the Opera; also referring to Rich, Doggett, Swiney, Heidegger, Cibber, Betterton, Tofts, Crosse, Nicolini, Handel, etc." What the auctioneer seems to have done is to pull out of the two quarto volumes those papers with appeal to autograph collectors. Items 169–215 are headed "Vice-Chamberlain Coke's collection

of Autograph Letters, original signed documents, etc." Comparison with the
Winston sale catalogue shows clearly that letters included in the two quarto
volumes in 1849 were now part of the "collection of Autograph Letters." In
all, the sale catalogue splits off sixty-one letters and documents, plus several
sets of signed receipts and item 199, "Owen Swiny's Operatic, etc. Correspondence, a most valuable and interesting collection of letters, signed and
holograph"—number unspecified. Lot 168 was bought by "Lee" for £4 10s.
The single lots went randomly to Lee, "Naylor," and "Harvey."

Phase 6: the documents dispersed late in the nineteenth century. Sometime after 1876 some of the Coke papers came into the possession of the music historian Julian Marshall (d. 1903), who used them in writing a number of
entries for *Grove's Dictionary*.[24] In 1882 Percy Fitzgerald cited bits of several
documents, especially those concerned with the Doggett row, and twice acknowledged "Mr. A. Harvey, [sic] of St. James's Street, whose knowledge and
taste as a collector are well known."[25] Trying to annotate Cibber's account of
the Triumvirate management quarrel in 1889 Robert W. Lowe cited six of the
relevant letters and documents specifically, saying that they were then "in the
collection of Mr. Francis Harvey of St. James's Street."[26] This is presumably
the "Harvey" of the 1876 sale catalogue annotations—a well-known book
and print seller born in 1830. His death was reported in the *Times* 16 February 1900; the Sotheby sale of his books 21 June contains no mention of Coke
manuscripts.

There is no clear pattern in the disposition of documents by the three
buyers at the 1876 sale. Several items bought separately by Lee (for example,
203, 204, 205, and 215) remained with the reduced collection; others (for
example, 172, 179, and 202) did not. Many of the items bought by Naylor
reappear in the sale of 1905—but not all of them (for example, our documents 52, 78, and 101). A substantial number of the many documents
bought by Harvey are now unlocatable, though the appearance at Harvard,
the Pierpont Morgan, and in the collection of Mary Hyde of documents
bought by Harvey argues against an en bloc disposition to a single source.

Phase 7: the sale of 1905. On 2 March 1905 Sotheby auctioned off a substantial number of letters and documents under the heading "Letters, &c.
from the Collection of Vice-Chamberlain Coke, 1706–1715" as part of a
larger sale of autograph letters from divers unspecified sources. Of the twenty-
five "Coke" items offered, one was unrelated (a 1748 letter by Heidegger);
most of the rest are described in terms taken verbatim from the 1876 sale

24. Specific references to Coke papers appear in his entries for Nicolini, Margarita de
l'Epine, Catherine Tofts, and Owen Swiney.
25. Fitzgerald, *A New History*, I, 309, 355.
26. *Apology*, II, 148–49.

catalogue. Item 712 is the reduced collection which wound up at Harvard—sold to Maggs for £4 5s. Seven other buyers bought one or more lots. Sotheby added a few items distinct from the Coke papers as listed, but related in authorship or theatrical interest. These additions include documents 133 and 140, otherwise known to us from Winston's transcriptions. A number of the documents sold in 1905 (including six of the eleven bought by Maggs) were bought at some point by A. M. Broadley, who put them in scrapbooks and grangerized editions. These then passed into various libraries which acquired Broadley's holdings, most notably the Folger and the Westminster Public Library in London.[27]

Phase 8: the reduced collection in the possession of W. H. Cummings. Between the 1905 sale and 1914 the residue represented in lot 712 drops out of sight. But on 20 January 1914 the well-known music historian W. H. Cummings addressed the Musical Association on "The Lord Chamberlain and Opera in London, 1700–1740."[28] Cummings began his talk by saying: "I have here a folio volume containing more than eighty papers which refer to matters connected with Drury Lane, Covent Garden, and Haymarket Theatres. There are letters, agreements, lists of salaries, receipts of various performances, autographs of Heidegger, Haym, Valentini, Owen Swiney; the Lord Chamberlain, the Marquess of Kent; the Vice-Chamberlain, Thomas Coke; and other notable people. The documents were originally in the possession of Coke the Vice-Chamberlain." What follows is a documentary history in the fashion of Percy Fitzgerald, the 1706–15 portions occupying some two-thirds of the space and drawing heavily on the papers now in the Harvard Theatre Collection. Cummings occasionally misdates the documents, and he had some problems with the handwriting (for example, reading "Valentini" for "Bolatri"), but certainly his article is a major step forward in the understanding of opera in early eighteenth-century England. Where or when he acquired the volume of papers he does not give us the least idea. In all probability he simply bought it from a dealer—he was a noted collector of music-related manuscripts. When Cummings died three years later the papers were sold with the rest of his library. Item 608 in the Sotheby, Wilkinson, and Hodge catalogue of *The Famous Musical Library . . . of the late W. H. Cummings* (17–24 May 1917) is "Drama. A collection of upwards of eighty Papers connected with the Haymarket Theatre, Covent Garden Opera House, etc. including Letters, Agreements, Tables of Salaries, Receipts taken at various Houses, etc. (the majority of which were at one time in the possession of Sir

27. First utilized by Ronald C. Kern, "Documents Relating to Company Management, 1705–1711," *Theatre Notebook*, 14 (1959–60), 60–65.

28. Published under that title in *Proceedings of the Musical Association*, 40th Session (London: Novello, 1914), pp. 37–72.

Thos. Coke, Vice Chamberlain, some bearing his address), some of the papers are in Owen Swiny's, J. J. Heidegger's, Haym's and Valentino's autograph, *all neatly laid down on stout paper*, in 1 vol. *new half morocco, g.e.* 4*to. c.* 1710." A sample list follows. The collection was bought by Dobell for £17.

Phase 9: arrival at Harvard. The reduced collection was given to Harvard by Robert Gould Shaw in 1928, where it is Harvard Theatre Collection fMS Thr 348. At some point between the 1876 sale and the time of Cummings' talk in 1914 someone removed the remaining documents from the two volumes mentioned by early sources and put them in the large scrapbook in which they now reside. A few extraneous oddments got added. The most important of these additions are six box-office reports for operas mounted by Handel in London between 1732 and 1734. These we have published elsewhere.[29] They may well have been separate acquisitions by Cummings, who was particularly interested in Handel, but if so he must have picked them up after the date of his talk, since they would have been highly relevant to his 1730s material, and they are not mentioned. We have also omitted "A Catalogue of Books Instruments &ca belonging to ye Music Club at ye Deanery taken ye 24th of January 1755," and an undated, untitled music inventory having nothing to do with Coke or the public theatre.[30]

Phase 10: known locations of Coke documents in the present day. Despite visits to many libraries, written enquiries to many more, personal application to scholars in the field, and public advertisements, we are unable to locate a considerable number of the documents known to have been at one time part of the "Coke papers." In some thirty instances we have had to rely on nineteenth-century transcriptions. Fortunately, both Winston and the transcriber of the Drexel manuscript are substantively very accurate indeed, as we have determined from comparison with originals we do possess. In eight cases we have had to report documents "missing," though one of these cases is probably a ghost, and for another the 1876 sale catalogue may well give us the whole text—but we cannot be certain.

The following table summarizes what we know about the location of Coke documents. Column 1 gives the document number in this edition. Column 2 gives the document number in the "reduced collection" now in the Harvard Theatre Collection—if the item appears there.[31] Columns 3 and 4 give page and folio numbers for transcriptions in Winston and NYPL Drexel MS 1986.

29. See note 13 above.
30. Also omitted is an undated summary of Novosielski's 1782 alterations to the Haymarket, said in a MS note by W.V.L. [William Van Lennep, formerly Curator of the Harvard Theatre Collection] to be in the hand of James Winston. We are dubious about this ascription.
31. fMS Thr 348 (Thr 464.4.15 * until it was recatalogued in 1981) is unpaginated. We have simply assigned numbers in the random order in which the documents appear.

(Numbering in the latter is extremely erratic: flagrant departures from order are indicated by quotation marks. Thus "41" means the folio misnumbered 41, and "42 fol. (s)" means the folio misnumbered 42 and the unnumbered folio(s) following. An entry such as 51v refers to the verso of folio
51. Column 5 gives the item number in the 1876 sale catalogue, if applicable. Column 6 gives the item number in the 1905 sale catalogue, if applicable. Column 7 gives the current location of a Coke original separated from
the main collection, or in some cases an alternative copy-text (e.g., LC 7/3).

Doc.	HTC	Winston pp.	Drexel fols.	1876 S.C.	1905 S.C.	Other
1	25	98–99	24	184?		
2	26	83	25	184?		
3	27			184?		
4	10	45	50			
5		59–60	84			LC 7/3
6	37	3–4	70			
7		51	134			Folger
8	47	51–53	"42" fol.			
9		84	"41"	185		
10	53					
11	14					
12	15					
13	60			204		
14				196	701	Harvard
15	12					
16		49–50	28	202	708	Broadley
17	18					
18	4					
19		70	26	187	695	
20	39					
21	40					
22	23					
23		3		197	702	
24	5					
25	77	47	126	189	696	
26		43	127	181?		
27		43	125	181?		Harvard
28	54	77–81	32 fols.			
29						Harvard
30	56	23–24	123			
31	45	44	124			
32						Broadley
33		81–82	37	191	697	Broadley

Doc.	HTC	Winston pp.	Drexel fols.	1876 S.C.	1905 S.C.	Other
34		4	34	190?	698?	
35	28	98–100	38–40	184?		
36		50	27	201	706	Broadley
37				180	691	
38				179		
39	50			203		
40	51					
41	11	46	54			
42	46	49	60			
43	69					
44	8					
45	49			205		
46		2	"40"	pt. of 209		
47		55	"43"	206	709	Pforzheimer
48	7	95				
49	3	86	56			
50	59	87	52			
51	29			184?		
52		71	44	199?		Harvard
53		75–77	45–46	pt. of 209		
54				193	699	
55	57a	88	53			
56	57b	89	55			
57	57c	90	51			
58	24/57d	91	51v			
59	58					
60	38					
61	72					
62		82–83	57			Pforzheimer
63		3				Morgan
64		32–33	58	207		
65	74					
66	48					
67	13					
68		92	132	182		Harvard
69	52			pt. of 204		
70		54–55	59	208	707	Huntington
71		34–35	49	198	703	
72	31			pt. of 184?		
73	42	87				
74				pt. of 199?	704	Broadley
75				194		
76	34	70	131			

Doc.	HTC	*Winston pp.*	*Drexel fols.*	*1876 S.C.*	*1905 S.C.*	*Other*
77	70					
78		40	63	pt. of 199?		Harvard
79		42		pt. of 199?		William W. Appleton
80		41 42	61	pt. of 199?		
81		38–40	71–72	pt. of 199?		
82	36	84				
83	66					
84				183	692	Broadley
85	67					
86		24–29	79 fols.	188		Hyde Collection
87		96–97	81	pt. of 199?		Broadley
88		37	122			
89	43					
90		64–65				PRO LC 5/155, p. 44
91		5	83	213		Harvard
92		69	85	pt. of 199?		Broadley
93				169	688	Texas
94	61	93–94				
95	44					
96	63	94 (part)				
97	62	93–94				
98	2	93–94	87			
99	65	91				
100	17	71–75	64–65			
101		53	62	pt. of 199?		Folger
102		66–67	90	pt. of 174?	690	Folger
103		68–69	91	pt. of 174?	690	Folger
104	1					
105	16	37	92			
106	22	23	93			
107	9	36	135			
108	21					
109	35	36	96			
110	71	85	98			
111	73	35	97			
112		47	80			
113		85	100	pt. of 215		
114	68			pt. of 215		
115	78			pt. of 215		
116	79a			pt. of 215		
117	6					
118	76			pt. of 215		
119	79			pt. of 215		

Doc.	HTC	Winston pp.	Drexel fols.	1876 S.C.	1905 S.C.	Other
120		6–9	101	172	689	Hist. Soc. Pa. & Folger
121				171		Harvard
122	55	63–64	136			
123	20					
124		5–6	121	170		Folger
125		56–57	107	209		Vanbrugh, *Works*, from
126		19	108	175?		Hyde Collection
127				211		
128		10–11	110	pt. of 214		Private Collection
129		12	111	pt. of 214		Private Collection
130				175		
131		12	112	212		
132		17	113	177		William W. Appleton
133		30–32	103 fol.		717	
134		44	115	210	711	
135		20–21	116	178		Morgan
136		21–23	109	176		
137		14–15	117	211?	716?	
138		13	120			
139		13	118	173		
140		14	120		713	
141	78	18	"102"			
142		15–16	119	192		
143		48	114	186	693	Broadley
144			138			
145			139–40			
146	19					
147		34	130	189		
148	41					
149				195	700	
150	33	61–63	following 151			
151	32	57–59	133			
152	30					
153				200	705?	

A few general remarks are in order. No very exact canon of "Coke theatrical papers" can be established. We have treated as "missing" anything enumerated in the 1876 sale catalogue for which we cannot find a text. All Winston transcriptions seem definitely to have come from Lamb's "Coke papers," but the compiler of the New York Public Library manuscript was much more eclectic. Most of his additions are from printed sources, but in two instances (documents 144 and 145) we have incorporated letters unique to that manuscript. Omission of a document by the two transcribers tells us nothing in itself. Neither attempted to copy French or Italian items; neither cared to grapple with orchestra rosters; and both shied away from numerical matters. Both seem to have copied somewhat randomly. Dates in the 1876 sale catalogue are so erratic that we cannot always be certain whether we have a particular document. Some items may have slipped out of the collection even before 1876. Document 7, for example, is recognizable in the 1849 sale catalogue, but does not appear in 1876 and is not in the papers which got to Harvard. Conversely, a few papers may well have been added along the way. Lamb's gleanings were certainly only a fraction of the theatrical papers which passed through his great-grandfather's hands between 1706 and 1727. Consequently we have not hesitated to add an item if it is obviously appropriate. Document 29 is an example—a letter from Vanbrugh to Coke now in another collection at Harvard. It was not copied by either nineteenth-century transcriber, and it is not in the 1876 sale catalogue, but it is directly related to Coke theatrical papers of January 1708, and to exclude it on canonical grounds would be silly. The chances are certainly very good that some of the documents which have continued to elude us are still extant, and we can only hope that the publication of this edition will someday help bring these and other relevant papers to light.

Finally, a legend should be laid to rest. A large part of W. H. Cummings' library went to the Nanki Music Library in Tokyo, and because Harvard's ownership of the reduced collection was long unpublicized, the story went out among scholars that the Coke papers had gone to Japan and been destroyed by bombing during World War II. This is, obviously, entirely untrue. (The story was probably fed by confusion with a fact—the British Library copy of the 1925 Nanki Library catalogue was destroyed during the blitz.) As recently as 1966 Mollie Sands could say of Cummings' Coke that "the present whereabouts of this collection is unknown."[32]

Editorial Policy

Our overall objective has been to create a readable documentary history of English theatre and opera during the period 1706–15. To this end we have dated as many of the papers as we could, set them in chronological order, and subdivided them into seasons, with a general explanatory headnote for each season.

32. Sands, "Mrs. Tofts."

Whenever possible, we have of course used the original document as our copy-text. Where we lack an original we have used Winston (British Library Add. MS 38,607), but we have checked his transcription against New York Public Library Drexel MS 1986, and we have occasionally adopted readings from the latter. All such variations from copy-text are recorded in the notes.

Spelling, punctuation, and capitalization of the original documents have been retained, with certain exceptions. We have felt free to insert a period and follow it with a capital where there is unmistakably a change of sentence and there is no punctuation at all. Raised letters have been lowered (except in French and Italian documents), and most abbreviations have been silently expanded. Thus "S^r" becomes "Sir" and "combina$\overline{con}$" becomes "combination." We have retained ampersand, Mr, Esq, and a few other conventional abbreviations—for example, 2d, 4ly, &ca, and tho'. We have transcribed "ye" literally because some of these writers use the form as distinct from "the," but in the few cases where the thorn is definitely used (y^t) we have rendered it "th." Abbreviations in names have been retained. We have allowed a word like "reservd" to stand, rather than treating it as an abbreviation. We have, however, followed copy literally when quoting a printed source—for example, Vanbrugh's *Letters*—except that we have silently lowered superscript letters.

We have regularized pound signs, printing "£" before the sum in question rather than preserving "*l*" and "*ll*" which are often raised, given with a line through them, and so forth, in the originals. We have also silently regularized the use of dashes and colons in columns of figures when the writer's inconsistency seemed both pointless and confusing (for example, in document 10). We have endeavored to follow the capitalization of the originals faithfully, though where size of the letters rather than their form is the determinant there are inevitably some awkward borderline cases.

Where we have qualms about the accuracy of our reading we have indicated our uncertainty with "reading doubtful" in the textual notes. Unfamiliar names can be particularly treacherous in this respect, and mangled names represent a further complication. "Mr cha" is evidently Mr Shaw, but is "Mi^s staf" Mrs Tofts? When we are not sure whether to read "Mr^s orm" or "Mr sorin" we have simply said so.

Brackets in the originals—[   ]—have been made parentheses, and brackets reserved for editorial interpolations. All documents in foreign languages are given in exact and uncorrected form, followed by a fairly literal translation. A few numerical doodles have been omitted, but only when we have bee unable to make any sense at all of them, and the omission is noted in each case. In a few instances when a manuscript contains verticals—for example, "trebles" written sideways against a list of musicians—we have silently rearranged them as horizontal subheads. Braces—for example those used to group musicians—have been carefully preserved.

All document titles have been supplied by the editors. The date which follows the title is editorial if in brackets, from the original if in parentheses. Textual problems are indicated by note symbols in the text, and explanations will be found following the document in question. In almost all instances canceled words or phrases have been removed from the text, and recorded in these separate textual notes. In a few cases, however, clarity seemed better served by showing the canceled passage in place in the text (for example, document 56). Cancellations in the nineteenth-century transcriptions are not recorded.

Prior to the text of each document we have included information from the back of the sheet or sheets. Coke—or his clerk—made a systematic practice of writing an identification for filing purposes on the backs of letters. "[Cover] Mr Swiney" means that the back of the item is annotated "Mr Swiney." Such cover annotations are in Hand A (discussed below) unless otherwise specified. "[Direction] To Mr Coke at St. James's Palace" means that the writer has written this direction on the outside of the folded sheet.

Under "Copy-text" we have explained in each instance what texts are available, and noted inclusion in the 1876 and 1905 sale catalogues. We have also provided for all original documents an indication of the handwriting. Analysis of the various hands represented in the Coke papers has helped us to identify some unsigned documents; it also helps to clarify the workings of the Vice Chamberlain's office.

Considered in terms of origin, we have four sorts of documents here. (1) Letters which were written by individuals in their own behalf (for example, Mrs Tofts, Nicolini). For the most part these are signed, and they come in a great variety of hands. They are often unique samples in this collection, and without an authenticated example of the individual's handwriting we cannot be certain that we are dealing with a holograph. (2) Letters and documents drawn up at one of the playhouses by a manager or one of his deputies. The identified writers include Christopher Rich, Vanbrugh, Swiney, Haym, and Collier. The deputies tend to be anonymous and unidentifiable. At least four members of the Haymarket staff supplied documents of particular sorts—for example, on matters having to do with the orchestra. (3) Letters or documents originating elsewhere which were copied by Coke or a clerk in the Vice Chamberlain's office, the original probably getting passed on to the Lord Chamberlain. (4) Letters and documents originating in Coke's office. Two distinctive hands recur in the office papers—evidently Coke's and Sir John Stanley's. The cover annotations normally appear to be in one of these hands, but since two or three words hastily scribbled for filing purposes make a poor sample for positive identification, we have simply dubbed them Hand A and Hand B in these instances. The recurring anonymous hands are as follows:

Hand A: probably Coke
Hand B: probably Stanley
Hand C: a clerk at the Haymarket box office
Hand D: a clerk or musician who reported orchestra rosters
Hand E: a clerk who was secretary to the Haymarket managers, perhaps the head office keeper or the prompter
Hand F: probably the dancer Desbarques—or another Frenchman reporting on dancers in 1708

The 1876 sale catalogue makes some very confident pronouncements about handwriting, as do some of the scholars who have worked with the manuscripts, Cummings in particular. A number of the manuscripts have penciled ascriptions (for example, "autograph of Owen Swiney") on them. All of these sources are so demonstrably unreliable that in the main we have simply ignored them.

In annotating the documents we have tried to be helpful without becoming prolix. We have given each document a "Comment" explaining its significance, discussing any special problems, and giving the basis for the date if we have assigned it. In a few instances we have added "interdocuments" where something outside the Coke papers seems particularly illuminating in conjunction with them. In supplying explanatory notes we have kept biographical matter to a minimum, especially where performers are concerned. With the *Biographical Dictionary* rapidly coming into print there seems to be no point in giving brief biographical sketches here. The bulk of the annotation has been devoted to other identifications, clarification of playhouse practices, and references to relevant material outside the present edition.

Vice
Chamberlain
Coke's
Theatrical Papers
1706–1715

SEASON OF

1705–1706

The season of 1705–6 saw heated competition between "Betterton's Company" (now under the direction of John Vanbrugh) and the Patent Company run by Christopher Rich. Vanbrugh had opened his fancy new Haymarket theatre in a semifinished state in April 1705, and after a summer back at Lincoln's Inn Fields his company found its new quarters complete. Rich spurned Vanbrugh's urgent proposals for a union of the two acting companies in June and July 1705; his success with *Arsinoe*—the first Italian opera staged in London—in the spring of 1705 doubtless encouraged him to think that he could stave off any challenge Vanbrugh might mount. Conversely the success of *Arsinoe* (originally to have been a Haymarket production) must have spurred Vanbrugh to answer opera with opera. He tried three, in varying styles. Granville's *The British Enchanters* (February 1706) was a fair success in the old English semiopera genre; *The Temple of Love*, an Italianate opera, failed in March, as did Durfey's *Wonders in the Sun* (April), a unique and peculiar extravaganza. Rich answered with a single opera, but a highly and lastingly successful one—*Camilla* (March).[1] The appearance of four new operas in the course of a single season was unprecedented in the history of the London theatre, and it is testimony to the rapidly increasing importance of music and concerts in the London entertainment world. Both companies found themselves embroiled in legal disputes with prima donna singers.[2] What is startling in this litigation is the sums involved: singers were trying to demand between £10 and £20 for each performance. Up to about this time the annual salary for a senior actor or actress had been between £80 and £150.

By 3 December 1706 Thomas Coke had become Vice Chamberlain of Her Majesty's household. His interest in music is reflected in the only three documents we possess for this season—all notes from Haym about private concerts he was arranging at Coke's house.

I

1. For Haym's contract with Rich for *Camilla* (dated 14 January 1706) see LC 7/3, fols. 86–87. For £100 Haym was to provide copies of the score and parts using an English translation made at Rich's expense, advise Rich on casting the opera and help rehearse it, and provide and perform other Italian music. The contract also specified that he would not assist the company in the Haymarket but would work to further Rich's interests.

2. See LC 7/3, fols. 89–90, for Haym's dispute with Vanbrugh and Congreve over money owed to "the Baroness," and fol. 88 for Dieupart's report of Mrs Tofts' claims against Rich.

1. Haym to Coke about a Private Concert

[Cover] Nicolini Hayams April 18th 1706.   (18 April 1706)
[Direction] to Mr Cook These

Sir

    Mr Ramondon, and ye Boy[1] cannot come to Night before ye Play is done[2] and if you Think that will be to Late you may have ye Baroness[3] to begin with her songs, and I am assurèd she will be very willing to serve you; but I wou'd not speak to her, before you send me word: I shall wait upon you to Night exactly at Nine. I am &c

Bow Street ye 18th of April   Sir
                                                           Your Most Obliging and
                                                           Obedient Servant
                                                           NICOLINO HAYM

Copy-text: HTC Coke 25 (Haym holograph). For nineteenth-century transcriptions see Winston, pp. 98–99, and Drexel MS, fol. 24. This letter was probably part of lot 184 in the 1876 sale catalogue.

Comment: Like documents 2 and 3 this is a note from Haym to Coke about arrangements for a private concert.

1. "The Boy" was advertised as such by Drury Lane this season. His identity is not certain, but he may well be the singer Henry Holcomb (fl. 1706–10), who was advertised as "the late Boy" at Dorset Garden on 1 November 1706.

2. The 1699 operatic form of *The Island Princess* was performed this day at Drury Lane, "With all the Original Songs and Dialogues," starting at 5:30.

3. Stage name of Joanna Maria Lindelheim, a protégée of Haym's who sang in London between 1703 and 1717.

2. Haym to Coke about Concert Performers

[Cover] Nicolini Hayams April 21st 1706.   (21 April 1706)
[Direction] To Mr Coke These

Sir
   This is to Let you know that Signora Margherita¹ desires the favour you wou'd pardon her for tomarow Morning she cannot come to you because she is obligèd to Learn ye part of Camilla by heart for Tuesday next.² I desire a further directions from you, to know wether I shall bring Mr Pepush a Long with me, and if it is necessary for me to find any Violins, or any Voice, and I assure you I shall ever be ready to obey your commands —

Bow Street ye 21th of April 1706   Sir
                                                     Your Most humble and
                                                     obbedient servant
                                                     NICOLINO HAYM

   Copy-text: HTC Coke 26 (Haym holograph). For nineteenth-century transcriptions see Winston, p. 83, and Drexel MS, fol. 25. This letter was probably part of lot 184 in the 1876 sale catalogue.

1. Margherita de l'Epine (usually spelled "Margarita" in these papers).

2. *Camilla* was performed at Drury Lane on Tuesday 23 April, and again on Tuesday 30 April. Haym's phrase could refer to either performance. The opera had received its premiere on 30 March with the temperamental Catherine Tofts as Camilla. Why de l'Epine was replacing Tofts on short notice we do not know, but Tofts was apparently not performing in May and early June. On 14 June Drury Lane advertised *Arsinoe* with "Mrs Tofts performing her own part," and the next performance of *Camilla* (5 July) was advertised with Mrs Tofts billed for the title role—something normally done at this time only when a change of cast was involved.

3. Haym to Coke about Plans for a Concert

[Cover] May 6th 1706   (6 May 1706)
[Direction] To Mr Coke These

Sir

    I have finishd the Ode of discord,[1] That you Commanded me to set to Musick, and I have tought it Mr Leveridge, and we were ready to Come and perform it at your house on Fryday Last; When Mr Pepusch told me, not to go; and Therefore I write this to desire the favour of you, if you please to Let me know what day will be most proper for us to wait upon you. The Wiolins part being very difficult, I beleive it will be necessary That Mr Gasperini shoud play ye first, and Mr Corbett ye second. I attend your Commands, and I remain &

London ye 6th of May 1706

                                       Sir
                                       Your very humble servant
                                       NICOLINO HAYM

    Copy-text: HTC Coke 27 (Haym holograph). This letter may have been part of lot 184 in the 1876 sale catalogue.

1. Unidentified.

SEASON OF
1706–1707

The unprofitable season of 1705–6 left Vanbrugh more anxious than ever for a union. Congreve had dropped out of the management of the Haymarket by December 1705, commenting that he had been "dipt."[1] In April 1706 he wrote to his friend Joseph Keally: "I believe the Play house cannot go on another Winter. Have heard there is to be a Union of the two houses as well as Kingdoms."[2] On 26 April the Duke of Montagu wrote to Lord Halifax, who was about to embark on a diplomatic mission, "Mr Vanbrooke, who is to waite of you to Hannover will perhaps delay his Journey as longe as he can . . . [because] he is now upon making an agreement betweene the two playhouses."[3] The *Poetical Courant* contains "A Prologue on the propos'd Union of the two Play-Houses," the British Library copy of which is dated in MS 22 June.[4] Efforts to promote a union evidently continued all summer. On 3 September the Newdigate Newsletter reported (inaccurately) that "her Majtie has ordered all her Servants belonging to the severall Play-houses to act in conjunction with those at the Haymarket."[5] Failing to achieve a union, Vanbrugh evidently changed his strategy and tried to arrange a genre split of the sort actually decreed in December 1708–but with the important difference that opera would have been confined to Drury Lane, plays to the Haymarket. (See documents 4 and 5 and the interdocument which follows.) Rich again balked, but eventually he acquiesced in a peculiar compromise partially described by Congreve in a 10 September letter. "The play-houses have undergone another revolution; and Swinny, with Wilks, Mrs Olfield, Pinkethman, Bullock, and Dicky ["Jubilee Dicky" Norris], are come over to the Hay-Market. . . . My Lord Chamberlain [Kent] approves and ratifies the desertion; and the design is, to have plays only at the Hay-Market, and operas only at Covent Garden."[6] What Congreve does not make plain is that in the event the augmented Haymarket company was enjoined from using adjunct musical performers even in entr'actes, but Drury Lane re-

5

tained the right to put on plays. The harried Vanbrugh appointed Owen Swiney manager at his theatre as of 14 August (see the interdocument of that date), and the rearrangement of September 1706 was evidently a trade-off fixed by Rich and Swiney: the Haymarket would give up music to Drury Lane in exchange for most of Rich's best actors. As Cibber tells us, Rich's "Notion was that Singing and Dancing, or any sort of Exotick Entertainments, would make an ordinary Company of Actors too hard for the best Set who had only plain Plays to subsist on." [7]

The two houses operated on these strange terms for a season and a half. When the Haymarket company wanted to mount its operatic success, *The British Enchanters*, it had to do so without singing and dancing—eliciting a protest from the outraged author (see document 7). The transfer of personnel created a squeeze at the Haymarket. Thus we find old George Bright in debtors prison, and his long-time colleagues in no hurry to extricate him (document 6). A note in PRO LC 7/3, fols. 94–95, tells us that John Downes, prompter since the 1660s, was forced out in this reorganization—but at least the management was willing to grant him a pension. During this season the Haymarket ran profitably with straight plays, while Rich appears to have enjoyed a tolerably good year relying largely on added musical attractions and operas. *Camilla* proved a sturdy prop, and Rich tried two new operas. The Addison-Clayton *Rosamond* in March was a failure, but Heidegger's production of *Thomyris* the next month was a solid success. Three of our documents for this season concern the financial details of that production.

1. *Letters & Documents*, no. 22.
2. Ibid., no. 23.
3. Drexel MS 1986, fol. 10 (nineteenth-century transcription). Ralph, Duke of Montagu (1638–1709), was reporting what Sarah, Duchess of Marlborough, had told him that morning. Charles Montagu, Baron, later Earl, of Halifax (1661–1715), had reformed the currency in 1695 while Lord Treasurer. He was one of the original subscribers to the Haymarket theatre building.
4. See Price, "The Critical Decade," p. 55, n. 60.
5. John Harold Wilson, "Theatre Notes from the Newdigate Newsletters," *Theatre Notebook*, 15 (1961), 79–84.
6. *Letters & Documents*, no. 26. "Covent Garden" here is Drury Lane.
7. *Apology*, I, 335.

INTERDOCUMENT.
Agreement between Vanbrugh and Swiney

August ye 14th 1706

Memorandum

That with the Consent and Approbation of the Right Honourable the Earl of Kent, Lord Chamberlain of Her Majestys Houshold, it is agreed between Mr Vanbrugh and Mr Swiny

That Mr Vanbrugh shall put into the Hands of Mr Swiny the Direction and Government of the Queens Company of Actors in Her Majestys Theatre in the Haymarket, for the Space of Seaven Years, commencing from the date hereof.

That Mr Swiny shall likewise have the free use of all the Stock Tho' without power of Selling, or disposing of any Part of it, Otherwise than for the Use of the Company. And at the Termination of the said Seaven Years, Mr Vanbrugh shall be entituled to the Stock, in the Condition it then shall be.

That Mr Swiny shall receive for his Own Use and Benefit, the whole and Entire clear Profits, that shall be made.

That Mr Swiny shall have the Power of receiving into the Company, Such Actors as he shall think fitt; But shall not discharge any of them without the Consent of the Lord Chamberlain.

That in consideration of this Power resign'd to Mr Swiny together with the Use of the House and Stock, He shall pay to Mr Vanbrugh, Five Pounds every day there shall be a Play Acted by the said Company during the Abovemention'd Term, either in London Oxford or else where.

That the said Five pounds shall be every Night deducted by the Treasurer out of the Receipts, preferable to any Other Charge, And paid by him weekly to Mr Vanbrugh.

That all Taxes and Repairs whatever, shall be paid by Mr Vanbrugh.

That the Ground Rent, (being fifty pounds per Annum) shall be paid by Mr Swiny; but he shall have the Advantage of the Fruit-money.

That if at any time there happens a Dispute, upon the meaning and Intention of any of these Articles, it shall be referr'd to the Decision of the Lord Chamberlain. And it is our Humble Request to his Lordship, that this Book may be kept in his Lordships Office, in the Custody of the Secretary.

J VANBRUGH
OWEN SWINY

Copy-text: PRO LC 7/2, fol. 1, scribal copy signed by Vanbrugh and Swiney.

4. Draft of an Order for Genre Separation

[ca. August 1706] [1]

[Cover]   Play house
          Order of Separation

Whereas by ye division of ye Comedians into two distinct Companys it has been found that the players have not suficient subsistence for their Encouragement & that the Plays are not always acted to ye best advantage And whereas the charge of maintaining Comedians & performers of Operas in the same house is now * become too great to be continued Therefore for the better regulation & support of ye Theatres [2] I do hereby order & require That for the future all Opera's & other Musicall Entertainments & dancing only att the Theatre in Drury lane or Dorsett garden [3] under ye Direction of ye Managers thereof with leave to receive & Employ any performers in Musick Dancing &ca they shall judge necessary and do hereby strictly charge & forbid ye Managers of ye said Theatres hereafter to represent any Comedies Tragedies or other Theatrical Entertainments that are not sett to Musick *upon pain of being silenced for breach of this my order*
    I doe hereby like wise give leave to the Managers of her Majesties Theatre in ye Haymarkett to recieve admitt & Entertain any Players & Actors of Tragedy or Comedy *&ca* tho they were before Entertaind in ye Play house att Drury lane &ca att the same time strictly charging & requiring them not to perform any Musicall Entertainments &ca upon the stage or to recieve into their service † any Dancers or performers in Musick other then such Instrumentall musick as are not Employ'd in ye Operas & are necessary for such Entertainments, [4] *upon ye like pain of being silencd for breach of this order*
    Given under our hand & seal

    * *now*: the underlining—here indicated by italics—is in the original ink, here and in the instances below.
    † *service*: word supplied from catchword.

Copy-text: HTC Coke 10 (Hand A). For nineteenth-century transcriptions see Winston, p. 45, and Drexel MS, fol. 50.

Comment: This document appears to be a draft version of the Lord Chamberlain's order for a new union of acting companies, finally issued 31 December 1707 (PRO LC 5/154, pp. 299–300, printed as an interdocument below). That order is substantively identical to this one, with a single major difference: Kent there assigns opera to the Haymarket, plays to the Drury Lane/Dorset Garden company. The date of the present draft is uncertain, but we are inclined to place it in August 1706—after Vanbrugh's efforts to arrange a union had failed, but before the completion of the partial actor transfer and compromise described by Congreve in his letter of 10 September (quoted in the headnote for this season).[5] A much-corrected initial draft in Hand B is preserved in LC 7/3, fol. 178.

1. On the dating problems, see the Comment.
2. What appears to be "Vide past" is written in the left margin at this point. The second word might be "Pat⁺": Winston reads "Patent." The transcriber of the Drexel MS ignores the marginalia.
3. "Qv[?] Lincolns in field" is written in the left margin. The reading of the first two letters is doubtful. The Lincoln's Inn Fields theatre had been vacant since 20 October 1705. A clearer meaning is obtained if the doubtful letters are read as "Or"—which in any case is probably the sense of the annotation. The earlier draft in LC 7/3 lists a third theatre at this point, "Little [Lincoln's Inn Fields?]." The page is torn in half at "Little."
4. I.e., to play "act music."
5. "1710 . . . Owen Swiney . . , Nov 6" has been penciled in the upper left hand margin of the first page in a twentieth-century hand. This date is incorrect: for the order of 6 November 1710, see the interdocument at that date below.

5. Vanbrugh's Justification for Denying Rich the Right to Produce Plays

[ca. August 1706]

If any body shou'd endeavour to possess the Queen That the Persons concern'd in the Patent (besides Mr Rich) wou'd be prejudic'd by an establishment That shou'd confine acting to one house, and musick to tother. It is so evidently otherwise That 'tis the only means left to Restore 'em to any advantage, for the money they have in that adventure; as will beyond all Contest appear when it is observ'd.

That in twelve years past,[1] That Mr Rich has had the management in his hands. (tho' 'tis notorious he has spent Vast sums himself) he has not divided to those concern'd with him, one single shilling.

That he own'd last year, he lost by his Players, what he got by his Opera;[2]

and by Consequence, his desire of keeping 'em on, can be for nothing, but to confound and embroil the Accounts and give him a Pretence to make no Dividend

That if he has the Opera single & Entire The Proffit must be so Certain, and the accounts will ly in so short and plain a Compass; That twill be impossible for him to deceive the People any Longer who have Claims to a share with him

Whereas; If he go's on, in this Confus'd jumble, of a Double Company, There is no manner of Reason to believe, They'll fare any better for twelve years to Come, Than they have done for twelve years Past.

Memorandum

To put Mr Riches design of Cheating the rest of the adventurers out of all question: There was an offer made him in August was twelve month,[3] to put the Whole thing into his hands, and He refus'd it. owning very frankly that 'twas better for him to have it as 'twas to himself; than by restoring the Patent to its former Condition to let in the Others to govern & share with him.

This may be prov'd upon Oath

Copy-text: LC 7/3, fols. 179–80 (Vanbrugh holograph, unsigned). Nine-teenth-century transcriptions exist in Winston, pp. 59–60, and Drexel MS, fol. 84, which must have been made from another version of this statement no longer part of the collection—most probably an office copy made for or by Coke, who passed the original on to the Lord Chamberlain. This document is here attributed to Vanbrugh for the first time.

Comment: This statement, in what appears to be Vanbrugh's hand, is evidently connected with his proposal for a genre split in September 1706 on terms which would have left opera to Drury Lane. Rich successfully opposed such an arrangement, retaining the rights to both forms. Vanbrugh's impression of the money to be made on operas came partly from the comparison reported in this document. Rich had avoided paying company shareholders since the actors' rebellion of 1694–95, claiming that there were no profits. In 1704 a group of shareholders led by Sir Edward Smith had brought suit against Rich, charging long-standing concealment of profits by systematic fraud. The case was apparently never resolved.[4] But profits made on operas financed by subscription would, according to the argument advanced in this document, be harder to conceal.

1. I.e., since the 1694–5 season. Rich actually assumed financial control of the United Company in December 1693, but Vanbrugh is evidently referring to the twelve seasons which have elapsed since the fragmentation of the company in the autumn of 1694.
2. A reference to the great success of *Camilla* in the 1705–6 season, and perhaps to *Thomyris*, for which a subscription of 1200 guineas had been collected in advance (see document 8 below).
3. I.e., in August 1705. We have no information about the precise nature of this proposal, which is entirely different from the terms reportedly proposed by Vanbrugh in June 1705, according to Gildon's *The Post-Boy Robb'd of His-Mail* (1706). For discussion, see Milhous, *Thomas Betterton*, pp. 201–3.
4. See PRO C8/599/74 and Milhous, *Thomas Betterton*, chapter 6.

INTERDOCUMENT.
Letter from Owen Swiney to Colley Cibber

Saturday Night October 5th 1706.

Dear Colley

I undertook the management of the playhouse in the Haymarkett by and with the advice of some who were Mr Rich's best friends but incensed against him because he trifled with 'em about Vanbrugh's businesse, he never really intending any thing (but the gaining of time) by the treaty, his old play. Well Whats that to me youl say— why I'll tell thee puppy. Know then that Rich was to make a union of the houses and I was to manage under him My Angel at 100 Guineas per annum Salary & I was to have a place at court and the Devil and all you know, upon this I quitted my post in the Army. In about a fortnights time after this I found that Mr Rich intended nothing but the going on his old way of paying Singers and dancers & not paying the Actors, I did not think it was my Interest to be Concerned on the wrong side, since I had no obligation to stay with Mr Rich, he discharging me of my promise the minute he broke of with Vanbrugh. Further my Angel I thought if I had reason to complain now I was not in his power I thought it wou'd be too late to seek redresse when ever I shou'd be so unlucky as to fall into his hands for you must know my Dear that Rich is as tyrannycall as Lewis Le Grand, and I have as many grievances to complain off as Prince Ragotzki,[1] I thought the best way of doing my selfe right was to take up Arms and declare for the liberty of the Actors who were oppressed by Singers and dancers (Jesuits of a play house). And I think I shall be as successfull as my Brother Princes who turn out another upon the pretence of Mal administration and secure themselves a greater power. But to be serious I will Exhibit a few Articles against my Late Soveraign viz.

1 He sent for me from my Quarters in the North, I was at a great charge in coming to town and you know it cost me a great deal of mony last winter, I served him night and day, nay all night and all day, for Nine Months. He sent me forty pound by Jack Hall[2] as a return for my vast services, I bid him carry back the mony to his Master with a bill of Jobs or porterage to whites Chocolate house, Lord Whartons, Mr Manwarings, & Mr Boyles, which at 2d a jobb came to above £50 13s and 4d.

2 It was impossible for him to have had the Opera of Camilla without me, he told me if I coud get a Subscription he woud give me £100 50. to be disposed off to a gentleman that was concern'd in the writing it, the other for the Industrious Mr Swiny. I applyd to Lord Wharton and his Grace of Richmond, the Subscription was gott and Rich told me in the Winter he woud let me have a part of a benefit from the performance of it one day, he not being in a Condition to keep his word with me tho' he received 1400. Guineas for it besides the Gallerys that time that the subscription was got by my Lord Wharton was for the Scotch Nobility. Item for a great parcell of Ill language at several times and places, but that I think he never got the better of me at Except when Collonel Brett was by. Successe will determine who is in the right.

I did design to have communicated this matter to you as soon as you came from Windsor and was with Mr Wilks at your house the thursday friday Saturday Sunday & Monday before the businesse was discovered, It was to have been kept Secret a fortnight longer till I had gott the people I had pitcht upon among whom was Mr Cibber among the Betterton's Wilks's Barry's &c the paper delivered to My Lord Chamberlain will be my Voucher, his Lordship was big of the plot and was afraid if any body shou'd let it be known at Court before him, he shou'd be Robbed of the glory of Establishing the Stage upon a foot of going on, he told it at the Dutchesse of Malbro's the same day Wilks & Oldfield signed and if I had not been pretty brisk the whole matter might have miscarried, for on Monday Mills Bullock Keen Newman & Norris Signed, so that you may see I had no such mean design of lowering the Actors or starving 'em into a compliance with me, I am satisfied that it can't be worse with the Actors any where than where they were as to their Salary, And to show you that I have a very great regard for Mr Cibber he shall be welcome to me when he sees which side is strongest tho' it shou'd be ours. Estcourt must be had tho' he has addrest Mr Rich. I think your first question is answered. As to your Second Mr Rich might have had the house for £3 or £3 10s a day. I have taken a lease for 7: yeares at £5 per day. I think your second is reasonably well answered. I have given every Actor greater Salarys than Rich did and most of 'em benefits paying * £40 charge. Now I've here yours answered, if you have any difficulties upon your mind if I can ease you by answering I will. I shall begin on tuesday 7: night and play the Earle of Essex or the spanish Fryar.[3] The Bellman has frightened me out of some other things which you shall have when I hear from you, My Duty to my Coll[4] and most humble respects in the most obliging manner you can to Madam[5] Brett Mr Brent &c

Unbeliever thine
OWEN SWINY.

* *paying*: MS reads "playing."

Copy-text: Holograph letter in the Osborn Collection, Yale University.

1. Francis Rakoczy II, Prince of Hungary, had been encouraged by Louis XIV to annoy the Emperor by demanding independence for Transylvania. France, however, failed to produce the subsidies that might have made Rakoczy an effective eastern ally. See Imre Lukinich, *A History of Hungary in Biographical Sketches* (1937; rpt. Freeport: Books for Libraries Press, 1968), pp. 176–80. Swiney is complaining that his mentor, Rich, has not fulfilled promises to him.
2. Possibly the John Hall mentioned in a *Daily Courant* ad 7 September 1708.
3. The Haymarket opened Tuesday 15 October 1706 with *The Spanish Fryar*.
4. Evidently Col. Henry Brett.
5. Reading of abbreviation doubtful, but the reference is probably to Brett's wife Ann, divorced wife of the Earl of Macclesfield, whom Brett had married in 1700.

6. George Bright's Petition

[Cover] Brights Petition [Fall 1706]

To the Honorable Henry Boyle Esquire[1] Chancellor of her Majesties Exchequer &c

The Humble Pettition of George Bright, Comedian—
Sheweth That your Petitioner being a Comedian, has for about 27 years belonged to Dorsett Garden, Drury Lane, Lincolns-Inn Fields, & ye Hay: Markett Theatres,[2] & that playing severall parts after Mr Noaks, & Mr Leigh, he became a Sharer in Lincolns-Inn Fields Theatre, & by ye Comand of ye Most Noble Henry Marquiss of Kent, Lord Chamberlaine of her Majesties Household, he went to performe at the Theatre in ye Hay-Markett, Where it was agreed your Petitioner should have 40s per weeke, tho' under pretence of ye Insufficiency of ye Receipts he was offten paid noe

more than 6s:8d per weeke, By reason whereof your Petitioner to support himselfe & family was forced to Contract severall Debts, for which he was arrested & Confined in ye Marshalsea Prison about 8 weeks, During all which time he Received noe Subsistance from ye Playhouse, his pay being Stopt by reason of such his Confinement (which never was done to any Actor in ye like Case;) During this his Confinement One Miles[3] with an Attorny brought an Instrument (in writing) to your Petitioner desireing him to joine with ye other Sharers in ye Sale of ye Cloaths & other Ornaments to Captain Vanbrugh for £500;[4] which if your Petitioner refused to Execute, they had orders to carry back ye mony they brought with them, and leave your Petitioner in Prison, (Altho' that mony was a Collection from all the Actors in Generall, & not a Tenth part from ye Sharers which did belong to ye Theatre in Lincolns-Inn Fields, But withall to Encourage your Petitioner; Acquainted him there would be more mony coming.

Whereupon your Petitioner to Obtaine his Enlargement did Execute ye Instrument But notwithstanding they have not paid him one penny since, And (Altho' your Petitioner is well Qualified to doe his business) have dismist him without any Cause alleadged; to his & his families Utter ruine.

In consideration whereof your Petitioner most humbly prayes your Honor of your great goodness & Charity to ye Distressed, will please to Interceade with ye Most Noble ye Lord Chamberlaine of her Majesties Household, that his Lordship will direct, As well ye Speedy payment of ye Arrears due to him for his Sallary, as his Reestablishment in his former business, Your Petitioner haveing delivered a Petition to his Lordship to ye same Effect.

And your Petitioner as in Duty bound shall ever pray, &c—

Copy-text: HTC Coke 37 (scribal fair copy). For nineteenth-century transcriptions see Winston, pp. 3–4, and Drexel MS, fol. 70.

Comment: This document must date from after April 1705, since Bright has been acting at the Haymarket. In his letter of 20 November 1713 (document 125 below) Vanbrugh implies that he bought the stock of scenery and costumes for £500 immediately upon the move from Lincoln's Inn Fields. However the use of John Mills as emissary implies a date after September 1706. The authors of the *Biographical Dictionary* (II, 340) date this document "probably . . . 1707–8," but Cibber tells us that the actors were—for a wonder—paid their full salaries in 1706–7 at the Haymarket (*Apology*, I, 336). We would conclude that old Bright got into debt during the bad season of 1705–6, and that after the influx of actors from Drury Lane in September

1706 the Haymarket company found no further use for him. Bright's only known appearance in London after 1705 was in Taverner's *The Maid's the Mistress* in June 1708. In a letter ostensibly addressed to the *Tatler* (i.e., 1709–10) Gildon tells us that "Mr. *Bright* . . . has been subject to the evil Fortunes of all great States, is fall'n into Banishment, and stroles about for a Living."[5]

1. Henry Boyle, Baron Carleton (d. 1725), was Chancellor of the Exchequer from 1701 to 1708. Why Bright appealed to him we do not know.
2. Bright's first known role in London was in *Troilus and Cressida* with the Duke's Company in April 1679. He acted with the United Company throughout its existence, and moved to Lincoln's Inn Fields as a sharer with the rebels in 1695.
3. Presumably John Mills, who came over to the Haymarket from Rich's Company in the reorganization of September 1706. Using him as an emissary seems particularly heartless: evidently Bright's long-time colleagues did not care to face him in person with this piece of blackmail.
4. For details of the sale of the scenery to Vanbrugh see document 125 below.
5. Charles Gildon, *The Post-Man Robb'd of his Mail* (1719; rpt. New York: Garland, 1972), p. 266.

7. Granville's Request for Suppression of *The British Enchanters*

[Cover] Swiny   [9 December 1706]
[Direction] For the Honorable Sir John Stanley Bart These

Sir;

    I am very much concern'd to find my self under a necessity to bring a Complaint to you, But so it is, that the Players in the Hay-market have put forth Bills for acting the British Enchanters to morrow without singing & dancing mauger the necessity thereof, which I can deem no other than a design to murder the Child of my Brain. Nevertheless when I revolve how happy I am in having so good a friend at Court in a station that gives him so immediate an Autherity over these Enemyes of Reformation, I chear my self with the hopes You will not refuse me a Cap[1] of your office in forbidding the same to be Acted till farther Order and in so doing you will very much oblige

                       Sir Your most humble & obedient servant
                       G GRANVILLE

Cockpit
Monday night

Copy-text: Granville holograph(?) bound into Folger Library V.b. 268, Bishop Gilbert Burnet, *History of His Own Time*, IV, 172–73. For nine-teenth-century transcriptions see Winston, p. 51, and Drexel MS, fol. 134.

Comment: The date of this letter is almost certainly Monday 9 December 1706. In the *Daily Courant* for that day the Haymarket advertised Granville's *The British Enchanters* (premiered in February 1706) for performance Tuesday the 10th, but *Hamlet* was acted instead. We presume that the substitution was a result of the unhappy author's protest to Stanley—who just happened to be Granville's brother-in-law. See *The London Stage*, Part 2, I, 134. The Hay-market was, of course, no longer able to offer singing and dancing. The company did perform Granville's semiopera in March and April 1707, specifying in ads that it would be played "With all the Original Scenes, Machines, and Decorations"—though still, evidently, without singing and dancing. Gran-ville continued to take an active interest in the fortunes of his piece, and over the summer of 1706 he had been busy adding to it. See Elizabeth Handasyde, *Granville the Polite* (London: Oxford Univ. Press, 1933), esp. pp. 96–97.

1. Granville apparently used "Cap" as short for "capias." A writ of capias can be of several sorts, but in modern usage we may say that Granville was asking for an injunc-tion against performance until he had a chance to argue his case.

8. Rich to Coke about Terms for *Thomyris*

[ca. January 1707]

[Cover] Mr Rich his Proposall for Mr Headances * Opera
[in another hand:] & Mr Heidegger

The Subscription to an Opera call'd Thomyris being 200d Guineas a day for fower hundred persons for Six dayes Mr Rich hath offered to have it perform'd at Drury Lane Theatre by the best Singers & Masters & well dress't designing to please the quallity in all things as well as he can & to prevent all differences with Mr Heidegger hath allready Proposed That he nominate two of the Nobility of the Subscribers & Mr Rich two others who will please to appoint the distribution of the Subscription money between Mr Heidegger & Mr Rich as they think reasonable and if such fower persons shall differ in any thing they will please to nominate an Umpire to decide it.

This Proposall hath been Rejected & Mr Rich presst by my Lord Chamberlain to make some other Proposall

Now Mr Rich further Proposes in order to make the Translation of this Medley Opera his own with the Score & parts To lay out 300d Guineas in the Dressing & Decoration of it & for Printed Books for the Subscribers [1] & that Mr Heidegger have all the Subscription money for the 4th day & sixth day it shall be perform'd being 400d Guineas & Mr Rich to have the rest of the money

And in such case Mr Heidegger to deliver the Score & parts to Mr Rich as soon as they shall be finished, a great part of the last Act not being yet done, nor the part for Signor Valentini altered for him

Mr Claytons Opera call'd Rosamond is finished & in all Probability may be [†] perform'd in 3 Weeks time, the parts being getting up by Mr Rich his performers. [2]

Mr Rich procured the Translation & Score of Camilla for less then £200 and he hath provided another Opera [3] which he is told is as good as Camilla for less then £200 and the last may be perform'd assoon or sooner then Mr Heideggers can, unless Mr Rich's singers & performers be hindred in getting of it up to learn up Mr Heideggers

So by this last Proposall Mr Rich Complyes to give more then double for this Opera called Mr Heideggers (which he hath not a good Opinion of) then he gave for Camilla or is to give for the fine Opera which may be ready to be performed next after Mr Claytons

Besides my Lord Chamberlain knows that Mr Rich was in a manner Engag'd in the presence of himselfe & my Lord Hallyfax to perform an Opera written by Mr Congreve & sett by Mr Eccles [4] before ever Mr Heidegger offered his Opera to Mr Rich who thinks himselfe hardly used to putt by other good Bargains meerly for Mr Heideggers Interest & profitt.

---

[*] *Headances*: The writer butchered Heidegger's name throughout this document. The name sometimes seems to read "Headance," sometimes "Headanres" or "Headacres," sometimes "Headames." Winston usually reads it as "Headane." We have followed the practice of the transcriber of the Drexel MS in emending to "Heidegger" throughout the document.

[†] *be*: "finished" was written and canceled after this word.

Copy-text: HTC Coke 47 (unidentified hand similar to Rich's but probably not his; cover annotations in the same hand, with additions in Hand A). For nineteenth-century transcriptions see Winston, pp. 51–53, and Drexel MS, fol. "42" and unnumbered folio following.

Comment: *Thomyris* received its premiere at Drury Lane 1 April 1707. The success of *Camilla* had evidently led to rapid escalation in the financial demands of the people responsible for these "medley operas." Compare Haym's terms with Rich for *Camilla* (discussed in the introduction to the season of 1705–6, n. 1).

1. I.e., libretti to be distributed at the theatre.
2. The Addison-Clayton *Rosamond* was given its premiere 4 March 1707 and died after three nights, betrayed by its music. "Three weeks" sounds overly optimistic. Cf. document 9 (dated 17 January 1707).
3. Identity uncertain, but perhaps *Love's Triumph* (February 1708) or Haym's *Pyrrhus and Demetrius*, which finally received its premiere in December 1708.
4. I.e., *Semele*, which remained unperformed in London until 1972 (Fiske, *English Theatre Music*, p. 38).

9. Heidegger's Terms for *Thomyris*

(17 January 1707)

I desire the whole receipts of the House without any deduction of the 3d and the sixt day of acting Thomyris and besides the 10. and the twentieth day paying the Charges of the House for which i give to Mr Rich the above said opera of Thomyris with all the parts drawn out and renounce any further advantage. January the 17th 1707

J J HEIDEGGER

Copy-text: Winston, p. 84. This note is item 185 in the 1876 sale catalogue. For another transcription see Drexel MS, fol. "41."

Comment: For the terms proposed by Rich, see document 8. Roger Fiske notes that most of the music was selected from the works of Scarlatti and Bononcini; recitatives were composed by Pepusch; a story and English words to fit the tunes were provided by Motteux.[1] Yet Heidegger is demanding payment far in excess of the usual author's benefits for himself. What Heidegger finally got out of Rich we do not know.

1. Fiske, *English Theatre Music*, p. 48.

10. Valentini's Bill for Costume Sundries in Connection with *Thomyris*

[Cover] M. Valentine   [ca. April 1707]
      £25:5:3
       0:12:0
      £25:17:3

Mémoire pour Mons.̣ Valentine pour la Royale Amazone:[1]

	£	sh	d
Pour 11. Verges 3/4 de satin couleur de cerise, à 3. Chelins et 9p la Verge	2:	4:	0
Pour 11. Verges et 1/2 de Satin Jaune à 4. chell et 6p	2:	11:	9
pour le canevas	0:	6:	6
pour deux piesses de Chenille	0:	5:	0
Pour 12. Verges et 1/2 de Taffetas blanc à 2: shell et 4p la verge	1:	9:	2
Pour 6. Verges et 1/2 de Mohere d'argent pour le Tonnelet[2] à 5. Chell et 6p la verge	1:	15:	9
pour la Fourure des habits	0:	10:	6
pour une paire de bas blancs	0:	16:	6
pour 6. verges de Mousseline à 3. chell et 8p	1:	2:	0
Pour les dentelles et galons d'argent	4:	8:	0
pour 3/4 de Taby[3] doré	0:	4:	3
pour huit verges de gase à 14p	0:	9:	4
pour 2. onces de palette*	0:	1:	6
Pour 12. Agréements brodés à 2. Chell et 6 p	1:	10:	0
pour les Agréements de devant	0:	12:	0
pour de la toile glassée pour doubler	0:	7:	0
pour la flanelle	0:	5:	6
pour la doublure des Chausses et poches	0:	4:	6
pour les boutons d'argent	0:	2:	0

Pour la façon de l'habit à la Perse   2: 10: 0
Pour les plumes ⎫
Pour le Turban ⎭   3: 10: 0
                                                                    ─────────
                                                                    £25: 5: 3
Pour les Brodequins ou Buskins   0: 12: 0
                                                                    ─────────
                                                                    £25: 17: 3

* *palette*: *paillette* in modern French.

Copy-text: HTC Coke 53 (Valentini's scribe).

Translation: "Invoice for Mr Valentini for *The Royal Amazon*. For 11 3/4
yards of satin, cherry colored, at 3s 9d a yard, £2:4:0; for 11 1/2 yards of
yellow satin, at 4s 6d, £2:11:9; for the canvas, £0:6:6; for two pieces of che-
nille, £0:5:0; for 12 1/2 yards of white taffeta, at 2s 4d a yard, £1:9:2; for 6 1/2
yards of silver mohair for the *tonnelet* at 5s 6d a yard, £1:15:9; for the fur
trimming, £0:10:6; for a pair of white stockings, £0:16:6; for 6 yards of muslin
at 3s 8d, £1:2:0; for the laces and silver braids, £4:8:0; for 3/4 of golden tabi,
£0:4:3; for 8 yards of [silk] gauze at 14d, £0:9:4; for 2 ounces of spangles,
£0:1:6; for 12 embroidered trimmings at 2s 6d, £1:10:0; for the front trimmings, £0:12:0; for glossy cloth for linings, £0:7:0; for flannel, £0:5:6; for the
linings of breeches and pockets, £0:4:6; for the silver buttons, £0:2:0; for the
making of the Persian costume, £2:10:0; for the feathers [and] for the turban, £3:10:0. [Subtotal] £25:5:3. For the boots or buskins, £0:12:0. [Total]
£25:17:3."

Comment: Valentini was a second-rank Italian castrato who proved an exciting novelty in London. In *Thomyris* he and the countertenor Francis
Hughes alternated in the role of the hero, Orontes. Valentini sang in Italian,
the rest of the cast in English.

1. I.e., *Thomyris*, first performed at Drury Lane on 1 April.
2. I.e., taffeta and trim for the skirt of the *habit à la romaine*, the conventional costume for classical roles.
3. I.e., tabi (watered silk).

11. Owen Swiney's Apology to Lord Tunbridge

[Cover: see document 12]   [August 1707]

Copy of Mr Swiny's letter to my Lord Tunbridge[1]

My Lord
   This letter I take ye Liberty to trouble your Lordship with, is all that's left
in my power to convince you I never had a thought of doing even the least
unmannerly thing to you much less so brutal & so barbarous an Action as I
have had ye hard fortune to be thought guilty of. 'Tis impossible on t'other
side to doubt but your Lordship must think you saw some thing or other in
my behaviour to provoke you to what happend. I am very unhappy from
this mistake, and the more so since tis of a Nature, that admitts of very few
ways for a man to clear himself tho never so innocent. I know but three,
One is ye Testimony of unconcernd persons who casually were by, an other
is the improbability of the thing that a Man should without any sort of
Provocation (for I own I had none) start into a Quarrel so certain to turn to
his disadvantage, if not utter destruction, and the third is ye making use of
all the Protestations a Tongue can utter, That if there was any thing even in
my looks, that seemd to offer the least afront or rudeness either to your
Lordship or the Gentleman with you 'twas wholly without my intention,
and is still without my knowledge. This being the sincere Truth, I both
hope & beg your Lordship will believe me more unfortunate then guilty in
this unhappy accident and that I am, with all the respects due both to your
person & Quality Your Lordships

                                             most humble
                                             and most obedient servant
                                             Owen Swiny

Copy-text: HTC Coke 14 (copy in Hand A, including signature).

Comment: This document, together with 12 and 14, form a set dealing
with a case apparently referred to the Lord Chamberlain because it involved
the theatre, even if only incidentally. Lord Tunbridge—perhaps in a state of
insobriety—appears to have picked a quarrel with the hapless Owen Swiney
outside the Haymarket theatre on the 15th of August. Swiney then not only
had to collect testimony from uninvolved bystanders, but had to apologize
abjectly for his "offence."

An undated holograph note by Swiney now in the Collection of William W. Appleton appears to have served as a cover note, at least for the affidavits in document 12. We presume that Coke was the addressee.

Sir

I did Expect your summons to attend you in order to the Examination of an unlucky accident that lately happen'd me in which I have suffered very much. I hope the inclosed affidavits will satisfie you I am not so much in the wrong as I am represented to be. I hope you will Excuse this trouble given you by your Honours most obliged and

most humble servant
OWEN SWINY

1. William Nassau de Zuylestein, Viscount Tunbridge, later Earl of Rochford (1681–1710), was aide-de-camp to Marlborough and brought the news of the victory at Blenheim to London. See the *Marlborough-Godolphin Correspondence*, p. 361.

12. Depositions of Thomas Dean and John Sympson

[Cover] Ye Affidavits of Dean   (22 August 1707)
        & Sympson
        Mr Swiny Letter
        to Lord Tunbridge
        1707.

Middlesex
          et } ss
Westminster

Thomas Dean of ye Parish St James's Westminster Victualler came this day before me one of her Majesties Justices of ye Peace for ye said County & liberty and made oath that he this Deponent upon Friday ye 15th of that instant August did see Mr Owen Swiny going into ye Play house in ye Hay markett in ye said Parish of St James's Westminster and he this Deponent did see two Gentlemen meet the said Owen Swiny who ask'd him what he would have, Mr Swiny answer'd I would have nothing upon which one of them drew his Sword and ye other laid his hand upon his Sword, but did not draw it and they both pursued Mr Swiny within the Gates of ye Play house but ye said Mr Owen Swiny did not draw his Sword or offer so to do or say any thing to provoke them and further this Deponent sayeth not.

The mark of
Thomas Dean

Jurat coram me Vicessimo
Secundo Die Augustii 1707
Jonathan Chase

Middlesex
  et } ss
Westminster

John Sympson of ye Parish of St Andrew Holbourn in ye County of Middlesex Jeweler came this day before me one of her Majestyes Justices of the Peace for ye said County and Liberty and made Oath That he this deponent did on friday ye 15th of this Instant August, see Mr Owen Swiny going into ye Play house in ye Hay markett in ye Parish of St James's Westminster, and that he this Deponent did see two Gentlemen meet ye aforesaid Mr Owen Swiny * one of whom drew his Sword and ye other laid his hand upon his Sword, and they both pursued the said Mr Owen Swiny within ye Gate of ye Play house, but one of ye two persons did not draw his Sword, and ye said Mr Owen Swiny did not draw his Sword nor offer soe to doe, or say any thing to provoke them, and further saith not

Jurat Coram me   John Sympson
22° die Augustii 1707
Jonathan Chase

* *Swiny:* "within the Gate of ye Play" written and canceled after this word

Copy-text: HTC Coke 15 (copy in Hand A, including signatures).

Comment: These are copies of depositions obtained before a magistrate by Owen Swiney from bystanders to support his story in the fracas with Lord Tunbridge. Cf. documents 11 and 14. The two depositions occupy 1r and 2r of a single folded sheet with the "cover" annotation on 2v. A squiggle between "Thomas" and "Dean" evidently represents Dean's mark.

13. Agreement between Motteux and Valentini for
Love's Triumph

[Cover] Mr * Valentin & Mr Motteux.   (22 August 1707)
        August 22d 1707.

Eu Egard a un accord fait Entre Le Sieur Pierre Motteux & moy le soub-
signe Valentino Urbani pour un opera apellé Il Trionfo d'amore dont je luy
doibs † mettre en main la musique & les paroles Italiennes, je prometz et
m'engage, en cas qu'il me delivre les paroles en anglois pour le dit opera
avant la fin de la presente anneé; de luy payer Cinquante Guineés le jour de
la première Representation dud ᵗ opera a Londres soit en anglois ou en Ita-
lien; Et en suitte je promets luy payer trente autres Guineés le jour de la
sixieme Representation par soubscription Le tout quitte de tous frais. Et
quant a l'Impression dud ᵗ‡ opera, cest a dire des paroles, soit en Anglois soit
autrem ᵗ sans la musique, je prometz d'en laisser tout le profit aud ᵗ s ᵗ Motteux, qui en poura disposer co̅m̅e bon luy semblera. M'engageant de n'en
point disposer a aucune personne que ce soit. En Foy de quoy j'ay signé &
scellé de mon Cachet le present accord. a Londres Le 22.ᵐᵉ Aoust 1707

Sign'd seal'd & deliver'd   Jo§ VALENTINO URBANI.‖
being first stamp'd with a double
stamp, in the presence of
    Susannh Burgess
    John Baselir

    * *Mr*: reading doubtful.
    † *doibs*: *dois* in modern French.
    ‡ *dud ᵗ*: *dudit*.
    § *Jo*: reading doubtful.
    ‖ *Urbani*: last two letters obscured by the remains of a red seal.

Copy-text: HTC Coke 60 (Valentini holograph?). This letter is part of lot
204 in the 1876 sale catalogue.

Translation: "According to an agreement arranged between Mr Pierre Motteux and myself, the undersigned Valentino Urbani, for an opera called *The
Triumph of Love*, of which I must give him the music and the Italian text, I
promise and commit myself, provided he delivers the text in English for the
said opera to me before the end of the present year; to pay him fifty guineas on

the day of the first performance of the said opera in London whether in English or in Italian; and then I promise to pay him thirty more guineas on the day of the sixth performance by subscription: all this free of any expense. As for the printing of the said opera, that is of the text either in English or otherwise, without the music, I promise to leave all the profit from it to the said Mr Motteux, who will have the right to use it as he pleases, and I engage myself not to dispose of that money with anybody whatsoever. In testimony whereof I have signed and sealed with my seal the present agreement in London, 22 August 1707."

Comment: *Love's Triumph* received its premiere 26 February 1708. For Motteux's receipt acknowledging payment see document 54.

14. Lord Mohun to Coke(?) about the Tunbridge Affair

[Cover] Lord Mohun letter   (13 September 1707)
      Swinny

Sir   London September ye 13 1707
   I thank you for the favour of yours & am extreamly sorry that you have so much trouble about this affair, I showed the affidavits[1] to my Lord Tunbridge who says itt is very true that Captain Ottway[2] did persue Mr Swiny into the play house butt that it was nott without provocation, which makes me observe that these fellows who were walking by, sware pretty boldly in pretending to say what was nott sayed or done by Mr Swiny, I won't trouble you with any more on this subject only to add that I don't att all doubt of your justice & friendship & that I am

                    Sir your most obedient humble
                    Servant
                    MOHUN[3]

Copy-text: Houghton bMS Am1631 (293) at Harvard. (Mohun holograph? Unique sample in this collection.)

Comment: This document was item 196 in the 1876 sale catalogue, which quotes all but the final words of the letter verbatim, a description repeated in item 701 of the 1905 sale catalogue. For other documents in the Tunbridge affair, see documents 11 and 12 above. This letter may well be holograph, but it lacks a direction or seal. The cover annotation is an office addition. A modern pencil annotation on the front of the letter says "Mohun to Owen Swiney," which is probably the source of the sale catalogues' error in making this assertion. Coke appears to have sent Mohun the copies in document 12 above as part of his investigation of the Tunbridge-Swiney affair because Otway served under Mohun.

1. I.e., the affidavits of Dean and Sympson, document 12 above.

2. Probably Charles Otway, a captain in Lord Mohun's Regiment of Foot. See Charles Dalton, *English Army Lists and Commission Registers, 1661–1714* (1898–1904; rpt. London: Francis Edwards, 1960), V, 265–66. (James Otway, a career officer active at the same time, has no documented connection with Lord Mohun.)

3. On Lord Mohun see Robert Stanley Forsythe, *A Noble Rake: The Life of Charles, Fourth Lord Mohun* (Cambridge: Harvard Univ. Press, 1928). Mohun and Tunbridge had gone together with the Earl of Macclesfield to present the Garter to the Elector of Hanover in the summer of 1701. A journalist who wrote an account of the trip in 1714 reported that Mohun was among the soberest and best conducted members of the delegation. Mohun is chiefly remembered for other things, but he was a Kit-Cat who sat for his portrait in 1707.

SEASON OF

1707–1708

T he season of 1707–8 is one of the strangest and most interesting throughout the entire eighteenth century. Little has been known about what happened in the immediate aftermath of the "Union of 1708," as it is popularly known. Happily, a very large number indeed of the Coke papers concern Vanbrugh's struggle to keep the opera afloat that spring.

The season started with the two companies in pretty much the state they had put themselves a year earlier. The Haymarket offered unadorned plays, while Drury Lane presented plays with music and dance, as well as opera. The fragility of this status quo must have become increasingly obvious as the fall wore on. Vanbrugh intended to seize control of opera; perhaps not altogether coincidentally Rich found his singers in a state of open mutiny by mid-November (see document 16). Vanbrugh was apparently tendering offers to singers well in advance of any official notice of the union (see document 15), and was busy lining up an orchestra (document 17). A breaking point was reached in late December. Pressure was brought on Rich to accept a generic split, and on 31 December the Lord Chamberlain issued the order which united the actors at Drury Lane under Rich and gave Vanbrugh his opera monopoly at the Haymarket.[1]

By December 1707 Vanbrugh had resumed control of the Haymarket, retaining Owen Swiney as a salaried manager. Vanbrugh spent early January frantically trying to get his singers under contract at reasonable prices, and discovering what the contracts he had taken over from Rich obligated him to (see documents 29, 35, 40, and 44). The opera company presented old productions of *Thomyris* and *Camilla* two nights a week from 13 January to 26 February, when they opened *Love's Triumph*. Receipts varied drastically, but by April it was clear to Vanbrugh that he was losing frightening sums of money, and that the opera would have to be run on a different basis if it were to survive. By 13 April the Duchess of Marlborough was writing to the Earl of

Manchester that the opera "is in so much disorder that I cannot undertake to answer for any promises they should make" to new foreign performers.[2] After unsuccessfully exploring the possibility of Royal subsidy, Vanbrugh gave up, and early in May he bailed out, leasing the whole operation to Swiney and ending his own financial liability (interdocument, 11 May 1708). The general outlines of Vanbrugh's disenchantment have long been known from letters published by Webb in 1928, extracts of which we have printed in chronological place below.[3] The mass of detailed material published here for the first time, however, makes clear just how impossible was the situation into which Vanbrugh had so eagerly precipitated himself.

1. For a full account of events leading up to the Union of 1708—a story which really begins in 1703—see Milhous, *Thomas Betterton*, chapter 7.
2. *Court and Society from Elizabeth to Anne*, ed. William Drago Montagu, 7th Duke of Manchester, 2 vols. (London: Hurst and Blackett, 1864), II, 337–38.
3. For a survey based largely on printed sources see Philip Olleson, "Vanbrugh and Opera at the Queen's Theatre, Haymarket," *Theatre Notebook*, 26 (1972), 94–101.

15. Vanbrugh's General Calendar for Opera

[ca. October–November 1707?]
[Cover] Heads of ye Proposall for ye year for ye severall Performers

To sing at ye Theatre in ye Haymarket twice a week for a year, to commence Christmass 1707 * & to have three monthes vacation, from ye midle of June to ye midle of September

* *1707*: "twice a week" written and canceled after this date.

Copy-text: HTC Coke 12 (Hand B).

Comment: This was evidently Vanbrugh's general schedule, to be written at the beginning of his proposal to each performer, with specifics of salary and terms to be added. At the time this formula was settled, Vanbrugh obviously expected to be in business by mid-December and performing by the end of the month.

16. Mrs Tofts to Coke about a Dispute with Rich

[Cover] Mr Tofts [*sic*]   (18 December [or 18 November? 1707])

Tuesday ye 18 December[1]

Sir

    I have seen ye orders you have sent to Mr Dieupart and am very sorry that I should be put to ye necessity of declining.* I am convincd that none but Mr Rich's friends could prevail upon my Lord[2] & you to have Thomyris don without having matters settled so that we may be seckeurd from farther trobles but if it is my Lords pleasure that I should be sylent I willingly submitt to his Lordships commands and am contented to wait for a better oportunity in hops that in case fresh orders should come that I must sing again 80 guines that I laid out last winter for Camilla's Cloths by ye order of a Noble man who is Mr Riches best friend[3] with Mr Rich's consent shall be payd to me otherwise I am resolv'd never to† sett my foot upon ye stage again since it is to my great loss that I have done it hitherto by reason of ye Expence that I have been att and must be daily to make a tollerable apearance since Mr Ritch won't allow necessary's. Therefore I humbly beg of my Lord Chamberlain not to depend upon my performance in Thomyris on saturday next since I am resolvd not to do it till I have 80 guineas sent to me by Mr Rich beside what I must have for my days Performance.

I am &ca
CATH: TOFTS

  * *declining*: MS reads "dining."
  † *to*: "sing" written and canceled after this word.

Copy-text: Broadley, p. 35 (copy in Hand A). This document is item 202 in the 1876 sale catalogue; it is 708 in the 1905 sale catalogue. For nineteenth-century transcriptions see Winston, pp. 49–50, and Drexel MS, fol. 28.

Comment: The date is problematical, but "Tuesday 18 December 1707" cannot be correct. *Thomyris* received its premiere in April 1707. The eighteenth of December came on a Thursday in 1707, and this letter cannot be later than that year on account of the union. *The London Stage* (Part 2, I, 161) reports a performance of *Thomyris* on Thursday 18 December, with Tofts in the cast "as formerly." A clipping from a dealer's catalogue with the MS dates the letter "Dec 18 1874," corrected in ink to 1714. A pencil annotation repeats the 1714 date, which is impossible since Mrs Tofts left the stage in 1709. The year must be 1707, but "Dec:" may be an error for November. The eighteenth was a Tuesday in November, and a notice in the *Post Boy*, 13–15 November, states that Mrs Tofts and Mrs de l'Epine do not intend to perform on account of a disagreement with the managers. The present letter is evidently part of the same dispute. *The Muses Mercury* for October 1707 (published around the beginning of December) reports that "There was a great Expectation of an Audience for the Opera of *Camilla* last Saturday [15 November], and they were all forc'd to return as they came; the Singers, the Women, and Foreigners especially, refusing to sing, without being secur'd such exorbitant Rates ev'ry Night for the whole Season, that not scarce any one could think they deserv'd for once only." Mrs Tofts was performing with the Drury Lane company again by Saturday 6 December in *Camilla*. Mrs Tofts had a history of disagreements with Rich. For some details of an earlier quarrel which went to the Lord Chamberlain's office for arbitration see LC 7/3, fols. 167–68 (ca. January 1706).

1. Abbreviated "Dec:"
2. The Lord Chamberlain.
3. Identity unclear.

17. List of Proposed Orchestra Members and Petitioners' Salary Requests

[ca. November 1707?]

[Cover] List of ye musick proposd & of ye musick who petition'd

15	Cloudio[1]	15			Persons who signd ye Petition		
15	Corbet	15			with ye Prices they askt for		
15	Banister	15			every night they are to play.		
15	Pepusch	15	} Violins		Dieupart		3–0
8	Roberts *	8			Claudio		1–10
10	Y: Babel	10			Paisible	P	1–10
10	Soyan	10–0			Banister	Q	1–10
8	Pitchford	8			Ayleworth		1–10
					Corbet	Q.E.	1–10
9–6	Smith	8	} Tenors		C: Babel	P	1–10
10	Armstrong	10			F. Goodsens		1–10

15	Lully	15	⎱ Houtbois	Chaboud		1–10
10	La Tour	11–0	⎰	Latour	P	1–5
15	Babel	15	⎱	Rogers		1–5
15	Pietro	15	⎬ Basson	Kytsch		1–5
7–6	Cadet	10	⎰	W: Babel	Q	1–5
24	Saggione	15	Double Base	Shojan		1–5
24	il Bolonese	30	Harpsicord²	Cadetts		1–0
30	N: Haym	35	⎱	Simpson		1–0
15	Paisible	15	⎬ Violoncelli	Waltser		1–0
15	Francisco³	15	⎰	C. Smith	Q	1–0
30	Pilotti			Armstrong		1–0
				T. Roberts	Q	1–0
				Linike		1–0
				Desabeye		1–0
				Davin		1–0

* *Roberts*: written in place of "15 Ayleworth," which was canceled.

Copy-text: HTC Coke 18 (Hand D; note overleaf in Hand A).

Comment: This list represents the orchestra for the Haymarket in the planning stage. Evidently some twenty-three musicians applied en masse, specifying the salaries they wanted in pounds and shillings (right column). The left column evidently shows a tentative orchestra roster with two sets of hypothetical salaries in shillings per night. There is no internal clue as to the meaning of "P," "Q," and "Q.E." David Lasocki suggests that "P" means "Prince of Denmark's musician," "Q" means "Queen's musician," and "Q.E." means "Queen's Emissary." This tallies with known rosters (save that Ayleworth was overlooked) and hence seems highly likely.

By 1 December 1707 the Lord Chamberlain was actively helping Vanbrugh set up an opera company. On that day he granted permission for fourteen prime musicians (all of them presumably under contract to Drury Lane) "to perform in the Operas at the Queens Theatre in the Haymarket" (PRO LC 5/154, p. 288). The musicians named are Banister, Paisible, Lully, La Tour, Le Sack, Elwart (i.e., Ayleworth),⁴ Soyan, Crouch, Babell, Francisco, Roger, Desabeye, Cadet, and Dieupar[t]. Ten of these men signed the "Petition" above. Nine of them (including seven Petition signers) are in the "Musick Proposd" here. One of the petitioners (Crouch) apparently never joined the orchestra. All of those "Proposd" eventually joined, though not all of them did so immediately. According to a protest dated 31 December 1707 (document 28) Banister, Le Sac, Lully, La Tour, Paisible, Babel, Roger, and Dieupart had forthwith been "turn'd out of Drury Lane Play house by Mr. Rich upon suspicion of being concern'd in the Project of Acting Opera's in the Haymarkett." Rich was not yet ready to bow to the inevitable.

For some sense of the extravagance of the petitioners' claims see Elizabeth W. Gilboy, *Wages in Eighteenth Century England* (Cambridge: Harvard Univ. Press, 1934), chapters 1 and 2, and John Burnet, *A History of the Cost of Living* (Harmondsworth: Penguin, 1969), chapter 3. At this date a skilled artisan could expect to make 2s.6d. for a day's labor.

1. I.e., Claudio Rogier.
2. In an isolated note overleaf is written: "il Bolonese Harpsicord." The reference is to Tomaso Gabrielli.
3. I.e., Francisco Goodsens (the "F. Goodsens" of the other column). See *Biographical Dictionary*, VI, 266–67.
4. We are indebted to David Lasocki for this identification.

18. Tentative Roster and Salaries of Musicians for the Spring of 1708

[ca. early December 1707?]

Violins 1st & 2d Trebles			
Mr Banister	40:0:0		
Mr Corbett	40:0:0		
Mr LeSac	30:0:0		
Mr Soyan	30:0:0	1st Trebles	200:00:0
Mr Dean	30:0:0		
Mr Simpson	30:0:0		
Mr Babel Junior	25:0:0		
Mr Robert	25:0:0		
Mr Smith	25:0:0	2d Trebles	150:0:0
Mr Manchip	25:0:0		
Mr	25:0:0		
Mr	25:0:0		

Hautbois[1]
Mr Luly	40:0:0		
Mr Latour	30:0:0[2]	100[*]	
Mr Smith	30:0:0		
Mr			

Tenors[3]
Mr	20:0:0		
Mr	20:0:0	40[†]	
Mr	20:0:0		
Mr	20:0:0		
a Trumpett Mr Davin	25:0:0		

Bases[4]
Mr Paisible	40:0:0	
Mr Francisco	30:0:0	
Mr Roger	30:0:0	
Mr Dasabeye	25:0:0	235:0:0
Mr Babel	30:0:0	
Mr Laroon	30:0:0	
Cadett	25:0:0	
	25:0:0	

805[5]

270[6]

1070:0:0

[A second list, without salaries, includes the following performers.]

5 1st Trebles: Banister, Corbett, LeSac, Sayon [only four are named]; 5 Second Treble: Babel Junior [only one named]; 2 Tenors: [none named]; 2 Double Bases: Saggione, Francisco; 4 other Bases: Heyams, Paisible, Roger, Laroon; 2 Harpsicords: Papusch, Dioparr; 2 Haut bois: Lully, Latour; 2 Bassons: Signor Pietro, Mr Babel; Trumpett [not named]. [Scratch figures follow—not transcribed.]

[*] *100*: written beside "110:0:0," which was canceled.
[†] *40*: written under "80:0:0," which was canceled.

Copy-text: HTC Coke 4 (Hand A).

Comment: This list of musicians is evidently a rough preliminary to the more fully worked out lists in documents 44 and 49 below. The present docu-

ment consists of three sheets comprising the roster printed above, a second
list without salaries (summarized above), and many numerical doodles which
we have made no attempt to reproduce. Scratch items of which we can make
sense are reported in the notes below. The crux of this document is the total:
Vanbrugh expected to pay his orchestral musicians a total of £1070 for a season which we know from other sources he estimated at sixty-four nights—or
close to £17 per night. "Ye Instrumental musike" at Drury Lane was paid £8
for a performance later this month (see document 28 below).

1. The calculation sheet lists three salaries for Hautbois: 40, 30, and 30—and cancels
another 30.
2. Changed from 40:0:0.
3. The calculation sheet lists only two tenor salaries—£50 and £40.
4. The calculation sheet enters only £190 for Bases, divided 40, 30, 30, 30, 30, 30.
5. The correct total is £800 (before corrections) or £750 (after corrections).
6. This figure is the approximate total for senior musicians "Heyams, Diopar, Papusch, Seggione" as calculated in documents 44 and 49.

19. Littleton Ramondon's Agreement with Heidegger and Dieupart

(2 December 1707)

It is agreed between John James Heidegger and Charles * Dieupart Gentlemen of one side & Littleton Ramondon Gent on the other that in consideration of ye sum of two pounds ten shillings a week which ye said Mr
Heidegger & Mr Dieupart oblige themselves to pay unto the said Littleton
Ramondon from this day 1st December † 1707 to the first day of May next
ensueing the date hereof the said Littleton Ramondon obliges himself to
sing in ye operas as they shall order him. In witness whereof ye said Parties
have sett their hands to this present Agreement this 2d December 1707.

Wittness   JJ HEIDEGGER
D RAMONDON [1]   L: RAMONDON

    * and Charles: Winston leaves a blank between "Heidegger" and "Dieu-
part." The Drexel MS adds "Charles" in brackets (cropped but legible).
    † December: abbreviated "Xber" here and below.

Copy-text: Winston, p. 70. For another nineteenth-century transcription see Drexel MS, fol. 26. This item is 187 in the 1876 sale catalogue; it is 695 in the 1905 sale catalogue. It was offered for sale (priced at £1 10s.) in an unidentified catalogue, a clipping from which is pasted in Broadley at page 43.

Comment: The relation of this agreement to the Haymarket venture remains conjectural. We would guess that Heidegger and Dieupart were gambling on signing up singers at a fixed rate, hoping then to sign them over to Vanbrugh at a higher rate. Whether this contract was honored we do not know, but if it was, the speculators probably lost substantially on it. They promise Ramondon 50s. per week, but in document 44 below he is set down in a Haymarket roster for a salary of 15s. per performance, or no more than 30s. per week.

1. D. Ramondon was Littleton Ramondon's father. See document 23 below.

20. Bill from Cherrier, Desbarques, and Mlle Desbarques for Opera Performances and Sundries

[December 1707?]

Memoire dés dépance faite pour Le Compte De monsieur éDéquer *

	Li#	chelins	sols
pour Deux péruque Longue	05	10	00
plus pour douse Boucle pour mademoiselle debargues	02	00	00
plus trois paire de souliers pour homme savoir deux paire ordinaire et une pour Le matelot	00	18	00
plus pour une paire de souliers pour femme	00	09	00
plus pour Labit de matelotes	01	05	00
plus pour six branche de fleur artifitielles pour La matelotte	00	01	08
plus pour deux paire de gant dhomme	00	04	00
plus pour douse rose de ruban blanc et rouie pour homme	00	14	00
plus pour Septs verge de ruban de Satin pour La Coifure et manche de mademoiselle debargues	00	08	00

plus pour 6 verge de ruban blanc		oo	o3	oo
plus pour avoir fait blanchir dés plume		oo	o4	oo
	monte	11	16	o8
		#	chelins	sols
il et du pour quatre jour de representations				
de l'opera mr cherrier		o6	oo	oo
pour mr debargues		o6		
pour mademoiselle debargues		10	oo	oo
		22	oo	oo
		#	ch	sols
nous avons ressu pour Lés avance paite[†]		1	oo	oo
réste		10	16	o8[1]
nous avons ressu Sur Lés quatre				
représantations de l'opera quatre guinee				
réste a paier En tout jusque a ce jour		#	chelins	
		28	10	o8[2]

   [*] *éDéquer*: i.e., Heidegger. Roughly three words following have been canceled and are now illegible.

   [†] *paite*: i.e., *paie* (payment) in modern French.

Copy-text: HTC Coke 39 (unidentified hand).

Translation: "Memo of the expenses made for Mr Heidegger's account. For two long wigs, £5:10:0. Plus for twelve bows for Mlle Desbarques, £2:0:0. Plus three pairs of shoes for men, namely two ordinary pairs and one for the sailor, £0:18:0. Plus one pair of shoes for a woman, £0:9:0. Plus for the sailor-woman costume, £1:5:0. Plus for six branches of artificial flowers for the sailor-woman, £0:1:8. Plus for two pairs of men's gloves, £0:4:0. Plus for twelve rosettes of white and red ribbon for men, £0:14:0. Plus for seven yards of satin ribbon for the hair and sleeves of Mlle Desbarques, £0:8:0. Plus for six yards of white ribbon, £0:3:0. Plus for having had plumes bleached, £0:4:0. Total: £11:16:8.

"Owed for four days of performances of the opera. Mr Cherrier, £6:0:0. For Mr Desbarques, £6:0:0. For Mlle Desbarques, £10:0:0. [Total:] £22:0:0.

"We have received for the advance payment £1:0:0. There remains £10:16:08.

"We have received for the four performances of the opera four guineas. There remains to be paid all together to this day £28:10:08."

Comment: This bill for performances and costume expense reimbursement is evidently to be dated December 1707 when Desbarques and Cherrier were advertised as dancing at Drury Lane. Rich was never one to pay bills willingly, and evidently he more or less stopped paying his opera performers when he realized that they were all proposing to decamp to Vanbrugh at the Haymarket. For other such bills see documents 21, 23, and particularly 28. The present bill probably wound up in the Vice Chamberlain's office because Rich disputed it or refused to pay it. Details of financial settlements and compensation necessitated by the transfer of personnel, scenery, costumes, and so forth, occasioned by the union are unknown.

This bill gives a good idea of the disproportionate incidental expenses of opera, especially when one recalls that no new production was involved. These dancers were evidently being paid by or through Heidegger, which is why the account is directed to him. In document 28 (31 December 1707), "The Dancers vizt. Monsr. Charier Monr. Debargues & Mle Debargues . . . desires [sic] that they may be reimburs'd the Expences that they have been at by Order, as it appears by their Bill delivered to Mr Heidegger."

1. The advance payment is here subtracted from the sundries total above.
2. The correct total is £28.12.08.

21. Undated Costume Bill for Women

[December 1707?]

L'habit de Mrs Tofts fournitures et façon se monte a[1]	£24 10 0
Lhabit de Mrs Marguerette se monte a	£27 5 0
Lhabit de Mrs Dabarg[2] se monte a	£12 0 0
Brous[3]	£63 15 0

Copy-text: HTC Coke 40 (unidentified hand; may be a copy).

Comment: Like the preceding document, this seems to be a bill unpaid by Rich in December 1707. These claims are exactly reiterated in document 28 (31 December 1707).

1. "The costume of Mrs Tofts: materials and making amount to . . . ." (etc.).
2. I.e., Mlle Desbarques, as she is termed when this claim is repeated in document 28. References in these papers and in newspaper bills (e.g., 7 February 1708) to "Mrs"

and "Mlle" Desbarques lead the authors of the *Biographical Dictionary* to say that "the evidence seems to suggest a husband, wife, and daughter, . . . not a confusion between the two latter" (IV, 341). But since we have never seen the "two" women referred to together, we are inclined to think that they are one and the same—presumably a daughter or niece of Mons. Desbarques.

3. *Brous*: Mr Brous was a tailor at the Queen's Theatre in the Haymarket in 1708 (*Biographical Dictionary*, II, 356). He also signed three invoices for trimming materials ("imbrodry," "purl," "fring") delivered to Drury Lane after 1714. The invoices are undated, but were approved for payment by Cibber, Wilks, and Booth (MS W.b.111 in the Folger Shakespeare Library).

22. Tentative Roster of Opera Performers and Their Salaries

[Cover] Opera Performers   [ca. late December 1707]

Mr Banister√	40-0-0		Mrs Tofts	500
Mr Corbett√	40-0-0		Mrs Margaritta	400
Mr Le Sac√	30-0-0		Sr valantino	400
Mr Soyan√	30-0-0		Sr Casani	300
Mr Dean√	30-0-0		Mrs Lyndsey	60
Mr Sympson√	30-0-0		Mr Hughs	60
Mr Babel junior√	25-0-0		Mr Lawrance	50
Mr Robert√	25-0-0		Mr Levdrige	80
Mr Smith√	25-0-0		Mr Ramondon	60
Mr manchip√	25-0-0		Mr Lody[1]	100
Mr	25-0-0		ye Baronesse	200
Mr	25-0-0		Mrs Sagione	100
Mr Lullie√	40-0-0		Mrs Crosse	100
Mr Smith√	Hautbois	30-0-0	Mr Lovett	40
Mr La Tour		30-0-0	Mr Turner	40
Mr Roussellett		25-0-0	3409	2470[2]
Mr Smith	Tenor	25-0-0	4000	995[3]
Mr		25-0-0		3465
Mr Paisible√		40-0-0		
Mr Francisco√		30-0-0		
Mr Roger√	Bases	30-0-0		
Mr Desabeye√		30-0-0		
Mr Laroon√		30-0-0		
Mr Haym√		xxxxxx[4]		

Mr Babel√		30-0-0
Mr Cadet√	Bassons	25-0-0
Mr La Sere		20-0-0
Mr La Borde√		20-0-0
Mr Sagione√		40-0-0
Mr Dieupart√		
Mr Darien * Trumpet√		25-0-0
		845 [5]

* *Darien*: probably an error for "Davin."

Copy-text: HTC Coke 23 (unidentified hand).

Comment: This list is a slightly improved version of document 18, with singers added in the right-hand column. Mr Roussellet (a mystery man), La Borde, and La Sere are new: none of them actually played with the orchestra that spring. The singers and their salaries are still tentative: Vanbrugh did not yet know about Cassani's contract (see document 42 below); Mrs Tofts' salary was lowered; Mrs Lodi did not join the company, and so forth. The significance of "3409" and "4000" under the right-hand column is not clear to us, and nor is the meaning of the checkmarks against many of the musicians' names. For lists of performers closer to the company as it actually took shape, see documents 44 and 50 below.

1. Probably an error for "Mrs" Lody—i.e., Anna Lodi. See documents 32, 33, and 34 below.
2. The correct total of singers' salaries is £2490.
3. This figure may represent the anticipated total for musicians—i.e., £845 plus £150 to be divided between Haym and Dieupart.
4. The salary for Haym is crossed out and illegible.
5. This total ignores blanks for Haym and Dieupart.

23. Petition by Ramondon against Rich

[ca. late December 1707]

A Petition from D Ramondon that his son should be paid he having left Rich last November. Signed D Ramondon.

Copy-text: Winston, p. 3. Item 197 in the 1876 sale catalogue probably describes this document: "Ramondon (D.) Petition, 1714. Names Rich,

Dieupart, etc. 1 page folio. holograph and signed, *rare*." The date is implausible. Date and description are repeated verbatim as 702 in the 1905 sale catalogue.

Comment: Winston gives only this summary. Ramondon's son signed a special contract with Heidegger and Dieupart on 2 December 1707 (see document 19). Document 28, "The Opera Performers' Complaint against Rich," dated 31 December 1707, specifies that Ramondon is owed £10 "pay for a month"—evidently by Rich. In another part of that complaint Ramondon implies that the agreement of 2 December is not being honored and that he has given the written agreement to Coke with a request for help in getting what is owed to him.

24. Vanbrugh's Rough Estimate of Expenses and Income for the Spring of 1708

[ca. late December 1707]

Trebles	350	Voices		
Hautbois	125[1]	Women	1450	
tenors & bases	330[2]	Men	1100	
four chief Bases	280		2550	
	1085		1085	
			3535[3]	
		Rent	370[4]	
120			3905	
64 Nights		Attendants &ca	395	
480			4300	
720		Dancers & Cloaths	700	
7680[5]			5000	
6000		2 New Operas	1000	
1680[6]			6000[7]	

```
 80              40                  2̶0̶    20
150              40                  5̶0̶     9
150              30     I ˢᵗ        1̶0̶0̶   180
380  Women Singers  30     &
400              30     2 ᵈ                         12̶  24
400              30                                 4̶0̶  24
 80              25                                      16
────             25              10                     ──
1260             25     Trebles   190    35             64
450              25              190                    80
300              25              120                    ──
 50  Men Singers  25              7                      00
 80              25             ───                    4820
 60      940     350             50                    3520
                 40                                    1300
────             30     Hautbois
2200             30                                    100
 70              30                                     60
 70                                                   ────
 70             ─────                              35  6000
 70  28  Cadet[?]  450                             36  4000
2480             25                                    2000
 800             40
3̶5̶2̶0̶             30                                         3235
                 30                                    H-   370
3̶5̶2̶0̶             30                          300  Dancers  800
2480             30                         2400  Candles  320
 755             30      100                 120         1000
3235             30      100                  64         5725
                 560  [correctly,           480          275
                       665]    120          720         6000
                  50             64         7680          640
                  40  Tenors    480                      6640
                 ───             84                      1040
                 755                                     7680
```

Copy-text: HTC Coke 5 (Hand A).

Comment: From similarities to figures in other documents we would guess that this set of figures is Coke's copy of a rough estimate of expenses and potential profits Vanbrugh made no later than late December 1707—cf. document 18. As of this time Vanbrugh was anticipating an average income of £120 a night for a season of 64 nights, and total expenses of £6000, or only about £94 per night. For the actual figures January–March 1708 see documents 49, 50, 55–58, and 62 below.

1. Only £100 is allowed for Hautbois in document 18.
2. In document 18 £40–90 is allowed for tenors, £90–235 for basses.
3. This total should be 3635.
4. This figure seems very low: £800 rent is allowed in document 44.
5. This figure represents estimated gross income for the season.
6. This figure represents estimated net profit for the season.
7. The grand total should be 6100.

25. Kent to Coke about the Union

(Tuesday [23 December 1707?])

[Cover] Duke of Kent about the two play houses
[Direction] To The Right Honorable Mr Vice Chamberlain[1]

Sir

I send you here a new proposall to satisfye both houses that neither of them may be ruined by the operas Leaving of them.

I shall say more to you about it when I see you next, in the mean time pray send to Mr Rich Estcourt to talk with them about it & to make them agree.

I am Sir
Your most Humble servant
KENT

tuesday morning
11 a clock

Copy-text: HTC Coke 77 (Kent holograph; cover annotation for filing purposes added in an unidentified hand). For nineteenth-century transcriptions see Winston, p. 47, and Drexel MS, fol. 126. This note was evidently part of lot 189 in the 1876 sale catalogue, and part of 696 in the 1905 sale catalogue.

Comment: The "proposall" is not preserved. If, as seems likely, this note is directly connected with the final negotiations in the Union of 1708, then it probably dates from 23 December 1707. The following Sunday Sir John Stanley (Kent's secretary) called a meeting for 11:00 A.M. Tuesday 30 December to discuss terms of a union (see documents 26 and 27). The order of union was issued Wednesday 31 December.

Two cruxes in the present note deserve consideration. "To satisfye both houses that neither of them may be ruined by the operas Leaving of them" probably means that both companies of actors are to be reassured, not that the opera is to be removed from both Drury Lane and the Haymarket. "Send to Mr Rich Estcourt" probably means "To Mr Rich and to Richard Estcourt," not just to Estcourt. The final line ("to make them agree") seems to make the double invitation definite. So does document 26 when Estcourt says, in begging off on account of illness, "Rich shall attend you." Estcourt's inclusion, however, does imply that he was serving as manager for Rich in the fall of 1707. For details of the actors' feelings about the situation see Colley Cibber's dedication to Kent of *The Lady's last Stake* (advertised in the *Daily Courant*, 29 December, as to be published "tomorrow").

1. The remains of a red seal are preserved near the Direction.

26. Estcourt to Stanley about the Union and His Benefit

(Monday [29 December 1707?])

Munday 10[1]

Honourd Sir

I never had such a cruell instance of Two upon one being Foul play for a Rheumatisme attended with a sneaking feaver seises me on saturday night and has confind me to the softest part of my Chamber ever since. But Sir [*] your letter came this morning tho dated on Sunday night. Rich shall attend you which I am sorry I cannot do. But I beg your Friendship in Relation to my benefit Play which I woud feign have out of the way before any alteration of affairs happen among us. It is my Northend[2] and makes me easy all the Summer. I beg my duty to my Lady and believe me

Honourd Sir

Your most obedient Servant
R: ESTCOURT

The sing at midnight and Colier† are on me.

To the Honourd Sir John Stanly

  * *Sir*: Winston abbreviates "S." Reading taken from the Drexel MS.
  † *Colier*: Drexel MS reads "Collier."

Copy-text: Winston, p. 43. For another nineteenth-century transcription see Drexel MS, fol. 127. This letter is probably one of the two Estcourt items mentioned in 181 of the 1876 sale catalogue: "Estcourt (R.) eminent actor. A.L.s. 1 page 4to (two specimens) 1714." The 1714 date may be discounted: Estcourt died in 1712.

Comment: This note is evidently a reply to an invitation to a meeting to discuss terms for the Union of 1708. Cf. documents 25 and 27. Estcourt is obviously disturbed at the prospect of a theatrical rearrangement depriving him of his benefit, a concern on which he expands in the following letter. We do not know what to make of "The sing at midnight and Colier are on me."

1. "Munday 10" presumably means 10:00 A.M. If "10" is taken as a date, it puts this letter in November, which seems too early.
2. Stanley's suburban retreat (cf. document 76)—by implication an estate which brought him an income.

27. Estcourt to the Lord Chamberlain about the Union and His Benefit

[Cover] Mr Estcourt   (Monday [29 December 1707?])
[Direction] To the most Noble Marquiss of Kent Lord Chamberlain

May it please your lordship
                  Munday from bed.
    I am the worst way prevented from the Honour of waiting on your lordship by being sick and lame in bed. This morning a letter came from Sir John Stanley ordering Mr Rich to attend you to morrow at eleven, I guess it brings with it some Method and Turne in our Affairs, and I humbly beg that my Benefit Play may be over, which is my great support, before any thing that may hinder me from it may happen. Tickets are out for it already and I

will dispatch it in the month of January. I beg your lordships favour in this and be pleased to forgive this unavoidable trouble from

> Your most Obedient servant
> R: ESTCOURT

I am then at your lordships service.

Copy-text: Harvard Theatre Collection TS 953.10F, Augustin Daly, *Woffington*, Vol. I, between pp. 26 and 27 of text, p. [141] of this extra-illustrated volume. (Estcourt holograph? Unique sample in this collection.) For nineteenth-century transcriptions, see Winston, p. 43, and Drexel MS, fol. 125. This letter is probably one of the Estcourt items mentioned in 181 of the 1876 sale catalogue.

Comment: On the dating, see document 26. Estcourt obviously believed (quite correctly) that a major upheaval was at hand, and was concerned about his benefit. We have no record of a benefit for him in the last days of Rich's old company at Drury Lane in early January, but he was allowed an out-of-season benefit on 12 February by "her Majesty's United Company of Comedians." Whether Kent needed to intervene on Estcourt's behalf we do not know.

28. The Opera Performers' Complaint against Rich

[Cover] Mr Dieupar relating   (31 December 1707)
to ye performers bargains
December 31st 1707 *

Seignior Valentino, Seigniora Margaritta and Mrs Tofts having declared in a Writing that was deliver'd to Mr Vice Chamberlain upon what foot they desired to be, to which they refer themselves.[1]—but as perhaps their demands may at first sight be thought Exorbitant.—They humbly beg leave to Represent, The shortness of the time wherein Opera's are perform'd, and how long they are without being Imploy'd, as also the great Expence they must be at to keep themselves in order to sing, This Climate being much wors than any other for voices, and in short the misery they undergoe if seiz'd with a cold, as well as the slavery they are at to prevent it.—All which considered they hope to meet with Encouragement suitable to their trouble.

But if Mr Rich, by reason of the Agreements he has made with other performers cannot come to any certainty with them, he may, if he pleases, paying them as he has done of late, call them to sing, only when he shall have occasion.

Seigniora Margaritta humbly desires that Twenty Guineys due to her by Mr Rich on her bargain of last Winter, should be paid, besides her having perform'd twice in the Opera after the time the said Bargain was out,[2] for which she has received nothing, & therefore desires that she may be paid in proportion to that agreement.

Mrs Tofts humbly begs leave to represent the hardness of her case, concerning the cloaths that she made for the part of Camilla,[3]—For tho' she may be thought Extravigant in laying out 80 Guineys, upon them, yet she hopes that no body will think it Reasonable that she should loose the whole summe, it being matter of fact that the cloaths that were made by Mr Rich for Camilla, & paid for by the nobility, were kept for Rosamond & paid for again out of the subscription money that did arise for the said opera of Rosamond.[4]

So that Mr Rich cannot say that he ever made more than 3 suits of cloaths for Mrs Tofts, tho she has perform'd in 4 opera's vizt, Arsinoe, Camilla, Rosamond, and Thomiris, every one of the said operas having been subscrib'd for, and money allow'd for cloaths & sceans. &c. The said cloathes are newly made up & will be delivered to Mr Rich when agreed for.

She begs leave also to represent that the Principal parts being given to her, she's thereby oblig'd to be at very great Expences for several things that the house never allow's for, as Locks for hair, jewells, ribbons for knotts for the head & body, muslin for vails, gloves shoes, washing of vails and head cloaths, and many other things, for which she may modestly afirm that one hundred pounds is not sufficient for the season.

Mr Ramondon, who was actually in Pay with Mr Rich, and had money owing him, which Mr Rich refused to pay when Mr Ramondon made his Agreement to come to the hay Markett. He therefore humbly begs that the said Agreement be made good, or else he must take his Course with them that Engaged him in My Lord Chamberlains name, that Agreement in writing is in Mr Vice Chamberlain's hands.[5]

The Dancers vizt Monsr. Charier Monsr. Debargues & Mlle Debargues who were prevented making an agreement with Mr Rich upon the project of goeing to the Hay Market Playhouse desires that their Agreement may be

made good and that they may be reimburs'd the Expences that they have
been at by Order, as it appears by their Bill delivered to Mr Heideger.

Those of the Instrumental Musick Vizt Mr Banister, Le sac, Lullie, La
Tour, Paisible, Babel, Roger and Dieupart who were turn'd out of Drury
Lane Play house by Mr Rich upon suspicion of being concern'd in the Project of Acting Opera's in the Haymarkett,[6] humbly represent that they who
are allow'd to be the best performers in their kind might desire some consideration for the time they have lost & their trouble being much greater than
formerly by reason of Opera's which require an attendance of 4 hours without intermissions besides practices, yet being not willing to be an hindrance
to the performance of Opera's by introducing Novelties, they only desire
that their former bargain with Mr Rich, may be punctually observ'd without
alteration viz.

	£ s d
Banister for 6 days acting of Playes	2 0 0
Le sac	1 10 0
La Tour	1 10 0
Paisible	2 0 0
Babel	1 10 0
Roger	1 10 0
Dieupar	4 0 0

But if Mr Rich cannot Act Plays or Opera's 6 days in the week, they
desire that when the Opera is perform'd, if but once per week, to receive 3
days pay for that one performance, and if twice per week, 3 days pay for
each Performance; Obligeing themselves to attend any other day of the
weeke, either Plays or Practices of Opera's, as occasion shall require.—and
if the Opera is perform'd above twice a week, they dont desire any more
than their six days pay, according to their former bargain.

The Performers in General Desire that some Consideration be made to
Mr Heideger, who to their knowledge, in several Articles has laid out a
Considerable summe of money in relation to this Project,—

Signor valantino's cloathes amounts to	25-17-03
Signora margaritta	27-05-00
Mrs Tofts	24-10-00
Mlle DeBargues	12-00-00
ye haymarketts play house Bill[7]	
the Dancers Bill	11-16-08

their pay for a month	44-00-00
Mr Ramondon's pay for a month	10-00-00
ye Instrumantal musike for ye Last time ye Opera was performd[8]	08-00-00
Mr heideiger desire	20-00-00

in All[9]

December ye 31 1707

* *December 31st 1707*: this date is written in another hand.

Copy-text: HTC Coke 54 (professional scribe with additions in an unidentified hand). For nineteenth-century transcriptions see Winston, pp. 77–81,
and Drexel MS, fol. 32 and two unnumbered folios following.

Comment: This bitter complaint—evidently put together by Dieupart on
behalf of all the performers—shows pretty clearly that Rich and his operatic
personnel had reached an impasse. We may also note that a number of performers (Ramondon, Cherrier, M. and Mlle. Desbarques) who had been
prompt in agreeing to desert Rich—were upset both at Rich's not paying
them money previously due, and at the failure of the Haymarket to start putting on operas. The reiterated request to the Lord Chamberlain that their
agreements "be made good" is a plea that he go ahead and permit the Haymarket to employ them. How these claims for back pay and costume reimbursement were settled we do not know. On this day the Lord Chamberlain
issued orders (printed following this document) uniting the acting companies
under Rich at Drury Lane and granting Vanbrugh an opera monopoly at the
Haymarket.

1. This implies that Valentini, Margarita de l'Epine, and Mrs Tofts made a joint financial proposal to Vanbrugh (via Coke?) in December. No such document has come
to light.
2. This claim evidently refers to the season of 1706–7. Following the row in November 1707 (see document 16) "Signora Margarita" apparently performed for Rich on 6,
9, 13, and 18 December.
3. On this dispute see document 16.
4. Performed at Drury Lane in March 1707. Whether this particular charge is true or
not, such accounting methods were highly characteristic of Christopher Rich.
5. Littleton Ramondon, having signed up with Heidegger and Dieupart (cf. document 19) protests here (a) that Rich has not paid him in full, and (b) that he is not yet

being paid by Heidegger and Dieupart. Of course the Haymarket was not yet a going operatic concern.

6. For a list of musicians who petitioned to join the Haymarket opera orchestra see document 17.

7. The significance of this phrase escapes us.

8. This presumably refers to the performance of *Thomyris* 18 December.

9. No total was written in: it is difficult to calculate. Margarita and Tofts claim 100 guineas between them, plus two nights' salary for Margarita. Miscellaneous claims total £197.8.11. Tofts' claim for another £100 seems to be more a matter of principle than one of past fact; she could not seriously have hoped to collect.

INTERDOCUMENT.
The Order of Union

(31 December 1707)

Whereas by reason of the Division of her Majestys Comedians into two distinct houses or Companys the Players have not been able to gain a reasonable Subsistance for their Encouragement in either Company nor can plays always be Acted to ye best Advantage And Whereas the charge of maintaining a Company of Comedians with performers of Opera in the same House is now become too great to be Supported Therefore to remedy those inconveniences and for the better regulation and Support of the Theatres I do hereby Order & require

That all Operas and other Musicall presentments be perform'd for the future only at her Majestys Theatre in the Hay Markett under the direction of the Manager or Managers thereof, with full power and Authority to receive Admitt and Employ any performers in Musick Dancing &ca whom he or they shall judge fitt for their Service and I do hereby strictly charge and forbid ye said Manager or Managers from & after the 10th day of January next to represent any Comedys Tragedys or other Entertainments of ye Stage that are not set to Musick or to erect any other Theatre for that purpose upon pain of being Silenced for breach of this my Order

I do likewise hereby give leave to the Manager or Managers of ye Theatres in Drury Lane & Dorsett Garden &a full power and Authority to receive and Admitt into their Company any players or Actors of Tragedy or Comedy they shall think fitt to entertain notwithstanding any Articles or engagements they may be under in any other play House at the same time strictly charging and requiring the said Managers not to performe any Musicall Entertainment upon their Stage or to receive into their Service any Dancers or performers in Musick other than such Instrumentall Musick as are not employed in ye Operas and are Necessary for such entertainments[1] upon ye like pain of being Silenced for breach of this Order. And for ye greater encouragement of ye Above nam'd Theatres I do further Order and Require

that no person Society or Company of Undertakers what ever do presume to erect
any other Theatre or to represent Comedys Tragedys Operas or other Entertainments
of ye Stage except ye Above Managers of ye Theatres in Drury Lane Dorsett Garden
and of the Theatre in the Hay Markett as is before Appointed as they shall Answer
ye Contrary at their perill Given under my hand and Seal the 31. December 1707 in
ye Sixth Year of her Majestys Reign

KENT

To the Managers of the Theatre
in Drury Lane & Dorsett Garden

Copy-text: PRO LC 5/154, pp. 299–300.

Comment: This order issued by the Lord Chamberlain on 31 December
1707 is popularly known as the "Order of Union" because it reunited the two
acting companies at Drury Lane. The marginal annotation is "Orders for the
Queens Theatre in the Hay Market."

1. I.e., to play "act music" and the like.

29. Vanbrugh to Coke about Performers' Salaries

[Cover] Mr Vanbrugh   (Wednesday [7 January 1708?])
[Direction] To the Right Honourable Mr Vice Chamberlain
                                                        Wensday

Sir
    In order to hasten the Performance of the opera (which I find a mighty
call for) twill be necessary to settle out of hand, the Rates to be allow'd the
People and that I doubt will take up more time than it shou'd do, without a
Little of your aid. If therfore you'd give your self the trouble, of one hours
time this morning, I'd wait upon you with a List of all their names, and
take your opinion what allowance may be reasonable to fix to 'em.
    If you please to name the time you shall be most at Leisure, I'll attend
you, & bring Mr Swiny with me. I am Sir

Your most humble Servant
J VANBRUGH

Copy-text: Vanbrugh holograph bound into *Theatres of London*, Harvard Theatre Collection TS 942.10 (extra-illus.).

Comment: This letter was first published by Howard P. Vincent in "Two Unpublished Letters of Vanbrugh," *N&Q*, 173 (1937), 128–29. This letter evidently postdates the Union, but probably not by much. Vanbrugh apparently realized that the performers were going to give him a hard time, but he did not yet have any idea how intractable they would prove. Cf. documents 46 and 47.

30. Petition of Verbruggen, Porter, Pack, and Bradshaw for Reinstatement

[early January 1708]

[Cover] Verbruggen, Pack &c their Petition¹

To the Most Noble the Marquiss of Kent, Lord Chamberlain of her Majesty's Household etca.

The Petition of John Verbruggen, and Mary Porter George Pack and Lucretia Bradshaw.

Humbly Sheweth—That your Petitioners having unhappily fal'n under your Lordships displeasure, Leaving the Haymarket Play-House, without your Lordship's Permission; and your Petitioners being very Sensible of their fault, humbly Request your Lordship, that out of your wonted Goodness you wou'd be Pleas'd to Pardon their Misdemeanor, and Restore them to their Employment, that they may be Partakers of the Union so happily Accomplish'd by your Lordship.

And your Petitioners as in Duty Bound shall ever Pray etca.

Copy-text: HTC Coke 56 (fair copy in an unidentified hand). For nineteenth-century transcriptions see Winston, pp. 23–24, and Drexel MS, fol. 123.

Comment: This is a petition for reinstatement presented to Kent by four renegade actors. Because all of them had jumped the Haymarket company without permission they were not covered by the blanket authority in the order of union allowing Drury Lane to sign whatever actors it wished. Although there is no record of action, Porter, Pack, and Bradshaw had all been reinstated by February 1708. Verbruggen had not. He had left London in the late summer of 1707 for Ireland, where according to Clark he was scheduled to play a part in a production of *The Spanish Wives* at Smock Alley, though he was replaced before it opened.[2] The last acting date we have for Verbruggen in London is 19 August 1707. This petition disproves Clark's assumption that he fell sick and died in Ireland. He appears to have returned to London some-time in the fall, but his roles had been reassigned, and he is not mentioned in advertisements until a benefit for his orphan is noticed, 26 April 1708.

Porter, Pack, and Bradshaw had all played with the summer company at the Haymarket in 1707. Porter's grievances go back to the 1706–7 season and are stated in a complaint of 22 October 1707 preserved in PRO LC 7/3, fols. 102–3. Basically she felt abused and unappreciated, and she did not perform during the fall of 1707. Pack and Bradshaw played with the Haymarket com-pany as late as 24 November. From PRO LC 5/154, p. 298 (31 December 1707), we can deduce that all four of the petitioners had moved to Drury Lane: the Lord Chamberlain's order notes that they had left the Haymarket without discharges and disallows the move. In all probability Rich was in-dulging in a bit of counter-tampering. For a special plea on behalf of Mrs Bradshaw, see document 31.

1. A pencil annotation says "Dec. 1707," but this dating ignores the reference in the petition to "the Union so happily Accomplish'd by your Lordship."
2. See Clark, *Early Irish Stage*, pp. 123–25.

31. Brett to Coke(?) on behalf of Mrs Bradshaw

[Cover] Mr Brett about Mrs Bradshaw *   [January 1708]

Dear Sir

I hope this will find you in a disposition to suffer Mrs Bradshaw to Play upon the terms she has agreed on with Mr Rich. She has convinc'd me she left Mr Vanbrug for reasons that will very well excuse her, and at least if you shou'd severely think there's no room for favour to her as a Player, I hope you will joine with me in not being able to refuse her any thing as Mrs Bradshaw. If I have been too sollicitous to you in this affair, I hope you'll

forgive me for preferring her interest and the interest of ye House to any
other consideration.

ffriday[1]   I'm Dear Sir your most faithfull
                                              humble Servant
                                              HEN: BRETT

* *Bradshaw*: Only the first three letters were written in ink. The name was
completed in pencil in an unidentified hand.

Copy-text: HTC Coke 45 (Brett holograph? Unique sample in this collection). For nineteenth-century transcriptions see Winston, p. 44, and Drexel
MS, fol. 124.

Comment: Henry Brett bought or was given Sir Thomas Skipwith's shares
in the Drury Lane company in the fall of 1707.[2] Lucretia Bradshaw evidently
appealed to him to help get her reinstated after she had left the Haymarket
company without permission in November (see document 30). Brett's note
tells us that she had agreed to terms with Rich but that she remained under
the Lord Chamberlain's displeasure. She was acting again with the Drury
Lane company by 4 February 1708

1. Friday fell on 2, 9, 16, 23, and 30 January in 1708.
2. See Hotson, *Commonwealth and Restoration Stage*, pp. 311, 386–97, and Fitzgerald, *A New History*, II, 443–46.

32. Memo about Anna Lodi's First Salary Proposal

[Cover] Mrs * Lodis Proposition   [early January 1708?]

Mrs Lodis proportion for 42 times till ye 13th of June next 200 Guineas if
more then twice a week to be paid proportionably for every time more.

		60	
200		4–10	
42	9	240	
	8	30	
	───	───	
	71	270-00-00	
	8 + 16 + 24 + 48 + 96	250-00-00	

* *Mrs*: MS reads *Mr*

Copy-text: MS in Broadley, p. v (Hand A).

Comment: This note evidently records a salary proposal (not otherwise preserved) in which Anna Lodi asked £5 apiece for forty-two performances. The numerical calculation to the right shows a total for sixty performances at £4 10s. each (£270). Forty-two performances at this rate would amount to £189 or 180 guineas. Vanbrugh evidently found the 200 guinea demand excessive. For a reduced proposal made on 10 January see document 33.

33. Anna Lodi to Coke about Her Revised Salary Demands

[Cover] Mrs Lodi   (10 January 1708)
        January 10th 1708/7
[Direction] For The Honourable Thomas Cook Esquire Vice-
        Chamberlaine of her Majesties Household
                                        These

Sir
    I shall be contented to sing the part of Media in the opera called Thomyris or the Amazon Queen[1] in my own Cloths on the stage for two or three days[2] and after to perform the part of Eurilla in Mr Valentin's Opera[3] as often as the said Opera shall be performed from the date hereof untill the 13th day of next June if my health will permit But noe other part in any other Opera during the said season except I shall be consenting thereto myselfe. And before [I] doe perform act or sing in either of the said Opera's Mr Vanbrugh must oblige himselfe by writing to pay to me one Hundred & ffifty pounds by weekly payments (vizt) seven pounds tenn shillings every week untill the said one Hundred & ffifty pounds be paid. If Mr Vanbrugh will agree to this I shall be ready & willing to perform the parts as above-mentioned who am

                                        Sir Your most obedient
                                        humble servant
January 10th 1707/8   ANNA LODI

    Copy-text: MS in Broadley, p. v (scribal copy signed by Lodi). For nineteenth-century transcriptions see Winston, pp. 81–82, and Drexel MS, fol.

37. A clipping from a dealer's catalogue with the MS offers it for 15s. This letter is item 191 in the 1876 sale catalogue; it is 697 in the 1905 sale catalogue.

Comment: This proposal is evidently a response to a negative reaction to an earlier proposition from Mrs Lodi (see document 32). The salary demand is here reduced by a quarter, but Lodi's insistence upon having the right to approve or disapprove all roles but one (and that in an opera yet untried) cannot have satisfied Vanbrugh. For evidence that he refused these terms see document 34.

1. The role of Media was created by Mrs Lindsey in April 1707, and she kept the part. Vanbrugh may have been trying to play one performer off against another.
2. I.e., until the new opera, *Love's Triumph*, is ready to open.
3. *Love's Triumph*, which received its premiere 26 February with the Baroness as Eurilla.

34. Anna Lodi to Coke about Her Terms

(6 January [or 11 January?] 1708)

Sir

If my Last proposition does not please you I shall never agree to no other, because I have maid thes Propositions against my Interests uopen your desire. If they dont think me fit to act I desire not to be put to a tryall and I am ready to deliver the parts[1] whenever tis your command.

> I am Sir Your most obedient
> Humble Servant

January the 6th 1707/8　　　ANNA LODI

To the Honourable Tho Coke Esq Vice Chamberlain
　　　　　　　These

Copy-text: Winston, p. 4. For another nineteenth-century transcription see Drexel MS, fol. 34. This letter may be item 190 in the 1876 sale catalogue and 698 in the 1905 sale catalogue. See the Comment below.

Comment: Both Winston and the Drexel MS transcriber give this letter as "6 January," but both the 1876 and 1905 sale catalogues list what appears to be this letter with the date "Jan. 11, 1707." This date seems likely in view of documents 32 and 33: Lodi had evidently made two proposals, and she was now sticking to her revised demands. Vanbrugh chose not to yield, and Lodi never appeared with the Haymarket company.

1. I.e., return copies of the parts and music she had been given to study.

35. Haym to Coke about Performers' Contracts and His Terms for *Pyrrhus and Demetrius*

[Cover] Mr Heyams proposition   (12 January 1708)
      January 12th 1708/7

Sir[1]

    I send you, what you was please to ask of me; but as for Mrs Lindsey, I have heard this morning, that she is in town, but I cannot find her; for Mr Leveridge, no body can tell me where to find him. I sent yesterday several times for Mr Rich, but I cou'd not speak with him; and so I had no time it being so bad weather to see Signor Saggione, but I'le endeavour to see him to day, and Let you know to morrow morning my self what he says. And I remain &

                    Sir Your very humble an obedient
                    Servant
                    NICOLINO HAYM

ye 12th of January 1708/7

Heads of ye Articles Signd between
    Mr Rich and Nicolas Haym
    Mr Rich is to have my opera of Pyrrhus & Demetrius in English, with all the parts written out, and I am to fitt it for representation so soon as possible.[2] I am also to alter for him the opera of Thomiris, and make those amendments in it as I shall judg necessary: there are some other articles which for brevity I pass over. & Mr Rich is to pay me £300 sterling.
    Mr Rich binds himself to pay Madam La Baroness £300 sterling Who is to sing thirty times for it, before a certain day in July next—
    Mr Rich is bound to pay, what has been agreed to be payd to Signore Cassanino,[3] and also to pay for his journay hither and back again to Italie;

to pay for his mantenance whilest here, and to make him a present at his
going away.—

All these agreements are to be performd by July next 1708.

My Pretentions are

That every time I play at the opera, I be payd two Guineas, and every
time I make a new opera, that I have a seperate bargain for it, as at present
I have for this of Pyrrhuss & Demetrius, are for this reason; that I have a
power to comand all the Musick: that be not obliged to goe to the tryals of
other opera's if I doe not judg it necessary, and that[‡] no one may comand
me besides the Protectors of the Theatre—

Madam La Barroness's demands are £300 sterling ascertaind to her for
singing 30 times, and if she[§] sings oftner to be payd after the rate of this
agreement; that she sing her part in Camilla, and another in my new opera
of Pyrrhus, she has Larnd a part in the new Pastoral viz. tha of Eurilla and if
desired will Learn the part of Thomiris.[4]—

In[‖] fine I humbly desire of ye Honourable persons, (or Lords and Gentlemen) concern'd, that I be not considerd Less, or made Second to any other
person of ye Musick, neither as to ye profit; nor any other matter, beliving
my self perhaps, not of inferiour merit to any of my Profession now in
England—particulary of ye foreigners. And as I have a part of Profit out of
ye Baroness's pay (according to agreement between her & me) it would not
be perhaps well, that she be Less considerd, then any of ye other Women
Singers. But I Leave this & every thing to ye judgement of those Honourable Lords, or Gentlemen, who are to be my Protectors, declaring at ye
same time that non of the propositions above be valid, without being signd
by the Persons concernd, and particularly without the Live of his Grace ye
Duke of Bedford, to whome I have the honour to be a Servant, & Master of
his Chamber Musick &c.

* *with:* "out" canceled at the end of this word.
† *to:* word added by editors.
‡ *that:* word repeated in MS.
§ *she:* MS reads "the."
‖ *In:* MS reads "I."

Copy-text: HTC Coke 28 (Haym holograph). For nineteenth-century
transcriptions see Winston, pp. 98–100, and Drexel MS, fols. 38–40. This
document may have been part of lot 184 in the 1876 sale catalogue.

Comment: This is a rather confusing document. It might at first inspection be taken as an agreement about an opera signed between Haym and Christopher Rich on 12 January 1708—thirteen days after the Lord Chamberlain had stripped Rich of the right to present musical entertainments. Puzzling over this, Curtis Price offers the comment that "there is evidence that even after Kent revoked his [Rich's] monopoly on opera in December 1707, he remained heavily invested in operatic productions at the Haymarket"—citing this document, "dated, remarkably, two days after the Lord Chamberlain's December 1707 order took effect."[5] However, no such secret investment theory need be postulated in order to explain this document.

As we understand the situation, the Lord Chamberlain's order freed all operatic personnel from existing contract obligations to Rich and Drury Lane, but said nothing about whom Vanbrugh should employ or on what terms. Vanbrugh asked Coke's help in establishing fair salaries and bonuses (see document 29). Various performers then wrote up their claims and proposals and delivered them to Vanbrugh or Coke. What we have here is not a new contract between Haym and Rich, but a summary ("Heads of ye Articles Signd between Mr Rich and Nicholas Haym") of an agreement for *Pyrrhus and Demetrius* signed before the Order of Union. As agent for the Baroness, Haym calls attention to her contract terms, and those settled for Cassani (not specified here—cf. document 42). Haym then enumerates and explains his "Pretentions"—that is, the terms on which he is willing to sign a contract with Vanbrugh to perform at the Haymarket.

In most cases the performers' "pretentions" were negotiable. We do not know to what degree Vanbrugh felt bound to honor the terms of Rich's contracts. The evidence is somewhat conflicting. In the case of Cassani, the full amount was allowed (though ultimately not paid)—perhaps because he was a special foreign import. For contract proposals from other performers see documents 32–34 (Anna Lodi), 36 (Tofts), and 39 (Valentini).

Haym seems to have served as a kind of impressario and agent. From the letter proper we would guess that he had been asked to get proposals from, or help negotiate terms with, Mrs Lindsey, Leveridge, and Saggione.

1. For clarity we have transposed the letter proper ("Sir / I send you, what you was please to ask of me. . . . Nicolino Haym") from the end of this document to the beginning.
2. *Pyrrhus and Demetrius* did not receive its London premiere until December 1708. The delay was probably caused by financial problems.
3. For Cassani's exorbitant agreement see document 42.
4. The Baroness sang Lavinia in *Camilla*; she took Deidamia in *Pyrrhus and Demetrius*;

and she duly sang Eurilla in the "new Pastoral"—i.e., *Love's Triumph*. She replaced Margarita de l'Epine in the title role of *Thomyris* on 10 April 1708.
5. "The Critical Decade," p. 72.

36. Terms Proposed by Mrs Tofts

[Cover] Mrs Tofts proposall [January 1708?]

In obedience to your Lordships command I humbly propose to sing upon ye following terms
1st I obleige my self to sing as often as required for twenty Guinneys each time
2d In Consideration ye Year is so far advanc'd I offer to sing as often as Operas shall be performd till ye first of July for four hundred Guinneys
3d I humbly propose to sing for tenn Guinneys A time till ye first of July next upon condition ye Undertaker obleige themselves to call me to sing twice a week
4ly * That I may not be debar'd singing at a Play which is comeing out upon condition it does not interfere with an Opera
All which is humbly offerd to your Lordships consideration by

> Your Lordships Most obedient
> Humble servant
> CATHERINE TOFTS

* 4ly: a large plus sign is inked by point 4. On its significance see the Comment.

Copy-text: MS in Broadley, p. ix (unidentified hand; signed by Tofts). For nineteenth-century transcriptions see Winston, p. 50, and Drexel MS, fol. 27. This letter is item 201 in the 1876 sale catalogue; it is 706 in the 1905 sale catalogue.

Comment: This letter was published by Ronald C. Kern in "Documents Relating to Company Management, 1705–1711," *Theatre Notebook*, 14 (1959–60), 60–65. For further analysis see Sands, "Mrs. Tofts," especially pp. 108–9. This letter seems definitely to be a proposal of terms for the spring of 1708. As Mollie Sands observes, "1, 2, and 3 appear . . . quite clearly as *alternatives*" (a point which escaped Ronald Kern). Curtis Price comments, apropos of the specially marked fourth point: "Mrs. Tofts was evidently un-aware of just how restrictive the new order would be."[1] Plays were now forbid-den at the Haymarket, and Drury Lane was strictly enjoined from employing adjunct singers.

Kern says that the handwriting is not Mrs Tofts'—and it does not resemble the signature. He tentatively identifies the scribe as Dieupart, who had served as Tofts' agent in recent seasons. But Dieupart's proposal of 28 January 1705/6 on her behalf, preserved in LC 7/3, fol. 88, is in yet another hand.

A pencil annotation dates this letter "1714." A clipping from a dealer's catalogue calls it an autograph signature to "an agreement circa 1750" and states the price: £1 4s. However, Mrs Tofts left the stage permanently in 1709.

1. "The Critical Decade," pp. 68–69.

37. Letter by Dieupart [Missing]

[December 1707 or January 1708?]

Known only from the 1876 sale catalogue (180): "A.L.s. in French, 1 page 4to. 1714; names Rich, Margarita, etc."

Comment: Mention of Rich and Margarita de l'Epine makes a date in the transition period December 1707–January 1708 likely.

38. Letter by Dieupart about *Love's Triumph* [Missing]

[January 1708?]

Known only from the 1876 sale catalogue (179): "Dieupart, celebrated composer. A.L.s. 4 pp. 4to. 1714, in French, naming 'Triomphe de l'Amour,' etc."

Comment: Reference to *Love's Triumph* (premiered 26 February 1708) makes the 1714 date (a favorite with the 1876 sale catalogue) highly im-probable. Dieupart composed part of the music for *Love's Triumph*, and adapted part of it from music by Scarlatti and others, fitting the music to

Motteux's English libretto.[1] This letter may well concern terms for his part in the opera.

1. See the *Biographical Dictionary*, IV, 400.

39. Valentini to Coke or Kent about His Terms

[Cover] Signor Valentin   [January 1708?]

Monseigneur

    Vôtre Grandeur m'à ordoneè de mettre par ecrit mes pretentions. Je dirais donc mes dernieres demandes, qui sont pour le 40 fois, que L'Opera se doit joüer 420 Guinées; cela n'estant que dix Guinées, et demy par soiré; j'espere que Vôtre Grandeur ne trouverà pas à redire à cèlà puisque je serais sur le Teatre à moitiè prix de l'année passée;[1]
    Pour mon Opera,[2] ceux qui sont engagez avec moy qui soit à charge des Messieurs Vanbruck et Suini; estant dejà certain qu'eux relacheront genereusement de son prix quand cela ne seroit qu'à mon exemple hormis L'Ecüyer de Monsr: L'Ambassadeur[3] à qui j ay promis La Somme de cinquante Guinees si L'Opera se fait; et pour moy même, L'Opera que je donnerais, et quelque depense que j ay fait, et pour La peïne que j ay eüe, et que j'aurois auparavant qu'elle soit sûr le Teatre, je demande La Somme de cent, et cinquante Guinées; Je n'en doute pas que Vôtre Grandeur,[*] ne trouve mes demandes trés Raisonnables, et avec un profond respect je suis.

De V: Grandeur
Vôtre tres humble et
tres obeïssant Serviteur
Valentin Urbani

[*] *Grandeur*: "mes" written and canceled after this word.

Copy-text: HTC Coke 50 (Valentini's scribe). This letter is item 203 in the 1876 sale catalogue.

Translation: "My Lord, Your Highness ordered me to write down my claims. Hence I shall state my latest proposals, which are 420 guineas for the 40 times that the Opera is to be performed: this being only ten and a half guineas per evening, I hope that your Highness will not object to it, since I shall be on stage for half the price of last year.

"For my opera: those who are hired with me under the direction of Mr Vanbrugh and Swiney are already certain that they will reduce their price, if only following my example, except for the Squire of the Lord Ambassador to whom I promised the amount of fifty guineas if the opera takes place. And for myself: I would present the opera whatever expense and effort it would take me, and would have taken me before it is on the stage; I ask the amount of one hundred and fifty guineas. I do not doubt that your Highness will find my proposals very reasonable and with profound respect I am

> of Your Highness
> your very humble and
> very obedient servant."

Comment: Valentini had presumably negotiated previously with Rich for *Love's Triumph*. The blank space on the page was used to make the calculations recorded in document 40 below. For the agreement reached on *Love's Triumph*, see document 45 below.

1. Valentini had performed at Drury Lane in the spring of 1707. We have no information about his salary then.
2. *Love's Triumph*.
3. Probably the Secretary of the Venetian Ambassador (the Mr Berti of document 45?) is meant.

40. Valentini's Terms and Preliminary Casts for *Pyrrhus and Demetrius* and *Love's Triumph*

[January 1708?]

> for Mr Valentin
> to sing 40 times 'till June ye [blank] next
> considering what he has had already
> to have 350 G ⎰ which is about 8G:1/2
> ⎱ per time

the Charge of the opera

for ye venetian Ambassadors secretary[1]	50G
for himself[2] a 3d night or	100
for Mr du Par for the scores	50
to Mr Motteux	20
	tottall 220

This will amount to about a 3d & 6th Night.[3]

Mr Heyams agreement with Mr Rich
pour Signor Cassano 250 besides his 2 Journeys
La Baroness for 30 nights   300
Mr Heyams for his Oper   300

Pyrrhus ⎱
         ⎰ coallo   Vanlentin
Demetrius   Cassano

Deidamia	Mrs Tofts
Clemene	La Baroness
Marius	La Margerita
Cleartes	Leveridge
Arbantes	
Doris or Brennus	a Comical part

Tryumph of Love

Eurilla	Baronness or Maria Gallia
Lycisca	Mrs Tofts
Serpetto	Mrs Lindsey
Liso	Mr Valentin
Olindo	Margarita
Neralbo	Mr Leveridge

Copy-text: HTC Coke 51, written on the same sheet as HTC Coke 50 (document 39 above) in Hand A.

Comment: This is a rough calculation of costs for *Love's Triumph* (words by Motteux, music arranged by Dieupart), and preliminary cast lists for both that opera and Haym's *Pyrrhus and Demetrius* (on terms for which see document 35). In January 1708 Vanbrugh was still expecting to mount premieres of both operas during the spring. When *Love's Triumph* opened 26 February the cast was as specified here, with the Baroness taking Eurilla.

When *Pyrrhus and Demetrius* finally received its premiere in December 1708 Nicolini (newly arrived) took Pyrrhus, with Valentini as Demetrius. Mrs Tofts and the Baroness swapped the roles specified here. Margarita de l'Epine duly took Marius. Leveridge was replaced by Ramondon.

For the contract finally agreed upon between Vanbrugh and Valentini see document 45.

1. The reason for this substantial gratuity is never specified.
2. Presumably Valentini.
3. Authors of plays were usually allowed the profits of the third and sixth nights of the first run. The projected fees for libretto and score are being checked to see that they are in line with normal practice.

41. Two Memoranda: Scenes for *Love's Triumph* and an Agreement between Cherrier and Santlow

[January 1708?]

[Cover] Mr Cherrier's agreement with Mrs Saint * Low
       Scenes † for ye Triumph of Love [1]

[Top of page]
    ye Wood of ye Perspective
    a garden with fountains and a Grotto
    ye Temple of Love with ye scene of a Wood

[Bottom of page]
    Mr Cherrier's Agreement with Mrs St Loe [2] for 5 years from ye time of her beginning to Dance ‡ which is 2 years now passing. He is to give her half of what he recieves for her dancing under ye mutuall pentalty of £100 forfeiture
    He taught her 2 years before she went upon ye Stage—

    * *Saint*: MS appears to read "Saitn."
    † *Scenes*: MS appears to read "Scences."
    ‡ *Dance*: "of" is written and canceled after this word.

Copy-text: HTC Coke 11 (Hand A). For nineteenth-century transcriptions see Winston, p. 46, and Drexel MS, fol. 54.

Comment: These notes appear to be entirely unrelated. Why Coke needed to know about part of the scenery for a production in progress we do not know. Recording Santlow's agreement with Cherrier was a routine part of working out salaries for the Haymarket.

1. I.e., *Love's Triumph* (1708), not *The Triumph of Love* (November 1712). Scene descriptions in the libretto of *Love's Triumph* say "The SCENE is a Grove with a Green, and a Village at a Distance" (p. 1), and "The SCENE opens, and discovers Eurilla seated in the middle of an Amphitheatre, adorn'd with Myrtles and various Garlands of Flowers" (p. 40).
2. I.e., Hester Santlow, as she is usually known, future wife of Barton Booth.

42. The Terms of Cassani's Agreement with Rich

[Cover] Casanano   [January 1708?]

Charges, and Coast of signore Joseph Cassano—

	£	s	d
salary agreed to him, one Thousand Roman Crowns, at 6s per Crown	300	—	—
Charges of Coming, & going bake 200 Pistols	87	10	—
Boarding & Lodging, for 8 Months, with alowance of one Bottle of Wine Every day [1]	50	—	—
	£437	10	—

A Present that Mr Rich had to make me, which was left to the decision of two noble men

Copy-text: HTC Coke 46 (Haym holograph). For nineteenth-century transcriptions see Winston, p. 49, and Drexel MS, fol. 60.

Comment: This statement details the agreement Rich had made with "Cassano" (Giuseppe Cassani) to come to England to sing—terms inherited most unhappily by Vanbrugh. Not only was Cassani's price inordinately high, but he performed only two nights at the Haymarket (7 and 10 February), and was met with fierce audience disapprobation. For Vanbrugh's comment on the

Cassani fiasco see document 70 below (14 May 1708). For an account of the bills the singer left unpaid, see document 72 below (8 September 1708). Surprisingly, Cassani did later return to England for two seasons (1710–12).

1. To judge from the figures in Gladys Scott Thomson's *Life in a Noble Household 1641–1700* (1937; rpt. London: Jonathan Cape, 1950), a bottle of wine would have cost one to two shillings. Over eight months this would amount to between twelve and twenty-four pounds, assuming the wine to be neither very cheap nor very expensive.

43. Terms Proposed by Saggione and Maria Gallia

[Cover] Saggione   [January 1708]

A di [blank]
Per Acordarsi nel Teatro Di Emarcht Io Ioseffe Fedelli Saggione, e che mi debba pagare pontual ogni [blank] per año Ghinee cento è Cinquanta al ano: lasiando che tre mesi siano di vacanza è noue mesi obligati cioe [blank] e saper da chi ho da eser pagto *

A di[1]
Per Recitar In Emarchet Io Maria Galia Saggione, che mi deba dare Il mio guadagno sicuro ogni tanto tempo. Per año, nove mesi obligati è tre di vacanza [blank] Ghinee settecento: e sicurarmi del mio dinaro doue e chi ha da pagarmi e se mi honora di dir se è tropo ò poco, io nõ uoglio manco prezzo sicuro che nesuna cioe di Margarita[2] e mi⁵ staf† il medemo‡ prezo, se li pai§ ch'io lo meriti. suplico di non farmi torto[3]

* *pagto*: i.e., "pagato."
† *mi⁵ staf*: reading doubtful. Probably a mangled form of "Mrs Tofts," though if it is read "mi' stab" some form of "stabilisca" could be intended.
‡ *medemo*: "medesimo" in modern Italian.
§ *li pai* (or "par"): reading doubtful. "Le pare" in modern Italian; the writer may be trying to use the equivalent of the subjunctive "paia."

Copy-text: HTC Coke 69 (Saggione holograph?).

Translation: "On the day [blank] By contracting with the Haymarket theatre, I Ioseffe Fedelli Saggione, must be paid promptly every [blank] each year, one hundred and fifty guineas per annum: allowing three months for vacation and nine months for service, that is [blank] and being apprised concerning by whom I will be paid."

"On the day [blank] For singing in the Haymarket, I Maria Galia Saggione, must be given my guaranteed earnings periodically. By the year, nine months of duty and three of vacation, seven hundred guineas: and guarantee me with respect to my money as to where and by whom I will be paid. And if you will do me the honor to inform me if it is too much or too little. I do not wish an established wage less than that of any other woman, for example than Margarita or Mrs Tofts[?] if it seems to you that I deserve it. I pray that you do not do me an injustice."

Comment: These papers are rough draft proposals of terms by Maria Gallia and her husband (a double bass player and composer). They are carelessly written with distinctly crude syntax: the translation is essentially literal. The salaries stated are outlandishly high. Compare documents 44 and 50.

1. The Maria Gallia proposal is written on a separate piece of paper.
2. I.e., Margarita de l'Epine.
3. Written sideways in Hand A on the same sheet: "Mr Sagione / 400 / 64 + 4."

44. Estimate of the Charges of the Opera Every Night

[January 1708]

[Cover] Estimate made of the Charges of ye Opera every night
    101-17-00 per Night
[Direction] Mr Arncourt[1] att his chambers in Lincolns inn

Mrs Margarita	300-00-00	
Mrs Tofts	300-00-00	
ye Baroness	120	to June [*]
Mrs Lindsey	60	or 30 shillings every time ye opera is acted
Mrs Seggione	120	ye same as ye Baroness
Mr Cassano	437	
Mr Leveridge	60	or 30 shillings every time ye opera

Mr Ramondon   50
Mr Lawrence   50

Mr Diopar   25 shillings a Time 5 shillings per Practice
Mr Heyams   25 shillings a Time 5 shillings practice
Mr Papuch   ditto & 5 shillings [†] practice
Mr Seggione   ditto

	per week		
Des barques	3-0-0	Mrs des barques	3-0-0
Cherrier	2-0-0	Mrs St Loe	2-0-0
des legarde		Mis Evans	
firbank or Labbe's Sc: [2]		Mis Norris	

Turn over [3]

Pirrhus & Demetrius				ye same at ye Triumph of Love		
450	413-10	15	309		200	90
22-10	103-10	148	150	148	1600	8
472-10	309 —	163	159		80	720
	59 —				36	36
					116	

Valentine	10-15-00	
Cassano	7-10-00	
Leveridge	1-10-00	
Ramondon	0-15-00	
Lawrence	0-15-00	20-15-00 [4]
Mrs Tofts	7-10-00	
Mrs Margarita	7-10-00	
ye Baroness	3-00-00	
Mrs Saggione	3-00-00	
Mrs Lindsey	1-10-00	22-10-00
Mr Heyams	1-05-00	
Mr Diopar	1-05-00	
Mr Papusch	1-05-00	
Mr Seggione	1-05-00	05-00-00

Instrumentall Musick

1st Trebles
Mr Banister	0-15-00
Mr Corbett	0-15-00
Mr Le Sac	0-10-00
Mr Soyan	0-10-00
Mr Dean	0-10-00

2d Trebles
Mr Babel	0- 8-00
Mr Simpson	0- 8-00
Mr Manchip	0- 8-00
Mr Smith	0- 8-00
Mr Robert	0- 8-00

Tenors
| Mr Smith | 0- 8-00 |
| Mr Lunican | 0- 8-00 |

Hautboys
| Mr Lully | 0-15-00 |
| Mr Latour | 0-10-00 |

Bassons
Mr Babel	0-15-00
Signor Pietro	0-15-00
Mr Cadett	0-10-00

Bases
Mr Paisible	0-15-00
Mr Francisco	0-15-00
Mr Roger	0-10-00
Mr Laroon	0-08-00
Des abey	0-10-00

| a Trumpett | 0-08-00 | 12-07-00 |

Rent of ye House att a proportion of £800 per Annum   13-10-00
Wax Candles   5 – 6 – 8
Attendants of ye Hous   10-13-4
The Practices of 2 New Operas

Dancers [5]

Mr Des Bargues	1-10-00
Mr Cherrier	1-10-00
Mr delagarde	1-00-00
Mr Firbank	
Mr Labbe's brother	
Mrs Des bargues	1-10-00
Mis St Low	1-05-00
Mis Evans	1-05-00
Mis Norris	

* *120 to June*: replaces "150 or 50 sh a Time," which is canceled.
† *ditto & 5 shillings*: MS reads "do 5& sh:"

Copy-text: HTC Coke 8 (Hand A).

Comment: These figures show Vanbrugh and Coke trying to project operating costs of the opera on a per-performance basis. The figures on the first
page (prior to "Turn over") note the basis on which major salaries were calculated. The rest of the list gives fixed expenses for each performance—salaries,
rent, candles, and so forth. As listed, the total is £98 10s., but if we allow £1
for each of the three dancers for whom no salary is specified the total is £101
10s., or just 7 shillings below the total given on the cover. This total does
not, of course, include the 5 shillings per rehearsal owed to at least some of
the musicians. Nor does it include "The Practices of 2 New Operas," for
which no sum is specified, or the considerable expenses of costumes and scenery which new productions entailed. Nothing is allowed for routine refurbish-
ment of sets and costumes.

The figure for rent (£13 10s.) seems high. In document 24 (late December?) only £370 is specified as rent. The £800 figure is repeated in documents
48 and 49. To some degree rent is probably an arbitrary figure. It was owed
by Vanbrugh to Vanbrugh, and above the level of debt service it would
have been money in his pocket, presuming that the venture was solvent.
Vanbrugh had built the theatre as a personal venture, with the help of contri-
butions from thirty society friends who received in return nothing but life-
time passes for themselves. [6] Vanbrugh did not, therefore, owe "rent" to
"building sharers" as had always been the case at Drury Lane and Dorset Garden. How much money he had to borrow in order to get the theatre built and
completed we do not know. Tentatively, we offer the hypothesis that £370
would at least have covered Vanbrugh's debt service, and that he boosted the

rent total as a way of minimizing his hypothetical profits at a time when, "Upon a Supposition that there wou'd be Immence gain,"[7] performers were demanding absolutely unprecedented salaries—and Coke was backing them up.

This document shows us one step in a series of escalating totals. In document 24 (late December?) Vanbrugh had estimated £94 per night. Here he calculated £101 (a difference fully attributable to rent). By 8 March the figure (now in actuality) was up to £110 and by 7 April to £116 (see documents 56, 57, and 62 below).

The present document is an "Estimate"—three salaries are not filled in, and the "Trumpett" is not named. Some of these salaries were not yet definite—Margarita de l'Epine and Mrs Tofts wound up at £400 rather than £300, the Baroness at £200 instead of £120, and so forth. Eager to get his venture going, Vanbrugh started opera performances at the Haymarket on Tuesday 13 January—well before he had settled terms with the performers. Consequently this financial estimate need not be dated before 13 January.

1. Evidently a lawyer or man of business.
2. "L'abbe's Scholar"? From the context we would suppose that this is "Mr Labbe's brother," mentioned below under "Dancers."
3. The figures which follow are on the back of the first sheet of this document. We have not been able to determine their meaning.
4. The correct total is 21-05-00.
5. The figures which follow differ somewhat from those given above.
6. See Milhous, "Vanbrugh's Haymarket Theatre Project."
7. See Vanbrugh's letter of 27 July 1708, an extract of which appears as an interdocument between documents 71 and 72.

45. Agreement between Vanbrugh and Valentini

[Cover] Mr Valentin's Agreement   [January 1708]

Accord fait entre Mr Vanbruck, et Valantin.

Que le dit Mr Vanbruck est obligè ly payer La somme de quattrecent Guinees pour La Saison c'est à dir du 13:me de Januier jusque aux 13:me du Mois de Juïn, outre Cent Guineés pour L Opera du Triomfe d'Amour; et le dit Mr Vanbruck est obligè encore payer pour La ditte Opera à Mr Mouteux et Mons: Berti[1] La Somme de cinquante Guinees chacun.

Receu par mon contract par La main de Mr Vanbruck deucent Guinees

c'est à dir tous les 13:me du moïs comme nous sommes restez d'accord d'ou
il m'est deû encore troiscent Guineés.

De cinquante Guinees de Mr Mouteux il en à reçeû vingt cinque en
Billet que Mr Vanbruck luy meme à donnè à son Valet d'ou il reste à Mr
Mouteux vingt cinque Guinees

et pour Mr Berti La Somme entiere, c'est à dire de cinquante Guineés

VALANTIN URBANI

Copy-text: HTC Coke 49 (Valentini's scribe). This document is item 205
in the 1876 sale catalogue.

Translation: "Agreement drawn between Mr Vanbrugh and Valentini.
That the said Mr Vanbrugh is obliged to pay him the amount of four hundred
guineas for the season, that is from the thirteenth of January to the thirteenth
of June, as well as one hundred guineas for the opera *Love's Triumph*; and that
the said Mr Vanbrugh is also obliged to pay for the said opera the amount of
fifty guineas each to Mr Motteux and Mr Berti.

"I received according to my contract from Mr Vanbrugh's hand two hundred guineas; [further payments will be made] every 13th of the month as we
had agreed; hence I am still owed three hundred guineas.

"Of the fifty guineas owed to Mr Motteux he received twenty-five in a note
that Mr Vanbrugh himself gave his footman; hence Mr Motteux is still to
receive twenty-five guineas.

"And for Mr Berti the whole amount, that is, fifty guineas [is still due]."

Comment: On preliminary negotiations see documents 39 and 40.

1. Mons. Berti is evidently secretary to the Venetian Ambassador.

46. Vanbrugh to Coke about Performers' Bargains

(15 January [1708])

[Direction?] To the Right Honourable the Vice Chamberlain
                                Thursday January ye 15th
Sir

I was to wait on you yesterday, but cou'd not Possibly to day. I wou'd fain
fix all these peoples Bargains, and, Am so far from desiring to squeeze any
thing out of their Demands To make a large profit to myself that I should be

extreemly pleased To find there would be room To give 'em all they ask—
I'll wait on you tomorrow towards Eleaven, and if you can then spare a little
time for Play house Dispatches— I wish you wou'd order Lindsey * to attend. If she has my Lord Whartons[1] [. . .][†] to be contented I believe we
shall agree

I am Sir
your most humble Servant
J VANBRUGH

To the Right Honourable Mr Vice Chamberlain in St James' Place
Thursday morning

* *Lindsey*: MS reads *Lindsey*; we have adopted our reading from the Drexel
MS.
[†][. . .]: this hiatus occurs both in Winston's transcription and in the
Drexel MS. A word such as "advice" is evidently missing or indecipherable.

Copy-text: Winston p. 2. For another nineteenth-century transcription see
Drexel MS, fol. "40" (misnumbered). This document was part of lot 209 in
the 1876 sale catalogue.

Comment: Vanbrugh's opera company opened on Tuesday 13 January with
Thomyris, attracting a house of £193.17.6. Here we see him trying to enlist
Coke's aid in making definite salary agreements with his performers. Com-
pare document 47.

1. Thomas Wharton (1648–1715), at this time Earl, later Marquis, of Wharton, in
November 1708 became Lord Lieutenant of Ireland, where he is credited with introducing opera. As director of court diversions he took with him Thomas Clayton, composer of *Arsinoe* and *Rosamond*. See Clark, *Early Irish Stage*, pp. 126–27.

47. Vanbrugh to Coke about Problems Reaching Terms with Performers and Competition from Concerts

[Cover] Mr Van brugh   (Tuesday [20 January 1708])
[Direction] To the Right Honourable Mr Vice Chamberlain

Tuesday night

Sir
    I endeavour'd twice today to wait on you—I hope you can spare an hour
to morrow, that some Conclusion may be made with these singers and musick; for without your Aid, nothing can be done with 'em. There was but

£150. last time and £120. to night. 'Tis impossible to go thorough with it, if the Performers are not reduc'd to Reason. I have Appointed severall of 'em to attend you to morrow—I'll likewise wait on you about ten a Clock and shew you what I have drawn up, which I think is all can possibly be offer'd em. There will be an other misfortune, a Great one if not nip'd in the Bud. I mean musick meetings. There's one given out to morrow at York Buildings, and the Bills larger & much more remarkable than usuall. I'm told, (and believe) Rich is in the Bottom on't. But I hope you'll move My Lord Chamberlain for an Order to stop their Performance. Which will be a great means to make our musitians both accept reasonable sallarys and be carefull in their Business. I am Sir

Your most humble servant

J VANBRUGH

Copy-text: Pforzheimer MS 117 (Vanbrugh holograph), published by per-mission of the Carl H. Pforzheimer Library. For nineteenth-century transcrip-tions see Winston, p. 55, and Drexel MS, fol. "43." This item is 206 in the 1876 sale catalogue; it is 709 in the 1905 sale catalogue. A typewritten tran-scription is to be found in Broadley, p. 3. The text of the Pforzheimer MS has been published in *A Catalogue of English Books and Manuscripts, 1470–1700*, 3 vols. (New York: The Carl H. Pforzheimer Library, 1940), III, 1058–59, and by Arthur R. Huseboe, "Vanbrugh: Additions to the Correspondence," *Philological Quarterly*, 53 (1974), 135–40.

Comment: Huseboe establishes the date from the box office totals of 17 and 20 January, and the date of the York Buildings concert.[1] (Kern er-roneously puts this letter in 1711.) By this time Vanbrugh was seriously dis-turbed about the financial demands of his singers. Whether Rich was indeed, as Vanbrugh charges here, trying to subvert opera at the Haymarket by en-couraging concerts we do not know. The advertised program names no opera singer, but does promise vocal as well as instrumental music.

At the great Room in York Buildings, on Wednesday the 21st of January, will be perform'd, A Consort of Vocal and Instrumental Musick, by the best Masters, viz. A full Piece of the famous Signior Bononcini by Mr. Dean, Sen, Mr. Beeston, and Mr. Luly, &c. A new Set of Airs for the Arch-Lute and Violin by the Two Mr. Deans, Compos'd on purpose by Mr. Dean, Jun. Singing to the Arch-Lute by Mr. Dean, Jun. A Solo of the famous Archangelo Corelli by Mr. Dean, Sen. Also several Entertainments of Singing in Italian and English by the Best Performers. Tickets are to be had at Robin's Coffee-House . . . [and] at White's Chocolate-House in St.

James's-street. Each Ticket 5s. Beginning exactly at 7 of the Clock.   [*Daily Courant*, 19 January 1708]

Vanbrugh saw clearly that if the singers and musicians could support them-selves with concerts he had little hope of getting disciplined performers at "reasonable sallarys."

1. See *The London Stage*, Part 2, I, 164. This concert was evidently postponed. The ads for 4 February specify "That the Tickets that were return'd at York-Buildings will not be taken, there being a Number of fresh Tickets issu'd out for Stationers Hall" (ibid., p. 165). The Lord Chamberlain probably stopped the performance of 21 January as a favor to Vanbrugh.

48. Two Memoranda: Shares in the Covent Garden Ground Rent and Vanbrugh's Projected Financial Totals for the Spring of 1708

[ca. January 1708]

[Cover] Proprietors of ye Ground Rent of Coavent Garden[1] House

Women	1370	Coavent garden Ground Rent	
Men	1030	in 36 shares	
4 Ch:[2] Bases	270	Mr Killigrew	9
other Instrumentall		Mr Morley	4 1/2
Musick	805	Mr Clayton	4
Musick	3475	Mrs Lacy	4
House Rent	800	Mr Kinnaston	1
Candles	320	Mr Ropper	1
Attendants to ye		Mrs Shepey	3
House	640	Mr Mordaunt	1
8 Dancers & their		Mr Stanhope	1
Cloaths	800	Mr Rich	
2 New Operas Cloaths		Mr Sherman	1
& scenes	1275	Mr Stone	1
	7310		

200
40
8000
7
150
60
9000

ye Lease upon ye union of ye 2 Houses
ye Rent of ye Coavent garden from £6
per diem to £3 per diem

Copy-text: HTC Coke 7 (Hand A). For a nineteenth-century transcription see Winston, p. 95.

Comment: The two parts of this document (separated by a fold) are unrelated. Why Coke wanted or needed a list of the sharers in the Drury Lane ground rent we can only speculate. (Rich notoriously did not pay such bills: conceivably Coke agreed to look into the claims of the sharers at the time of the 1708 union.) The list as given here totals 30.5: presumably Rich held the balance of the 36 shares. The reduction in rent referred to below the right hand column (actually from £5 14s. to £3) occurred at the time of the 1682 union.[3]

The figures on the left are similar to the totals in document 49. The calculations at the bottom of the column appear to show a projected £8000 gross income if the house averaged £200 per night for 40 performances, or £9000 for a £150 average over 60 performances.

1. I.e., Drury Lane.
2. "Chief"?
3. For earlier lists of sharers and the 1682 rent reduction see Hotson, *Commonwealth and Restoration Stage*, pp. 282 and 322.

49. Vanbrugh's Financial Commitments for 1708

[late January 1708?]

[Cover] List of Performers for ye Opera & their Salary's

Performers in ye Opera for 1 year including ye Vacation from ye Middle of June to the Middle of September ye year beginning & ending att Christmas.

Mrs Margarita	400:0:0	
Mrs Tofts	400:0:0	
Mrs Lindsey	90:0:0	
The Baroness	200:0:0	1370:0:0
Maria Gallia	200:0:0	
Mrs Cross or some other woman	80:0:0	

Signor Valentin
    to ye 13th June   430:0:0
Signor Casanino
    or £300 to ye time
    of his agreement   400:0:0
Mr Ramondon   50:0:0   1030:0:0
Mr Lawrence   50:0:0
    & if he learns a thro
    Base by ye End of ye
    Year to have £10 more
Mr Leveridge   100:00:0

Mr Heyams *   70:0:0
Mr Diopar   70:0:0
Mr Papusch   70:0:0   280:0:0 [1]
Mr Sagione   70:0:0 [2]
a Theorbo—

                             Turn over

Women singers	1370:0:0
Men singers	1030:0:0
Chief Bases	2801o:0 [3]
ye Rest of ye Instrumentall Musick	750:0:0 [4]
House Rent	800:0:0
Wax Candles & sweet Oyl	320:0:0 [5]
attendants to ye House &ca	640:0:0
8 Dancers & their Cloaths	800:0:0
2 New Operas Cloaths & scenes	1275:0:0 [6]
	7260:0:0 [7]
Printing ye Bills	60:0:0
	7320:0:0

* *Mr Heyams:* Two words were written above this name and smeared out.

Copy-text: HTC Coke 3 (Hand A). This sheet bears an address in an unidentified hand which is evidently unrelated to the contents: "To The Right
honorable Thomas Coke Esquire Vice-chamberlain to her Majesty In st.
James-place present." Coke seems to have written his list of performers and
salaries on a cover sheet from something else. For nineteenth-century transcriptions of his notes, see Winston, p. 86, and Drexel MS, fol. 56.

Comment: This could well be Coke's copy of the list Vanbrugh has "drawn up" to show to him, mentioned in document 47. A couple of items are still tentative ("Mrs Cross or some other woman"), but this comes close to the company as it tried to operate in the spring of 1708 (see documents 50, 55, and 56). A penciled note on this document dates it 1711–12, but that is out of the question, as reference to rosters in *The London Stage* quickly shows. The *London Stage* list for spring 1708 at the Haymarket lacks Cross, Ramondon, and Lawrence—but because we do not have full casts for *Thomyris* and *Camilla* that means almost nothing.

If we assume that Vanbrugh planned to mount a 64-night season (cf. document 24), these figures would yield a daily charge of £114—which is close to what actually happened in March and April (cf. document 62). But of course Vanbrugh did not achieve his £150 per night projected income, and in fact the Haymarket offered only 29 performances during the spring of 1708—one of them after Vanbrugh sold out in May.

1. Changed from 270:0:0.
2. Changed from 60:0:0.
3. Changed from 270:0:0.
4. Changed from 800:0:0.
5. Changed from 300:0:0.
6. Changed from 1270:0:0.
7. The correct total is £7265.

50. Haymarket Salaries for the Spring of 1708

[late January 1708]

[Cover] Hay markett Account January 1707[1]

A List of Persons hereafter named under sallary

Singers	per diem			Instrumental Musick	per diem		
Mrs Tofts	7	10	0	Mr Haymes	1	5	0
Margarita	7	10	0	Dieupart	1	5	0
Barroness	3	0	0	Papusch	1	5	0
Mrs Lindsey	2	0	0	Sagoni	1	5	0
Valentine	7	10	0	Bannister	0	15	0
Leveridge	2	0	0	Passible	0	15	0
Romondon	0	15	0	Lully	0	15	0

		£	s	d		£	s	d
	Lawrence	0	15	0	Corbett	0	15	0
	Turner	0	10	0	Babell	0	15	0
34 10*	Seignora Sajony²	3	0	0	Dean	0	10	0
					Petro	0	10	0
	Dancers				Soyan	0	10	0
	Debargues	2	10	0	Dessabaye	0	10	0
	Cherrier	1	10	0	Cadett	0	10	0
	Delagard	0	12	6	Latour	0	11	3
	Mrs Debargues	1	3	4	Rogere	0	11	3
	Santlow	1	3	4	Lesac	0	11	3
	Evans	1	3	4	Francisco	0	11	3
	Alloway	0	10	0	Babell Junior	0	8	0
	Shaw	0	10	0	Laroon	0	8	0
	Brous³	0	7	6	Simpson	0	8	0
	Cadett	0	7	6	Manship	0	8	0
		44	7	6	Smith	0	8	0
					Smith Junior	0	8	0
					Robert	0	8	0
					Lunican	0	8	0
					Davain	0	8	0
						£17	2	0

Mrs Saggione to have 20 Guineys
Saturday towards her bargain⁴

* 34 10: "31 10" written above this and canceled. £34 10s. is correct.

Copy-text: HTC Coke 59 (Hand E, with additions in Hand A). For nine-teenth-century transcriptions see Winston, p. 87, and Drexel MS, fol. 52 (both misdated).

Comment: This list appears to have been copied from the theatre's books recording daily salaries (per performance) as agreed upon in late January 1708. Unlike documents 44 and 49, this list has no gaps to indicate negotiations still in progress, and the salaries are less uniform than in those lists. One puzzle which remains is the absence of reference to Cassani. Possibly the Lord Chamberlain ruled that his lump-sum contract would have to be treated specially. A set of scratch figures below the left column is omitted in our transcription.

1. I.e., 1707/8.
2. I.e., Saggione/Maria Gallia.

3. Presumably the "Mrs Bruce" who had performed at the Haymarket in 1706. See *Biographical Dictionary*, II, 370.

4. This annotation is in Hand A, as are the omitted figures.

51. Haym to Coke about a Bassoon Player in *Camilla*

[Cover] Mr Nicolini Heyams   (27 January 1708)
      January 27th 1708/7
[Direction] To The Honourable Mr Coke's Vice Chamberlain
      in St James's Place

Illus^{mo}: Signore

   Sarei venuto in persona, a Incommodarla, mà come spero di finire questa Mattina La parte per il sig^r Cassanino nella Camilla, Li Mando La presente; et prego V.S. Illus^{ma} di farmi sapere, per il Latore di questa, se il signor Pietrino,[1] dell' Duca d'Ormond, deue sonare il bassone questa sera nella Camilla, ò nò; acciò io Lo possa fare auuertire; et supplicandola di perdonare L'Ardire et L'incommodo, fò fine, e resto &c.—

    Di V.S. Illus^{ma}:   Umiliss^{mo}: et deuotis^{mo}: seruitore
                                      NICOLINO HAYM

Li 27 Gennaro 1707/8

   Copy-text: HTC Coke 29 (Haym holograph). This letter may have been part of lot 184 in the 1876 sale catalogue.

   Translation: "Most Illustrious Sir, I would have come in person to inconvenience you, but since I hope this morning to finish the part for Mr Cassanino in *Camilla*, I send you this letter; and I entreat Your Illustrious Lordship to inform me by way of the bearer of the present letter whether Mr Pietrino[1] [in the service] of the Duke of Ormond, may play the bassoon tonight in *Camilla* or not, in order that I may have him informed; and begging you to forgive my boldness and the inconvenience, I make an end, and remain your most illustrious lordship's most humble and devoted servant, Nicolino Haym. The 27th of January 1707/8."

   Comment: Haym was evidently copying out—and probably adding to— the part of Metius in *Camilla* (previously sung by Ramondon in English) for Cassani. Cassani, newly arrived from Italy, performed in *Camilla* on 7 and 10 February and was shockingly ill-received—a great disappointment to Vanbrugh.

1. "Signor Pietrino" is Pietro Chaboud (or Schaboud—cf. document 72), often listed in these papers by his first name only. He petitioned for a place in the Haymarket orchestra (document 17), and was included in one early roster (second part of document 18). He was omitted in document 22, but does appear in documents 44 and 50 the latter probably from just about this date. We deduce that the orchestra roster was still in some flux. Why the question was referred to Coke rather than to Vanbrugh we do not know. The Duke's permission may have been needed in order for Chaboud to play that evening.

INTERDOCUMENT.
The Muses Mercury *on the Effects of the Union*

[early February 1708]

Since we took any notice of the *Theaters* in our *Mercuries*, there has been a Revolution, with which all Lovers of *Opera's* are very well pleas'd. For the Masters and Performers imploy'd for the Stage, have at last prevail'd, that the House in the *Hay-Market* should be taken up wholly for *Opera's*, and that in *Drury-Lane* for *Plays*. At that in the *Hay-Market*, *Opera's* will be perform'd twice a Week for 9 Months in the Year, and *Plays* as usually at the Theater in *Drury-Lane*. Perhaps the Distance of the House in the *Hay-Market* from the Scene of Business in the City was to its Disadvantage: For 'tis very certain, that a very good part of the Audience for *Plays* came from that Part of the Town, where Mr. *Collier's* Arguments prevail'd most. As for *Opera's*, the Expence of that Diversion is a little too great for such as declare for exact Oeconomy; and as the *Great* chiefly incourage them, they are now nearer than ever to their Protectors. Before this Agreement was made, there were Divisions among the Performers, which prevented any *Opera's* being play'd till 'twas late in the Season: But now 'tis hop'd they will understand their mutual Interest so well, as by doing Justice to one another, enable themselves the better to do Justice to the Town. The *Opera* has been always crowded since it has been under the present Management, and is now in a fairer way to live than ever. As for *Comedies*, there has been no new one but Mr. *Cibber's*, call'd, *The Lady's Last Stake, or the Wife's Resentment*: Part of which, the Epilogue, met with universal Applause; and Seignior *Ciberini's* artful acting it, was with Reason lik'd by all that saw it. The Humour indeed was new, the pretended Grievance it expos'd, by some thought crying, and the Pleasure the Audience took in it was answerable. But what is very extraordinary; the Subject of that Epilogue takes as much after it as it did before, and the same Persons clap both Seignior *Ciberini*, and Seignior ———. . . .[1]

The *New Opera's* are late, but ready, and will perhaps be the more welcome, for the Delays they have met with. The Pastoral *Opera*,[2] introduc'd by *Signior Valentini*; the Words written by Mr. *Motteux*, will be first perform'd, and the *Dido*,[3] or the *Pyrrhus* of *Scarlati*, the next.[4] 'Tis certain, the Former was ready several Months before either of the others; and the Musick, as we are inform'd, is more adapted to the *English* Taste, than that of the *Pyrrhus*: which however has its Merit. But since Mr. *Leveridge*, who introduces the *Dido*, has the good Fortune to be an *Englishman*, it may be hop'd, when he is to be judg'd by *English-men*, he will not be post-pon'd, unless his Musick is the Occasion of it. —We know this is no Argument in good Sense; Merit is of all Countries. But still 'tis the Argument the *Italians* and *French* make use of against the *English*, who are tame in nothing, so much as in the Arts, in which they are too apt to submit to their Inferiours.

Comment: This commentary on the state of affairs in the first month after the Union, though in an issue dated "December 1707," was actually published in *The Muses Mercury* in early February 1708.

1. *The Lady's last Stake* received its premiere 13 December 1707 at the Haymarket. Cibber's epilogue—in which he imagines his success as an Italian singer, Seignior *Cibberini*—is a fairly harsh comment on the popularity of Valentini.
2. *Love's Triumph*, which received its premiere 26 February.
3. This work remains a mystery. Whether Leveridge had composed a *Dido* of his own, or whether he had revamped Purcell's *Dido and Aeneas* (1689) we do not know. The work was evidently never performed.
4. *Pyrrhus and Demetrius* (performed in December 1708), with a libretto by Swiney, and music arranged by Haym, mostly selected from Scarlatti.

52. Swiney to Coke about a Schedule Conflict

(19 February 1708)

[Cover] Mr Swiny February 19th 1707. [1707/8]
[Direction] For The Right Honourable Mr Vice Chamberlain these.

Sir

Mr Cibber told me you desired him to let me know you wou'd not have me begin the opera[1] on Mr Betterton's day, we cannot perform it sooner so that we must loose above £50 by not playing above once that week, I have writt to Mr Betterton to lett him know the reasons why we can't ly by that day, and have advised him to take Tuesday next which will be the same thing to him. I * am Your Honours most obliged & humble Servant

OWEN SWINY.

Thursday Night
ffebruary 19th 1707[1707/8]

* *I* replaces "and" erased

Copy-text: HTC TS 992.31.7 (36). Swiney holograph. For nineteenth-century transcriptions see Winston, p. 71, and Drexel MS, fol. 44. This letter was probably among those offered in lot 199 of the 1876 sale catalogue.

Comment: This letter is a reply to Coke's objection (reported via Colley Cibber) to scheduling the premiere of *Love's Triumph* for 26 February, apparently already announced as a benefit day for Betterton at Drury Lane. Betterton seems to have cooperated by moving his benefit to 11 March. Swiney was writing in his capacity as deputy to Vanbrugh. His dilemma was this: writing on a Thursday, he realized that *Love's Triumph* would not be ready Saturday, and he wanted to get it on the boards Tuesday the twenty-sixth rather than the following Saturday. *Thomyris* had drawn a mere £96.18.9 on Tuesday the seventeenth and *Camilla* was to achieve just £125.15.6 on Saturday the twenty-first: only a new opera could put box-office receipts up to a profitable level. *Love's Triumph* drew a heartening £240.6.9 its first night, but totals of £101.1.9 on 28 February and £84 7s. on 2 March must have come as a shock and disappointment to Vanbrugh.

1. I.e., hold the premiere of *Love's Triumph*.

53. Vanbrugh's Proposal for Subsidy by the Queen

(21 February 1708)
February ye 21st 1707 [1707/8]
Sir
    The inclosd is a Copy of what I have given my Lord Chamberlain who disires you will call upon him tomorrow morning. I am

Sir Your most humble Servant
J VANBRUGH

To the Right Honourable Mr Vice Chamberlain In St James Place

    The regulation under which the Queen has been pleased to rescue the Two Theatres By seperating the Singers from the Comedians having already had many good effects not only by putting an end to those heats which have disturbd the Towne for several years past but by improving both kinds of Entertainments; and putting both houses into a capacity of supporting themselves very tollerably: there seems nothing more wanting to compleat their settlement, And to make it answer all that is wishd for by it. But that the Queen would please by her Bounty to contribute to the bringing over from Italy, one man and one woman Singers of the first Rate, with one of the best masters for the direction and Government of the Orchestra. Three such persons being absolutely necesary, to make the opera creditable to the nation and thoroughly entertaining to the Towne.

But the extraordinary charge of procuring them is so great, that tis, impossible for the House alone to support it.

Tis therefore humbly offerd That to this end the Queen woud be pleasd for the next year, to allow a Thousand Pounds, to be applyd as My Lord Chamberlain shall see occasion. The proposals to his Lordship being these

That Nicolini and Santini[1] may be the two Singers fixd on (if to be had) and Manchini[2] the Master of the orchestre.

That the two former may receive from the Queen four hundred pounds each, and the latter Two Hundred. In consideration of which allowance they shall come over as Servants Extraordinary to her Majesty, and by her orders perform in the opera. What they are more to receive from the House, being by way of present, as shall be adjusted with them before hand.

Copy-text: Winston, pp. 75–77. For another nineteenth-century transcription see Drexel MS, fols. 45–46. This document was part of lot 209 in the 1876 sale catalogue.

Comment: By this time Vanbrugh certainly knew (brave front notwithstanding) that the opera was in deep trouble, but he evidently hoped that importing a couple of major stars from the Continent would solve the problem. In essence he is suggesting that the Queen pay a top salary to two singers and an orchestra leader of renown, in addition to which the "House" would add a substantial sum to be agreed on in advance. The dream of royal subsidy (which had haunted Dryden in earlier years) was to go unrealized until the establishment of the Royal Academy of Music in 1719, and even then it was a token contribution to expenses.

1. Nicolini was Nicola Grimaldi (1673–1732), the male contralto Burney called "the first truly great singer" to appear in Italian opera in London. We have not been able to identify Santini satisfactorily. For one candidate see "Maria Santini," in Robert Eitner, *Biographisch-Bibliographisches Quellen-Lexikon der Musiker und Musikgelehrten christlicher Zeitrechnung bis Mitte des neunzehnten Jahrhunderts*, 11 vols., rev. ed. (Graz: Akademische Druck-U. Verlagsanstalt, 1959), VIII, 421.

2. Francesco Mancini (1679–1739) was an Italian composer. His *Idaspe* (*Hydaspes*) was brought to the Haymarket by Nicolini in March 1710.

INTERDOCUMENT.

Letter from Vanbrugh to the Earl of Manchester

(24 February 1708)

. . . at last I got the Duke of Marlbor: to put an end to the Playhouse Factions, by engaging the Queen to exert her Authority, by the means of which, the Actors are all put under the Patent at Coventgarden House,[1] And the Operas are Establish'd at the Haymarket, to the generall likeing of the whole Towne; And both go on in a very Successfull manner; without disturbing one an Other. This Settlement pleases so well, that people are now eager to See Operas carry'd to a greater perfection, And in Order to it the Towne crys out for A Man and Woman of the First Rate to be got against Next Winter from Italy. But at the Same time they declare for the future against Subscriptions,[2] and have not come into any this Winter. I have therfore (with Severall to back me) laid before my Ld Marlborough the Necessity there is for the Queen to be at Some Expence, And have such an Answer both from him and my Ld Treasurer, as makes me write this Letter to yr Ldship, to Acquaint you, that if Nicolini and Santini will come Over (my Ld Hallifax telling me this morning yr Ldship very much desired they shou'd) I'll venture as far as A Thousand Pounds between 'em, to be either divided equally, or More to One and less to tother as yr Ldship shall think fitt to adjust it with 'em, if you please to give your Self the trouble of making the Agreement. This Money I propose to give 'em for Singing during the Next Season, which as things are now Regulated begins the Tenth of September, and ends the Tenth of June. The Opera is very rarely perform'd above twice a Week, and in the begining and latter part of the Season, not above Once, so that their Labour won't be great. If yr Ldship cou'd engage 'em for Pistolls or Louis d'ores instead of Pounds, 'twou'd be so much Saved to two of your humble Servants, Mr Bertie[3] and my Self, We being now the Sole Adventurers and Undertakers of the Opera, for I have Bought Mr Swiney quite out: Only pay him as Manager. My Affairs are all thank God in a much more prosperous state than When yr Ldship left London.

Copy-text: Vanbrugh, *Works*, IV, 16–17.

1. I.e., the Drury Lane theatre.
2. Between 1701 and 1707 the managers experimented with advance subscriptions as a means of subsidizing expensive new productions both of operas and plays. In essence this arrangement gave advance ticket purchasers special seating privileges for a specified number of performances. On subscription practices see *The London Stage*, Part 2, I, lix–lxi. In a letter of 27 July (printed as an interdocument between documents 71

and 72), Vanbrugh laments that "the Towne having the Same Notion of the Profitts ['a Supposition that there wou'd be Immence gain'], wou'd not come into any Subscription."

3. Identified by Summers and by Webb as Peregrine Bertie (see document 70, note 3), but the *Biographical Dictionary* (II, 66) suggests another candidate: Montague Bertie, second Earl of Abingdon (ca. 1673–1743).

54. Receipt from Motteux to Valentini for Payment in Connection with *Love's Triumph* [Missing]

(6 March 1708)

Known from the 1876 sale catalogue (no. 193): "Motteux, Composer. 'Receu de Monsieur Valentino Urbani la somme de cinquante trois Livres quinze chelins pour ce qui m'est deû par accord pour l'Opera appellé "Love's Triumph," dont je le tiens quitte et de toutes autres demandes & prétentions quelqu'onques jusqu'a ce jour. Fait a Londres, Le 6 Mars, 1708,' *holograph and signed*. Motteux's signature is of singular rarity."

This may well be the document in its entirety. The entry is repeated verbatim as no. 699 of the 1905 sale catalogue.

Translation: "Received from Mr Valentino Urbani the amount of fifty-three pounds and fifteen shillings for what is owed to me by agreement for the opera called *Love's Triumph*, so that he is now free of it and of any other demands and claims of any kind to this day. Done in London, 6 March 1708."

Comment: For the original agreement between Motteux and Valentini see document 13. *Love's Triumph* had received its premiere on 26 February.

55. House Servants at the Haymarket in March 1708

(8 March 1708)

off & belonging to ye Queens Theatre March 8° 1707/8

Women Dressers	per diem
Mrs Brown	0 5 0
Steed	0 5 0
Cotton	0 5 0
Peryn	0 5 0

Cuthbert	0	5	0
Verbrachen	0	5	0
Pendry	0	5	0
Dressers			
Shermon	0	1	6
Wyatt	0	1	6
Burch	0	1	6
Sabin	0	1	6
Ray	0	2	6
Peer	0	4	0
Bill Carriers			
Cleeter	0	4	0
Miller	0	4	0
Soule	0	4	0
Simpson	0	4	0
Pitt			
Selby	0	2	8
Thomas	0	2	8
Shaw	0	2	8
Maund	0	2	8
Gallery			
Plumner	0	2	8
Goode	0	2	8
Mathews	0	2	0
Williams	0	2	0
Miles	0	2	8
Mrs harris	0	2	8
Wardrobe			
Goble	0	5	0
Lopru	0	3	0
Shermon	0	5	0
Archey	0	3	4
	£ 5:5:2		
Boxes			
hollinsworth	0	5	0
Curry	0	4	0
Brown	0	4	0
Barber	0	7	6
Peplo	0	5	0
∫ Wharton &	0	7	6
∖ Wife			

Darrell	0 5 0
Mr hall *	0 10 0
Tom	0 3 6
Scane-men	
Porter	0 10 0
Marsh	0 7 6
Potter	0 7 6
Powell	0 7 6
Smith	0 10 0
	£ 4:14:0

* Mr hall: reading of "Mr" doubtful.

Copy-text: HTC Coke 57(a) (Hand E). (This MS comprises four essentially distinct documents from 8 to 10 March 1708. We have separated them for clarity.) For nineteenth-century transcriptions see Winston, p. 88, and Drexel MS, fol. 53.

Comment: According to this list Vanbrugh's expense for house servants was £9 19s. per night, or about £600 for a season of 60 performances. Comparison with the 1703 "Company Plan" (probably devised by Vanbrugh as a rough sketch for a united company) shows that he then expected to pay about £620 per annum for roughly the same set of house servants—though of course that was for a company which would have acted six times per week, not twice.[1]

1. PRO LC 7/3, fols. 161–64 (printed by Nicoll, History, II, 276–78, but misdated 1707).

56. The Daily Charge of an Opera

[ca. 8 March 1708]

A particular Account of ye Daily Charge of an Opera

Singers & Dancers	44 17 6
Instrumentall Musick	17 2 0
Office keepers & Attendants	9 19 2
Incidents	6 7 10

Rent & Stock	15	0	00
Candles	3	0	00
Ditto Wax	3	0	00
Oyle	1	1	00
Printer	2	5	0
Mannagers &a	8	5	0

£101 2 6

Constant daily Charge is *   107:2:6
110:17:6

The Small Bills have hitherto
amounted, one night with
another to per night   £10:–:–

Two new Operas a Year, at
£600. Charge each, (if the
Opera is perform'd 60 times)
comes to per night   £20:–:–

So that the Daily Charge
One day with another at
60 times performance is   £140:17:6

Memorandum   The Receipts hitherto (tho' the best of the
Season)[1] amount one night with an other, but
to £140.

So that, shou'd there be 24 Performances
more this Season (which is impossible)[2] and
the Receipts shou'd mount to £100. a night
(which there is no hopes of) the Loss for the
rest of the year wou'd still be £891
1021

Besides £130 upon a Private
Agreement   £130
£1021

Note
Mr Heydeggers Pretention is
not included

* From this point on, the writing is Vanbrugh's.

Copy-text: HTC Coke 57 (b) (Hand E, with additions by Vanbrugh). For nineteenth-century transcriptions see Winston, p. 89, and Drexel MS, fol. 55.

Comment: This part of HTC Coke 57 peters out inconclusively, but if we accept Vanbrugh's impossible hypotheses—24 more performances at £100 receipts per night, and a "Daily Charge" of £140—his loss would be £3360 minus 2400, or £960. Ignoring the £20 allowed daily toward new productions, the loss would be about £480. On the next page of the manuscript, Hand A calculated that Vanbrugh had already lost £600 on the first sixteen performances (see document 57 below). What the "£130 upon a Private Agreement" was we do not know.

1. December, January, and February were regarded as the most profitable months of the theatrical season. See The London Stage, Part 2, lxviii and xcvii.
2. The Haymarket had mounted 16 performances as of 6 March; it managed only 13 more during the rest of the spring.

57. Daily Receipts at the Haymarket 13 January Through 6 March 1708

[ca. 8 March 1708]

A particular Account of ye daily Receipts of ye Opera's begining ye 13° January 1707/8 and ending 6° March 1707/8 Inclusive

January	13 Received at Thomiris	193: 17: 6
	17 Received at Ditto	153: 19: 6
	20 Received at Ditto	127: 0: 0
	24 Received at Ditto	159: 6: 6
	27 Received at Camilla	170: 5: 0
	31 Received at Ditto	137: 3: 6
February	3 Received at Ditto	89: 5: 6
	7 Received at Ditto	53: 15: 3
	10 Received at Ditto	77: 17: 6
	14 Received at Thomiris	155: 7: 9
	17 Received at Ditto	96: 18: 9
	21 Received at Camilla *	125: 15: 6
	26 Received at Loves Triumph	240: 6: 9
	28 Received at Ditto	101: 1: 9

	Received of Mrs White for Ticketts	
	by her delivered out for Camilla	
	when Seignor Cassani Sung[1]	175: 11: 6
March	2 Received at Loves Triumph	84: 7: 0
	6 Received at Ditto	101: 14: 3

Receiv'd in all[2] £ 2243: 13: 6

16 Days Performance[3] att ~~107:2:6~~	
110:17:6	1774[4]—8—0
The New Opera	~~250—0—0~~
Practices for it	42—0—0
a new scene	20—0—0
Bills for Cloths &ca	763—7—6
Total Charge to ye 6th of March	2848—15—6
2849—15—6[5]	
Receipts to Ditto	2243—13—6
Loss per Ballance	~~549 14 0~~
	~~598 2 0~~
	606 2

Memorandum By ye State of the Accounts ye 6th of March,
the Loss is About ~~£598~~ 606—2—0[6]

2849—15—6
2243—13—6
606— 2—0

---

* *Camilla*: "Ditto" was written and canceled, then "Camilla" was written and canceled, and then "Camilla" was written again.

Copy-text: HTC Coke 57 (c) (Hand E with additions as noted below). For nineteenth-century transcriptions see Winston, p. 90, and Drexel MS, fol. 51.

Comment: Unlike Vanbrugh's earlier profit/loss calculations this one includes no hypotheses or forecasts. Actual daily costs (as calculated in document 55) plus specific expenditures (mostly in connection with *Love's Triumph*) are subtracted from actual receipts—the result showing a substantial loss: £606, or nearly £38 per night. By this time Vanbrugh must have realized his predicament. The failure of *Love's Triumph* to set the venture on a solid footing left him only two options. He could make an expensive gamble and mount *Pyrrhus and Demetrius* late in the season, or he could renew his pleas for subsidy and try to reorganize the financial basis of the enterprise. Very sensibly, he did the latter. See documents 62, 63, and 64.

1. Cassani performed in *Camilla* on 7 and 10 February. The receipts recorded above for those dates are startlingly low, especially for the first night of an exotic foreign attraction. This note implies that tickets were sold in advance at White's Chocolate House (a standard arrangement: see documents 47 [Comment] and 110). If we divide the £175.11.6 evenly between those performances the totals would be about £141 and £165. In all probability the actual sums were higher the first night and lower the second, but however unpopular Cassani proved, the total receipts for these nights were not as low as the uncorrected figures in *The London Stage* suggest.
2. This phrase was added by Vanbrugh.
3. Beginning with this line, the next eight were added in Hand A.
4. Changed from 1766.
5. This—the correct total—is written in beside the other.
6. This memorandum was added by Vanbrugh before the eight lines above in Hand A. He gave an approximate loss because he did not yet have all the figures. After Vanbrugh had sent in his list of Tradesmen's Bills (document 58), that information was filled in and the total corrected from those figures in Hand A.

58. A List of Tradesmen's Bills to 10 March 1708

[Cover] Bills of ye Playhouse   (10 March 1708)
          Haymarkett March 10th 1708/7

Tradesmens Bills to March ye 10th 1707/8

Pyke Upholsterer	£ 5: 3: 6
Lepine, Tayler	£ 7: 2: -
Ditto	£ 29: 1: -
Ditto	£ 69:19: -
Brous * Tayler	£ 65:17: 6
Ditto	£ 46:14: -
Mr Halls Bill for stuffs &c	£ 27: 5: 8
Ditto	£ 29:16:10
Ditto	£271:17: 6
Browns Bill	£ 7: 3: -
Griffins Bill	£ 2: 2: -
Collops Bill[1]	£ 2: 7: -

James's Bill	£ 5:10: -		
Steeds Bill	£ 1: 3: 6		
	£571: 2: 6		
The small Bills amounted to	£160: -: -		
Paid Mrs Tufts for her Cloaths	£ 32: 5: -		
The Cloaths in all come to	£763: 7: 6		

	107-2-6	
Performances	16 Days	
	0-8	
	1-12	
	642	7
	107	4
	1714	280
New Opera	250	
	1964	300
Practices	42	
Scene	10	120
		3-5
	2016-0-0	110-7-6
Bills	763-7-6	~~40~~
Charge	2779-7-6	16
Receipts	2243-13-6	4 8
	535-14-0	2-0
		660
		110
		1766 8

* *Brous*: HTC Coke 57(d) appears to read "Brew Tailour."

Copy-text: HTC Coke 24, which is in Vanbrugh's hand. Information from it was copied onto HTC Coke 57(d) in Hand A. One minor variant in a name is recorded above; the figures are all identical. For nineteenth-century transcriptions, see Winston, p. 91, and Drexel MS, fol. 51v.

Comment: This list of tradesmen's bills is part of Vanbrugh's financial stocktaking in early March 1708. The calculations below the list are a rough preliminary form of the figures in document 57 (face date of that document notwithstanding), which show a loss of £535.14.0 rather than £606.2.0.

Vanbrugh uses here the daily total £107.2.6 canceled in documents 56 and 57 and replaced there by £110.17.6. The rest of the difference in total loss is accounted for by the new "Scene" being listed at £10 here versus £20 in document 57.

1. In the early years of the Triumvirate, Eileen Collup worked àt Drury Lane as a seamstress, washerwoman, and dresser. See Folger Shakespeare Library scrapbook W.b. 190, Drury Lane receipts. She is not noticed in the *Biographical Dictionary*.

59. An Enumeration of "Small Bills" for One Night

[Cover] Play house incidents   [ca. 8 March 1708?]
An Account of One Nights Incidents

£ s d

Supernumerary bill for Guards & ⎱
   other Attendants   ⎰
Constables & Beadles
Coach-hire for ye Treasurer
Chorus People & Extraordinary Musick
Bill Setters ye Days not playing *
Ditto Printer
Washing & Mounting of Feathers
Loan of Wiggs in Camilla above Twenty Shillings
putting ye Opera in ye Daily Courant
Tuneing ye harpsicord
Trumpetts, Washing Veils &c
Candlesticks &c
Weekly Wardrobe bills for mending &
   altering cloaths &c
Property bill & house bill for petty disbursments

  * *playing*: MS reads "playling."

  Copy-text: HTC Coke 58 (Hand E).

  Comment: This appears to be an explanation—without the figures giving a precise breakdown—of the "Small Bills" which amount to £10 each night "one Night with another" (see document 56). We have assigned a tentative date on the supposition that this is part of Vanbrugh's financial reappraisal in early March 1708.

60. Dancers' Bill Submitted by Desbarques

[Cover] Monsr des Bargues   [ca. 8 March 1708?]

Memoire De ce quil et Deu
a mr cherrier mademoiselle Debargues
et moy Debargues Deux moy; mondte *
pour mr Cherrier   24 Livre sterlin
pour malle Debargues et
moy Debargues   48 Livre sterlin

fourni pour Le Dernier oupera nouvau[1]
    pour Deux Chapo Darlequin   00-08-00
    pour une paire Soutier   00-05-00
    pour Deux paire pour Le petitcha   00-08-00
                                                  ———————
                                                    01-01-00
Reste a paier a mr charier pour
    Le petitcha   01-10-00
                       68-00-0
                        2-11-0
                      ————
                      70-11-0[2]

* moy; mondte; i.e., "mois; monte" in modern French.

Copy-text: HTC Coke 38 (Hand F).

Translation: "Memo of what is owed to Mr Cherrier, Mlle Desbarques, and me, Desbarques, two months, total: for Mr Cherrier, 24 pounds sterling; for Mlle Desbarques and me, Desbarques, 48 pounds sterling.

"Provided for the latest new opera: for two harlequin hats, 8s.; for a pair of shoes, 5s.; for two pairs [of shoes?] for the little cat, 8s. [Total:] £1.1.0. Remains to be paid to Mr Cherrier for the little cat, £1.10.0."

Comment: The date can probably be established by the reference to two months and the salary claimed. According to the second part of document 44 each dancer was owed £1 10s. per night. Thus we can deduce that this bill concerns 16 performances. The sixteenth performance at the Haymarket in the spring of 1708 (the only time these three dancers performed together there) was 6 March. We suspect, therefore, that this bill is part of the financial information which went to Coke about 8–10 March when Vanbrugh began to realize the extent of his problems.

1. I.e., *Love's Triumph*, premiered 26 February.
2. The correct total is £74.11.0.

61. Sherman's Bill for Cloth and Sundries

Mr Sherman his Bill—1707[1]   [March 1708?]
Layed out by Mr Edeter order

	£ s d
ffor 18 yeards of Lase att 2s per yeard	01:16:00
ffor 10 yeards of Broad Lase att 4s yeard	02:00:00
ffor 16 Dosine of Chaine	02:00:00
ffor 6 yeards of Buckerum	00:06:00
ffor half A yeard of Cherey culerd Satten[2]	00:02:00
ffor Thred and Silke	00:02:00
ffor Skower Silke	00:02:00
ffor Washing and Mownting of To Spanish Fethers	00:07:06
ffor 3 dayes worke for 3 Men and Breakfasts and Candles	00:17:06
Som is	07:13:00

There are other Expences on this account which amounts to[3] ·····················

Copy-text: HTC Coke 72 (unidentified hand).

Comment: We have tentatively dated this document March 1708 on the supposition that it is part of the financial reassessment made then. This item does not appear in the 10 March list of tradesmen's bills. A "Shermon" is listed as a dresser and another under "Wardrobe" in document 55. Possibly this bill covers expenditures by one of them.

1. I.e., 1707/8?
2. I.e., "cherry colored satin"; pencil annotation: "cord Satin."
3. This sentence is written in a different, unidentifiable hand.

INTERDOCUMENT.
Letter from Vanbrugh to the Earl of Manchester

(16 March 1708)

Since there is hopes of being quiet at home, I may think again of Operas. I had written to your Ldship a little before I rec'd your Letter, to desire you wou'd engage Nicolini & Santini for Next Winter, if a Thousand Pistols, (or Pounds if Pistols wou'd not do) between them wou'd be Sufficient, wch My Ld Dorset tells me will plentifully do. But they must perform the Whole Season wch is from the 10th of Sept: to the 10th of June. So that they must if Possible be here in August, Unless to have the Advantage of coming wth yr Ldship, they shou'd stay something longer, wch in that Case, to encourage 'em, one wou'd dispence with. Now cou'd there be a Third, some Young Agreable Person of a Woman, who not yet in great Vogue, yet promis'd fair to grow to it. who wou'd come for an Allowance of 80. or 100 pounds a Year, it might be of great Service to bring downe the Pride & Charge of Our Present Singing Ladys, who Cost the House four hundred pounds a Year apeice. Stanhope tells me of Such a One at Leghorn, that he believes wou'd Come. Her name is Redjana. He commends her extreamly.

Copy-text: Vanbrugh, *Works*, IV, 18–19.

62. Vanbrugh's Statement of the Opera Account

[7 April 1708]
[Cover] Mr Vanbrugg state of ye Opera Acount April ye 7th 1708

The Dayly Charge of an Opera is,

For Singers and Dancers	£ 44:17:-
Instrumentall Musick	£ 17:12:-
Office Keepers and Attendants	£ 9:19:2
Rent and Use of the Stock	£ 15:—:-
Incidents one night with an other	£ 6:10:-
Small Bills one night with an other	£ 10:—:-
Candles and Oyle	£ 7: 1:-

Printer	£ 2: 5:-
Managers	£ 3:—:-
Totall dayly Charge	£116: 4:2

Which in 23 times the Opera has been perform'd this Season is	£2672: 15:8
The Bills for Cloaths & Scenes	£ 815: 12:-
The new opera	£ 334: 10:-
Extraordinary Allowance to V.[1]	£ 107: 10:-
Allowance to Cassanini	£ 40:—:-
To Mr Heydegger for Thomyris	£ 120:—:-
Totall Expence this Season	£4090: 7:8
Rec'd in 23 nights	£2943: 13:6
Loss	£1146: 14:2

By this Account it appears. That Altho' the Queen shou'd be pleas'd to allow a Thousand pounds a Year toward Salarys; And that the Towne shou'd by Subscriptions take off the Load of Cloaths & Scenes: the Daily Charge wou'd Still rise to full a hundred pounds a day: Which is the most the House can ever hope to receive the Season throughout one Performance with an other

Copy-text: Pforzheimer MS 118 (Vanbrugh holograph), published by permission of The Carl H. Pforzheimer Library. For nineteenth-century transcriptions see Winston, pp. 82–83, and Drexel MS, fol. 57. There is a rather inaccurate typed transcription in Broadley, p. 2.

Comment: In the seven performances since 6 March[2] Vanbrugh's figures show the opera taking in exactly £700 while total loss mounted from £606 to £1146 (cf. document 57). About £112 of the further loss is attributable to daily expenses. Forty-two pounds is accounted for by clothes and scenery; the amount charged to the "New Opera" (*Love's Triumph*) rises to £334. The last three items suggest that Vanbrugh was paying some part of the sums owed on special contracts to Valentini, Cassani, and Heidegger.[3]

1. Valentini?
2. Only six opera performances are recorded between 6 March and 7 April in *The London Stage*. The discrepancy may be accounted for by lack of an ad in the *Daily Courant* on Tuesday 16 March. The Haymarket probably did perform an opera that night.
3. Probably connected with "Mr Heydegger's Pretention" in document 56.

63. Vanbrugh's Profit-sharing Proposal for 1708–1709

[Cover] Mr Van brugh   [ca. 14 April 1708]
      shares

If seignor Valentini, Mrs Tofts, Mlle Margarita Mr Dieupart, Mr Hayms
& Mr Papusch come into shares instead of salarys; The daily Charge
(Cloaths &c excepted which must be furnish'd by subscription) may be re-
duc'd to £70. per day

The Receipts this season have amounted to £125 per day, one day with
an other

But shou'd the Receipts next year rise to but £115 the Proffits wou'd then
be £45. per day. Two thirds of which going to the Performing sharers,* vizt
£30. each share wou'd be worth £450—dividing their £30 per day in four
parts

    one to Vall:
    one to Mrs Tofts
    one to Marg.
    & one divided in 3 between the men

  * *sharers:* "wou'd" written and canceled after this word.

Copy-text: MS in the Pierpont Morgan Library (Vanbrugh holograph). For
a nineteenth-century transcription see Winston, p. 3.

Comment: We have assigned a date of about 14 April from Vanbrugh's
statement that receipts have averaged £125. If we add two performances at
£100 each to the figures in document 62 we arrive at that average and a date
following the performance of 13 April.

We see Vanbrugh casting about here for a way to reduce the fixed daily
expense of the opera, or at least to reduce his own liability. He is hoping to
cover costume expense by special public subscription, and in essence he is
proposing to make Valentini, Tofts, Margarita de l'Epine, and three senior
musicians limited partners in profit, reserving one-third to himself. Unfortunately, the performers wanted no part of any scheme in which their salaries
were not guaranteed in full.

64. Vanbrugh to Coke about Financial Problems and the Need for Subsidy from the Queen

[ca. mid-April 1708]
Thursday Morning

Sir

I found a letter from you last night. I hope you will not doubt of my Entire disposition to comply with whatever you think right in this unhappy affair as far as the stretch of my power will go and I will accordingly make a very hard shift to clear Valentinos second month;[1] but must beg a little time for the Tother. For really tis not yet in my power. You are Sensible the daily Receipts of the Opera are not near sufficient to answer the Daily and monthly demands and whenever they fail, there will be a full Stop: So that I am forc'd to apply all other money I have, to keep touch in that point and this Distresses me to the last Degree, All kinds of income being very backwards. However I hope to receive very suddenly a large arrear[2] out of which I will certainly make good all you have promisd I shall: But methinks if ever my Lord Chamberlain will move the Queen, now should be the time, since he can never be furnishd with more pressing arguments: amongst which, that of the impossibility* the House at present is under, to make good the Bargains made with Foreigners, woud move both the Queen and my Lord Treasurer more than one coud plead: Besides, the Venetian Ambassador[3] was by at My Lord Chamberlain when both my Lord Treasurer & Marlborough Declard it woud be right, for the Queen to give a Thousand Pounds a year towards the opera support, and Ill lay my Life she comes readily into it whenever she is apply'd to which I therefore earnestly beg you will press my Lord Chamberlain to do, And when he has once (as the proper officer) movd the Queen in it I'll take the trouble off of his hands to solicit it. Ill wait upon you some time to day & am

Sir your most humble Servant
J Vanbrugh

To the Right Honourable Mr Vice Chamberlain in St James's Place

* impossibility: MS reads impossibly.

Copy-text: Winston, pp. 32–33. For another nineteenth-century transcription see Drexel MS, fol. 58. This letter is item 207 in the 1876 sale catalogue, where it is erroneously dated "Nov. 1713."

Comment: By this time Vanbrugh was barely able to keep the opera going on a day-to-day basis, and he was well aware of the impossibility of fulfilling "the Bargains made with Foreigners." Whether he hoped that the Queen would help with the immediate financial crisis or only with the next season is not clear.

We have placed this document in advance of 17 April on the hypothesis that the benefit for Valentini on that date is a response to prodding by Coke acknowledged in this letter. Also on 17 April Luttrell reported that the Venetian ambassador had begun preparations for departing England, having been forbidden the court (*Brief Historical Relation*, VI, 290–92).

1. This seems to imply that Valentini has been paid in full only for the first month of his agreement. The benefit arranged for him 17 April (see document 66) may well have been an attempt to catch up on what was owed him.
2. The likeliest source for this "large arrear" is tickets sold specially through an outside agent—cf. document 57, where Vanbrugh records £175 received from "Mrs White for Ticketts by her delivered out for Camilla when Seignor Cassani Sung."
3. Luttrell calls him Seignior Cornaro.

65. Dancers in *Love's Triumph*

[April? 1708]

Mr cherrier et Monsieur Debargues
Disposeron Le balet Du trionffe De Lamour
Comme il suit sauoir [1]

I acte
Monsieur cherier . . . . malle Sinteloo [2]
Monsieur Debargues . . . . . malle aloay [3]
mr cha [4] . . . . malle Cadet [5]
mr Lagarde . . . . malle iuens [6] pour Seuls [7]

2 acte
mr cherrier . . . . malle Sinteloo
mr Lagarde . . . . malle iuens
mr cha En peysan . . . . malle Cadet paysanne
. . . .
mr Debargues . . . . malle aloay pour Seul

3 acte
Monsieur Debargues . . . . . malle iuen
Monsieur Lagarde . . . . malle aloay
mr cha . . . . malle Cadet
        . . . .
mr cherrier . . . . malle Sinteloo   Seul

Copy-text: HTC Coke 74 (Hand F).

Comment: see document 66.

1. "Mr Cherrier and Monsieur Desbarques will arrange the ballet of *Love's Triumph* as
follows, namely. . . ."
2. Hester Santlow.
3. Alloway (cf. document 50).
4. Shaw.
5. No Mlle Cadet is recorded by the *Biographical Dictionary*.
6. Evans.
7. "By themselves."

66. A List of Dancers for *Love's Triumph*

[Cover] Order of ye Dancers *   (17 April [1708])
        Saturday ye 17th April

premier acte
Monsieur cherrier   Malle Sinteloo
Monsieur Debargues   Malle aloay
mr cha   Cadet
mr Lagarde   iuens Seuls

2 acte
monsieur cherrier   Mlle Sinteloo
mr Lagarde   Mlle iuens
mr cha   Mlle Cadet
mr Debargues   Mlle aloay Seulle

3 acte
mr Debargues   Mlle iuens
mr Lagarde   Mlle aloy
mr charrier   Mlle Sintelo Seulle

* *Dancers*: MS reads "Danc"

Copy-text: HTC Coke 48 (Hand F).

Comment: Documents 65 and 66 are almost identical, though 65 contains an extra entry for the third act. The performance of 17 April was a benefit for Valentini, which may account for the concern of the Vice Chamberlain's office about the details of the program.

67. Preliminary Financial Estimates for the 1708–1709 Season

[ca. April 1708]

[Cover] Heads for ye Plan* for ye opera for ye next year 1708/9

<pre>
  60   The Opera att Venice   35
  15   160
 300   60 Carraltadouri¹ who pay about 15 guineys   195²
  60
 ───   a piece for ye first Expences of the stage
 900   every year which is 900 guineys
                20 Boxes att 50 guineys a year 1000 guineys
 100   that persons who come in to pay ye Charge
  20
────   of Going in besides³
2000
</pre>

100 Subscribers att 15⁺ guineys a piece
      each years—2000
20 Boxes att 50 guineas a year 1000 guineys
      ye persons who come in to pay ye Charges
      of going in besides

<pre>
                                 2000
                                 1000
                                  150
The Subscribers Ticketts to   50
be free Entrance for every   25
body they give it to   £3225⁴
</pre>

To have ye Roes of five boxes a piece each side ye lower & second to make up the particular Boxes the others to be lett out every night together or in particular places

* *Plan*: reading doubtful (word cropped).

† 15: "20" appears to have been written messily over another figure (15?), and "15" was then written clearly above it.

Copy-text: HTC Coke 13 (Hand A).

Comment: Investigating ways to put the opera on a sound footing in 1708–9, Coke and Vanbrugh evidently looked to a foreign model for ideas. The facts about opera in Venice recorded here may have come from Seignior Cornaro, the Venetian ambassador in London (contact with whom is reported in document 64), or from Vanbrugh's friend the Earl of Manchester, who was Ambassador to Venice.⁵

We would hypothesize that only the first part of this document (above the line) refers to Venetian practice, and that the rest represents a scheme Vanbrugh hoped to try in London. Subscribers at £15 per annum (with transferable tickets) and annual boxholders are in fact part of the usual arrangement for opera in London in the 1720s and 1730s.

1. Carraltadouri: i.e., "cavalcatori," a class of knights.
2. We do not see the relevance of this calculation.
3. This appears to mean that the people who rent boxes on an annual basis must also pay for admission to the performances they actually attend.
4. This total assumes 100 subscribers at 20 guineas (rather than 15). The source of the three small items in this list is unspecified.
5. Julian Marshall, who once owned this document, suggested Nicolini as a source in his Grove entry on the singer. But Nicolini did not come to England until the fall of 1708.

68. Margaret Farquhar to Coke about a Benefit

[Cover] Mrs farqhuar¹   [May 1708?]
[Direction] To the Honourable Mr Vice Chamberlain

Sir

The exaction of the play house maks me very uneasy but hope through your authority and goodness it may be greatly Qualifyd, I have made a through search into ye rates and am well assurd that poor Mr ffarquhar allowed 35 for the Charges of the house² tho he was promisd by Mr swinney who was ther ∗ manager of the new playe house that he should have it free. Mr Wilks did then justify the same to Dr Shadwell³ who acquainting my Lord Chamberlain therewith, who orderd him another benifitt day but thro mismanagement it provd of no advantage to him, the players I understand usually allowd 40 for[†] their benifit play but still I hope thro your powerfull mediation it may be reducd to a much less sume, for ye Cheif actors I presume may be easily prevaild to quett their own charges upon Mr ffarquhars account who has bin so Serviceable to them. I hope Sir to have ye honor of Seeing you a Sunday and shall wholly submitt to your Commands in that affair who am

Sir your most humble Sarvant
MARG: FFARQUHAR

[*] *ther*: Winston reads "then."
[†] *for*: "your" written and canceled after this word.

Copy-text: Houghton Library bMS Am 1631 (132) at Harvard (Margaret Farquhar holograph? unique sample in this collection). This letter is no. 182 in the 1876 sale catalogue. For nineteenth-century transcriptions see Winston, p. 92, and Drexel MS, fol. 132.

Comment: This appears to be the original letter sent to Coke. It is neatly copied, probably by the author, who signed it. The letter cannot be dated with any certainty. There are two plausible possibilities. (a) Early May 1707. Farquhar's last play, *The Beaux Stratagem*, had its premiere at the Haymarket on 8 March 1707, the author receiving benefits the thirteenth and twentieth. Farquhar received another benefit on 29 April (the eleventh night—quite irregular). This might be "another benifitt day" as ordered by the Lord Chamberlain. Farquhar died about 18–21 May and was buried the twenty-third. No further benefit is recorded for him or for his survivors that spring. (b) May 1708. Two pieces of evidence point to a date about a year later than the first hypothesis. "Mr swinney who was ther manager of the new playe house" appears to suggest that he is no longer manager—that is, to a date between January and mid-May 1708. Second, among the irrelevant jottings on the cover of this letter is scrawled a date: "May ye 7th 1708." Farquhar's *The Constant Couple* was performed by the acting company (now at Drury Lane) "For the Benefit of the Author's Widow and Children" on 25 May. This benefit might well be a response to Margaret Farquhar's plaints.

There are two sets of numerical jottings on the cover. One says:

226-0-9	132-4-11 1/4	
150-0-0	76	[corrected from 86]
76·0 9	66	

The second says:

> May ye 7th 1708
> 2 bills to Mr John Perkins of £20 one payable
> as soon as he has money ye other of £23 ye
> 24th of June.

Below this passage is written "to Mr Weeks ye Joyner 106-00-00."

A clipping from a dealer's catalogue with the letter ascribes it to "Mary" Farquhar with a date of "*circa* 1705." A partial transcription contains some major errors—for example, "Grainney" for "swinney."

1. [*sic*] In a different hand.
2. "House charges" are the daily operating costs of the theatre, customarily deducted from benefit proceeds to cover overhead. If some or all of the actors performed gratis this charge could be reduced, and for highly favored beneficiaries it was occasionally waived altogether.
3. Sir John Shadwell (1671–1747), son of the dramatist Thomas, was a young doctor making his way toward an appointment as Physician-in-ordinary to the Queen. He was knighted by George I in 1715. Why he had interceded with the playhouse on Mrs Farquhar's behalf we do not know.

Interdocument.
Letter from Vanbrugh to the Earl of Manchester

(11 May 1708)

I have Two Letters from yr Ldship, of ye 16th of March & the 20th of Aprill. And am (as well as the Towne) oblig'd to you, for the endeavours you use to improve the Opera here. What yr Ldship says of having one or two of the Top Voices, is most certainly right; As to my Self; I have parted with my whole concern to Mr Swiney; only reserving my Rent: So that he is entire Possessor of the Opera And most People think, will manage it better than any body. He has a good deal of money in his Pocket; that he got before by the Acting Company; And is willing to Venture it upon the Singers. I have been severall times wth him lately in Consultation wth the Vice Chamberlain Coke, (who being a great Lover of Musique And promoter of Operas; My Ld Chamb: leaves that Matter almost entirely to him. I have Acquainted him wth what yr Ldship writes; And Mr Swiney has engag'd before him, to Allow a Thousand pounds for Nicolini, to stay here two Winters; That is, to be here in Sept: And at Liberty to go away again the May come twelve month after. A Thousand pounds, I think makes about 1200 Pistols; which undoubtedly he

may Carry away clear in his Pocket; for he can't fail of Advantages otherways Sufficient to defray his Expences over and over. As for Santini Mr Swiney offers the
Same Conditions to Her, if yr Ldship can prevail with her to come; Or if She won't,
and you think Rejiana wou'd do as well, he leaves it to yr Judgment, and will Allow
her the Same, If neither of these Women will come He wou'd venture at half this
Allowance, Vizt: 600 Pistolls for Something more, as yr Ldship shall think reasonable) for the two Winters, if a Young, improving Woman cou'd be found that had a
good Person and Action, and that might be esteem'd as good a Singer as Margarita.
If yr Ldship can get any of these People over, on the Terms here Mention'd, Mr
Swiney desires me to Assure you of punctuall performance on his Part; Nor is there
any reason to doubt him; for he has behav'd himself so as to get great Credit in his
dealings with the Actors And I know the Vice-Chamb: do's not the least Question
his making good all he Offers on this Occasion; Besides, he has Power Sufficient to
Oblige him to it, the License being only during the Queens Pleasure. I have not yet
had an Oportunity to discourse My Lady Marlborough, about yr Ldships proposition
to her for Manza. But I find no Disposition at all in Other People. to promote his
Coming at any great Expence; And by a Letter Mr Dayrolls[1] has sent me from him,
I find he expects 600. Guins: a Year, wch is not to be thought on. 'Tis Voices are
the things at present to be got: And if these Top ones come over, 'twill facilitate
bringing the Queen into a Scheme, now preparing by my Ld Chamb: and Others, to
have Concerts of Musick in the Summer at Windsor, twice a Week in the Appart-
ment. There is no doubt, but by some such way as this, if the best Singers come,
they will tast of the Queens bounty: for every body will Solicite for 'em that they
may go away Content, and encourage Others to come over hereafter: So that I hope
upon the Whole, yr Ldship will be of Opinion, you may Safely perswade a Couple of
'em to Undertake the Voyage: for 'tis most Certain the People of Quality will find
some means or Other, to send 'em home in good humour. I must give yr Ldship one
Caution by the Way: which is; That I have good reason to believe that Valentini
(tho' he pretends to wish for Nicolini's Coming) will underhand do all he can to
discourage him for he has link'd himself with Mrs Tofts (who is wonderfully im-
prov'd) And in order to make a great bargain for themselves for next Winter, will
certainly play some trick, to hinder both Nicolini and a Woman from coming over;
if yr Ldship don't Apprise 'em ont.

Copy-text: Vanbrugh, *Works*, IV, 20–21.

1. Luttrell identifies a Monsieur D'ayrolles or Mr Ayrolles as "the British secretary at
the Hague" in May 1710 (*Brief Historical Relation*, VI, 528, 585).

69. Valentini to Coke about Money Due to Him

[Cover] Monsr Valentin   (13 May 1708)
        May 13th 1708.
[Direction] A Monsieur
        Mons:^r le Vice Chambellan

                                                le matin 13 May 1708.

Mons:^{ur}
   Je n'ay point manquè selon L'ordre, que vous m'auez donnèz d'ecrir à M:
Vanbrugh, et de la reponse de son Billet comme vous verrèz vous meme ces
intentions n'etant pas pour me payer le reste de mon argent de 150 G^uinees
entre le mois de May comme nous en sommes convenus; maisde me chi-
caner de long tems M:^r j'espere de votre generositè, et de votre protection,
que davant votre depart vous etablirèz les choses ensi bon ordre, comme
vous en auez toujours usè entoute occasion èn-uers moy, par un ecces de
votre bontè et enccores baisant tres humblement les mains je suis

                                                M:^r *
                                        et trés affectionnè
                                        [Valenti]n Urbani

   * M:^r: part of the closing formula and signature is torn away.

   Copy-text: HTC Coke 52 (scribal fair copy signed by Valentini). This letter is item 204 in the 1876 sale catalogue.

   Translation: "Sir, I have not failed to write Mr Vanbrugh according to the
order that you gave me, and from the answer in his note, as you will see for
yourself, his intentions are not to pay me the rest of my money of 150 guineas
within the month of May as we had agreed, but to squabble for a long time.
Sir, I hope from your generosity and your protection that before your departure you will arrange matters in good order, as you have always done on all
occasions concerning me thanks to an excess of your goodness, and again
kissing your hands very humbly, I am, Sir, . . . and very affectionate. . . ."

   Comment: For the original agreement see document 45. For Vanbrugh's
view of the situation see document 70.

70. Vanbrugh to Coke about Financial Settlements at the End of the 1708 Season

[Cover] Mr Vanbrugh   (14 May [1708])
                                                 Friday. May ye 14th

Sir

I am forc'd to be gone for Blenheim, without time to wait on you But do in all I can Comply with what your Letter desires. I had before I rec'd it made up the Accounts, and with much difficulty given Mr Swiny money to pay the Ballance to All the Singers & Dancers except Val: Margt: and Mrs Sagioni: which Account he will wait upon you with and shew you. I believe there is nobody dissatisfy'd with it but she who has the least reason: I mean the Barroness, she never came to any Agreement at all, and she is paid for every time the Opera has been perform'd in Proportion to what you thought was reasonable to allow her: which has sattisfy'd even Mrs Tofts[1] & every body Else. Mrs Sagioni shall have her Twenty pounds to morrow. Val: has had half this last month advanc'd to him long ago, tho' his day[2] did not produce it, and I have let him know he shall have the other half as soon as Mr Bertie[3] comes to Towne which will be the end of next Week. The rest will be provided for him I hope, by the time 'twill be due. Mr Dieupart and Seignor Berti *[4] will likewise soon be taken care of: But what to do about Cassani I don't well know. Though something shall: not that I really think he has a Claim to almost any thing; for take the two Audiences together and they were a great deal short of what has been rec'd on Common Occasions, And there was an Expence of near £30. for his Cloaths; with a Cruell Clamour & Disgust of the Towne against the House for Imposing such a Singer: which gave the Opera a very mischievous shock.[5] I therfore think charity is his Chief Plea, which is of full as much force to the Lords who seem'd to Patronize him, as to me who am so Vast a Sufferer by this Years Adventure. I shall be out of Towne but about ten days; what I am able to do, (either by my self or others for him at my return) I will; And Mr Swiny will in the Interim, lend him something to keep him from Distress. I must upon the whole, beg you to believe, That on any of these Occasions, 'tis my nature & my principle to overdoe, rather than leave the least pretence for Complaint. But I am so hard run in this unhappy Business, that there is no room left for Generosity; If I can at last comply with what in rigour I ought, 'tis the utmost I can hope for, I therfore beg you will have a favourable opinion of my Intentions in all these Struggles; And if in any perticular I come something short of what you think shou'd be; lay it to my want

of Power to do better; for as far as that will reach, I will readily be determin'd by you; having all the reason in the World to declare my self satisfy'd
with your whole proceedure in this thing, and very much Oblig'd for the
perpetuall trouble you have been so willing to give your self about it, for
which I shall ever be Sir

> Your most faithfull & most
> humble Servant
> J VANBRUGH

* *Seignor Berti*: the MS reading (literally: Seig^r: Berti) seems clear, though
Winston appears to read "Seig^r Berls" and Rosenberg reads "Serg^t Berti."

Copy-text: Huntington Library manuscript HM 6833 (Vanbrugh holograph). For nineteenth-century transcriptions see Winston, pp. 54–55, and
Drexel MS, fol. 59. This letter is item 208 in the 1876 sale catalogue. It is
707 in the 1905 sale catalogue (where it is misascribed to Catherine Tofts).
The text of the Huntington MS has previously been published by John Bar-
nard in "Sir John Vanbrugh: Two Unpublished Letters," *Huntington Library
Quarterly*, 29 (1965–66), 347–52, and by Albert Rosenberg in "New Light
on Vanbrugh."

Comment: Having sold out to Swiney (see the letter of 11 May, part of
which is printed as an interdocument between documents 68 and 69), Vanbrugh is here trying to wind up his obligations to his ill-fated company. For
his attitude toward the whole fiasco see his letters of 27 July and 17 August,
which appear as interdocuments between documents 71 and 72. We have no
record of the terms on which he paid off his performers, but presumably most
of them got far less than had been agreed upon in January.

1. Mrs Tofts was celebrated for avarice, among other things. The poem "On a hand-
som *Singer*, covetous and proud" (later published as "On Mrs T——s") jokes:

> So bright is thy beauty, so charming thy song,
> As had drawn both the beast and their *Orpheus* along;
> But such is thy av'rice, and such is thy pride,
> That the beasts must have starv'd, and the Poet have dy'd.

(Alexander Pope, *Miscellany Poems* [London: Lintot, 1727], I, 222. For a denial of the
attribution to Pope see Alexander Pope, *Minor Poems*, ed. Norman Ault and John
Butt [London: Methuen, 1954], p. 413.)
2. Presumably the benefit of 17 April.

3. Presumably Vanbrugh means his partner, usually identified as Peregrine Bertie, Vice Chamberlain preceding Coke from February 1694 until late in 1706 (see Luttrell, *Brief Historical Relation*, III, 271, and VI, 113). The second son of Robert, third Earl of Lindsey, he was long Vanbrugh's intimate friend. See the letter of 24 February, which appears as an interdocument between documents 53 and 54; Downes, *Vanbrugh*, p. 12; and *Collins's Peerage of England*, ed. Sir Egerton Brydges, 9 vols. (London: F. C. and J. Rivington et al., 1812), II, 19–21.

4. Vanbrugh consistently distinguishes between his partner and "Seignor" or "Mons:" Berti, who was evidently secretary to the Venetian Ambassador (see documents 40 and 45). As of September 1703 a "M. Jouberti" signed documents as secretary to the Venetian Ambassador (*Calendar of State Papers, Domestic Series, of the Reign of Anne, Preserved in the Public Record Office*, edited by Robert Pentland Mahaffy, 2 vols. [London, 1916–24; Nendeln, Liechtenstein: Kraus Reprint, 1968], II, 324).

5. On the Cassani fiasco, see document 42.

71. Swiney to Coke about Nicolini's Contract and Other Theatre Business

[ca. July 1708]

Sir

I have enclosed left you a Copy of my proposals to Signor Nicolini, I think he can have no objection to em, I desire that a speedy end may be put to it that I may know what I have to trust to. If other bargains are to have so much ceremony wait upon 'em as he has had already I am likely to have more trouble than I will or am able to undergo, but these Italian Gentlemen think it makes em look very great but they'll find that I shall never give up any reasonable point to make their bargains better— I hope youl excuse the impertinent trouble I am forcd to give your honour contrary to my inclinations who am

Your Honours most obligd & humble Servant
OWEN SWINY

If you please to let me know when I may have leave to wait upon you I have a great deal to say concerning the right methods of bringing Rich &c to reason.[1]

The muscovite Princes being gone I hope youl not think it troublesome to enquire how I must apply for the money for their Box.[2]

Copy-text: Winston, pp. 34–35. For another nineteenth-century transcription see Drexel MS, fol. 49. This letter is item 198 in the 1876 sale catalogue; it is 703 in the 1905 sale catalogue.

Comment: We have assigned this date in view of the state of negotiations with Nicolini and the deferential request for help with payment for a box used by "muscovite Princes." The last opera performance at the Haymarket this spring took place 20 May. On 24 July Luttrell reported that two days earlier "the Muscovite envoy, who is leaving this kingdom, was arrested in his coach in the Hay Market for a debt of 360l., which he has since paid, but complained to her majestie of the affront, who ordered the officers to be prosecuted, and promised him all possible satisfaction." The case dragged on for months after the ambassador departed. The arrest raised questions about diplomatic immunity which the courts found difficult to answer. (See Luttrell, *Brief Historical Relation*, VI, 330–32, 407, and 517.)

1. This implies either continuing friction between the Haymarket and Drury Lane, or (more probably) disagreements between Rich and his actors. As a former manager for Rich, Swiney knew a good deal about how to handle him.
2. The Muscovite Princes were the party of His Excellency Andreas Artemonides Mativeoff, Ambassador from His Imperial Majesty the Czar of Muscovy, whom the *Daily Courant* of 3 June announced would attend a performance of *Bury Fair* that day. Mativeoff must have done a fair amount of opera and theatre going during his extended stay in England. In PRO LC 3/53, fol. 71, is a record of a warrant for £89.12.9 "To Mr Owen Swinny for the use of a Box in the Theatre in the Haymarket for the said Princes," dated 8 July 1709 (i.e., a year later). On the same day the government paid a bill of £29.9.6 for the Russians' use of a box at Drury Lane. (We owe this reference to the kindness of A. H. Scouten.)

INTERDOCUMENT.
Letter from Vanbrugh to the Earl of Manchester

(27 July 1708)

I lost so Much Money by the Opera this Last Winter, that I was glad to get quit of it; And yet I don't doubt but Operas will Settle and thrive in London. The occasion of the Loss was three things, One; that half the Season was past, before the Establishmt: was made. And then, My Ld Chamb: Upon a Supposition that there wou'd be Immence gain, Oblig'd us to Extravagant Allowances; An Other thing was, That the Towne having the Same Notion of the Proffits, wou'd not come into Any Subscription; And the 3d was, That tho' the Pitt and Boxes did very near as well as usuall the Gallery People (who hitherto had only throng'd out of Curiosity, not Tast) were weary of the Entertainment: so that Upon the Whole, there was barely Money to Pay the Performers & Other daily Charges; and for the Cloaths & Scenes they fell upon the Undertakers. I might Add a Fourth Reason which is, That I never cou'd look after it my Self, but was forc'd to Leave it to Managers. Mr Swiney has now Undertaken it himself, And I believe will go through with it very well Nor will he want Subscriptions to help him; I don't doubt but Nicolini will be mighty well rec'd. . . . My Ld Chamb: is in a Tottering way, I know he expects to be out which he has not a mind to.[1]

Copy-text: Vanbrugh, *Works*, IV, 24–25.

1. Kent's position as Lord Chamberlain was far from secure: Queen Anne had considered replacing him the previous August. His ambitions for a Garter were regarded as presumptuous by some people, but when he was finally forced out in 1710, he was rewarded with a dukedom. (See the *Marlborough-Godolphin Correspondence*, pp. 895, 972, and 1467.)

INTERDOCUMENT.
Letter from Vanbrugh to the Earl of Manchester

(17 August 1708)

[Postscript] I doubt the Composer yr Ldship Speaks of bringing won't turn to Acct: neither to the Opera nor himself For People will never believe him good, unless they had heard of him, as a most Famous Man; besides. there are So many Operas now in being, wch are translated ready to be performed, that there will be no want of New Compositions in Many Years. But if yr Ldship brought a perfect good Violin to Lead & Govern the Orcastre, 'twou'd be of great Service. Nicolini that belong'd to the Duke of Bedford & is now at Rome, is thought by the Skilfull here, to be as good as any in Europe for that perticular Service.

I hope Nicolini the Singer continues his Resolution, for they have cast all their Affairs depending on his Coming And 'tis absolutely Necessary he shou'd be here as soon as possible or the best part of the Season will be lost.

Copy-text: Vanbrugh, *Works*, IV, 26.

72. An Account of What Signore Cassani Owes

(8 September 1708)

[Cover] An account of what Signor Cassani ows.
     September 8th 1708.

Illus.^{mo} Signore

Riceuei La sua cortesissima dei 4, La quale mi hà posto in estrema con-
fusione, à causa delle cordialissime espressioni d'affetto, ch'in essa s'è de-
gnata mostrarmi, conoscendo il mio poco merito; come anche per La gran'
bontà che hà per il Sig^r Cassani, per La Sig^{ra} Baronessa, e per me, che non
può che farci dichiarare infinitamente obligati di V.S. Illus.^{ma} et rendermi
ambitioso d'una tal protettione qual'è La sua verso di me.

Essendo Io di partenza per Bedford Shire, hò consegnato La presente al
Sig^r Cassani per renderglila, con La quale trouerà annesso il conto dei Cre-
ditori, à fine che habbia maggior' campo di colmarlo di gratie; et in Vero
non poteua V.S. Illus.^{ma} mostrare un più grande amore per La Musica, che
dichiararsi il Sostentatore di questo Virtuoso infortunato, doppo hauere à
tutti noi della professione concesso L'honore di decantarla per il nostro
Mecenate. Mà Conoscendo che Le mie parole non possono che far cono-
scere Le infinite obligationi che gli deuo, stimo meglio il tacermi, e con
somissione mi sottoscriuo—

   Di V.S. Illus.^{ma}

                    Umiliss.^{mo} oblig.^{mo} et
                    deuotiss.^{mo} Servitore
   Londra Li 8 Settenbre 1708   NICOLINO HAYM

               Nota di quello che il Signor Gioseppe Cassani
               è in obligo di pagare qui in Londra
               a i suoi creditori come segue—

	ll	sh	d
Al Sig^r Gius. Miglorucci per danari fattogli pagare in Italia al Sud^{to} Signor Cassani	22	19	3
All Signor Pietro Schaboud che Stà con il Duca d' Ormond pagati per parte del Suo viaggio	29	00	6
Al Sartore per due Abbiti fattoli subbito il suo arriuo à Londra	14	00	0
Per Camisce, Crauatte, e Fazzoletti &c	6	00	0
Per Perucche &c	4	00	0
All Sig^r Giu. Como Mercante per denaro fattoli pagare in Holanda per prosseguire il viaggio	5	00	0

Per altri debbiti che hà contratti doppo partito
dalla Casa del Sig^r Corticelli per il suo
Mantenimento &c   6 00 0
                               In tutto   86 19 9

Copy-text: HTC Coke 31 (Haym holograph). This document may have
been part of lot 184 in the 1876 sale catalogue.

Translation: "Most Illustrious Sir, I received your most courteous letter of
the 4th instant, which has left me in a state of extreme embarrassment due to
the very cordial expressions of esteem which you have seen fit to bestow on
me, although you are aware of my paltry deserts; and also because of the great
kindness which you entertain towards Mr Cassani, the Baroness, and towards
me, which cannot but cause us to declare ourselves infinitely obliged to your
Most Illustrious Lordship and to render me solicitous for the same kind of
protection [for Cassani] as that you have given me.

"Being on the point of departure for Bedfordshire, I have entrusted this
letter to Mr Cassani in order that he convey it to you, to which you will find
attached his creditors' bill, so that you will be aware of the full extent when
bestowing your favor on him; and indeed your illustrious lordship cannot
show a greater love for music than by declaring yourself the protector of this
ill-starred virtuoso, after having given all of us in the profession the honor of
hailing you our Maecenas. But in the knowledge that these words cannot fail
to make known the infinite debt of obligation that I owe you, I deem it best
to say no more, and with humility I subscribe myself your most illustrious
lordship's most humble, obliged and devoted servant, Nicolino Haym.
London the 8th of September 1708.

"Notice of that which Mr Gioseppe Cassani is under obligation to pay here
in London to his creditors as follows: To Mr Giuseppe Miglorucci for monies
advanced in Italy to the aforementioned Mr Cassani, £22.19.3; to Mr Pietro
Schaboud, who resides with [is in the service of] the Duke of Ormond, paid
for part of his trip, £29.0.6; to the tailor for two suits of clothing made for
him immediately upon his arrival in London, £14; for shirts, cravats, and
handkerchiefs, etc. £6; for wigs, etc. £4; to Mr Giuseppe Como, merchant,
for money authorized to be paid to him in Holland so that he might continue
his trip, £5; for other debts that he has contracted after his departure from the
house of Mr Corticelli for his upkeep, etc. £6. In toto: £86.19.9."

Comment: The recipient is unspecified. Coke himself is the likeliest candidate: cf. document 51 for the same hyperbolic courtesies in a letter definitely
addressed to Coke. For other papers bearing on the ill-starred Cassani see
documents 40, 42, 44, 49, 50

SEASON OF

1708-1709

The opera company at the Haymarket spent a quiet and orderly season under Owen Swiney's direction during 1708–9. Indeed our near-total lack of documents connected with the opera is testimony to the peace which settled over the company after its stormy beginnings under Vanbrugh. Not surprisingly, Swiney did not get under way early in the fall, and the suspension of acting for mourning after the death of Prince George (28 October–14 December) further delayed the opening of the season, which finally occurred with the premiere of *Pyrrhus and Demetrius*. Swiney had succeeded in bringing the celebrated Nicolini to London, and the company seems to have done well during the winter and spring. Swiney repeated *Pyrrhus and Demetrius* and the popular *Camilla* until 2 March, when he opened *Clotilda*. We possess no financial details at all for the Haymarket this season: apparently Swiney was doing well enough that he did not have to supply financial summaries to Coke as a part of begging for assistance or mediation. We do know that the first six nights of both new operas pit and boxes (except stage boxes) were by subscription only. And the first time Nicolini appeared in *Camilla* (25 January) Swiney advertised that admission to pit and boxes would be "by Printed Tickets at half a Guinea each Ticket, the Number not to exceed 460." (The limited number was to guarantee that there would be no overcrowding.) If Swiney sold all the tickets the gross would have been 230 guineas, plus income from stage boxes at half a guinea, first gallery seats at 5s., and second gallery seats at 2s. Nicolini is said to have "got 800 guineas" at a benefit 19 January,[1] which suggests good public support for the star. *Clotilda* was no great success—it managed only seven performances in a month, and was not revived until 1711—but Swiney was doing well enough to afford some frills. On 2 April *Pyrrhus and Demetrius* was advertised "With an entire set of new Scenes, Painted by two famous Italian Painters (lately arrived from Venice)"—the sort of costly extra Vanbrugh had been in no shape to underwrite a year earlier.

Meanwhile at Drury Lane the actors, predictably enough, were not getting along at all happily with Christopher Rich. As early as the summer of 1708 they seem to have been thoroughly discontented. Some of the actors performed privately for Richard Norton of Southwick during the summer, and in a complicated prologue spoken at Drury Lane sometime in September they expressed the hope that Norton might "Buy out these sordid *Pattent-Masters,* / And make a *Free Gift* of it to the *Actors.*" "CONSTANT PAY" (as the prologue concludes) was their great aim, and they were not going to achieve it under Christopher Rich.[2]

At what point they hatched the plot which was finally to drive the hated patentee out of the theatre we have no hard evidence to tell us.[3] At some point during this winter the Lord Chamberlain entered into a conspiracy against Rich.[4] On 4 March Mrs Oldfield protested against Rich's detaining £71 (instead of the usual £40) from her benefit.[5] On 30 April the Lord Chamberlain got around to ordering Rich to pay "Comedians who had benefit plays . . . the full receipts of Such Plays."[6] This order seems, however, to have been no more than a blind. Even before it was issued Swiney was hard at work signing contracts with Rich's actors to perform in plays at the Haymarket. John Mills signed on 30 March, William Bullock on 4 April, Benjamin Johnson on 11 April, Mrs Oldfield on 21 April, Penkethman on 30 April, and others right on through the spring and summer.[7] The generic split so triumphantly engineered by Vanbrugh came unstuck in less than a season and a half. On 6 June, having allowed the actors to support themselves through all but the tag end of the regular season, the Lord Chamberlain sprang his trap. Sir John Stanley was evidently dispatched to prevent further performances at Drury Lane under the following order.

Whereas by an order dated the 30th day of Aprill last upon the Petition of Severall Players &c. I did then direct and require you to pay to the respective Comedians who had benefit plays last winter the full receipts of Such Plays And whereas I am informed that in contempt of the Said Order you still refuse to pay and detain from the Said Comedians ye profits of ye Said benefit plays I do therefore for the Said Contempt hereby Silence you from further Acting.[8]

A month later, on 8 July, the Lord Chamberlain granted the actors permission to perform plays at the Haymarket four days per week.[9] Rich tried what expedients he could. In July his treasurer, Zachary Baggs, issued a pamphlet suggesting indignantly that the actors were rapacious twisters already making immense amounts of money, and Rich attempted to sue for breach of contract—but to no avail.[10] When in September Drury Lane advertised a performance the authorities intervened and the audience had to be dismissed. Rich stayed silenced. And the upshot of six years of intrigue and reshuffling was the establishment of something like the united company originally envisaged by Vanbrugh when he planned the Haymarket.

1. Letter cited in *The London Stage*, Part 2, I, 183.
2. For discussion see Price, "The Critical Decade," pp. 69–70. The prologue has been reprinted from the original broadside (collected and annotated by Luttrell) by Emmett L. Avery, "Some New Prologues and Epilogues, 1704–1708," *Studies in English Literature*, 5 (1965), 455–67, esp. 463–67.
3. For discussion of the events involved in the "silencing" of Drury Lane in June 1709 see Price, "The Critical Decade," Barker, *Mr Cibber*, pp. 75–78, and Judith Milhous and Robert D. Hume, "The Silencing of Drury Lane in 1709," *Theatre Journal*, 32 (1980), 427–47.
4. Watson Nicholson suggests that an Order in Council for the investigation of the Patent Company, 18 February 1709, marked the beginning of official action against Rich. See *The Struggle for a Free Stage in London* (Boston: Houghton Mifflin, 1906), p. 13. But Nicholson's source was British Library Add. MS 20,726, so the date of the order should be 1709/10.
5. PRO LC 7/3, fol. 104 (4 March 1709).
6. PRO LC 5/154, p. 417. (The usual £40 house charges were still permitted.)
7. The contracts are in LC 7/3.
8. PRO LC 5/154, p. 437.
9. Ibid., p. 446.
10. See *The London Stage*, Part 2, I, 175–76, and Barker, *Mr Cibber*, pp. 77–78.

73. Musicians in the Opera Orchestra

[Season of 1708–9?]

A List of ye Musick belonging to Operas
per diem

Monsieur	Dieupart	1:15:0
√	Haymes	1:15:0
√ +	Papuch	1: 5:0
√ +	Sajoni	0:15:0
√ +	Bannister	0:15:0
√	Corbet	0:15:0
√ +	Clodio	0:15:0
√ +	Lulÿ	0:15:0

√	Babel Senior	0:15:0	8 Violins
√ +	Peitro	0:15:0	2 Tenors
√ +	Paisible	0:15:0	2 Hautboys
√	Francisco	0:15:0	3 Bassons
√ +	Latour	0:11:3	1 Double Bass
√	Rogers	0:11:3	1 Harpsicord
√ +	Soyan	0:11:3	3 Bass Viols
√ +	Babel Junior	0:10:0	1 Trumpet
√ +	Armstrong	0:10:0	
	Disabaye	0:10:0	
	Kaite	0:10:0	
√	Cadet	0:10:0	
	Craig	0:10:0	
	Simpson	0: 8:0	
	Walters	0: 8:0	
√	Smith	0: 8:0	
√	Roberts	0: 8:0	
+	Lunican	0: 8:0	
	Manship	0: 8:0	
	Devon	0: 8:0	
	Vinum	0:10:0	
		£19: 9:9	

Copy-text: HTC Coke 42 (Hand E with notes in Hand A). Winston has a summary (without names), p. 87.

Comment: We have tentatively assigned this list to the season of 1708–9. It is quite similar to the list of musicians given in PRO LC 5/155, p. 3, and dated 24 December 1709 (see Nicoll, *History*, II, 278–79). By that date Manship has left the orchestra. Vinum appears neither in the 1707–8 lists nor in any list after this one. Both this roster and that of December 1709 include Craig, who was replaced about 1710. Armstrong, Kytch, Walter, and Clodio are all additions to the original 1708 rosters. Ayleworth, who was one of the original petitioners and was crossed out of the tentative list (document 17), later joined the orchestra, but is not yet listed here.

Twenty-nine musicians are entered on this roster, though the number specified in the right-hand column is only twenty-one. Nineteen names are checked; twelve have a plus sign written by them. We do not know the significance of these symbols.

74. Terms Proposed to Nicolini by Swiney

[ca. April 1709]

Proposals to Signor Nicolini.

1st The Engagement to be for three years.

2d He shall not perform in any place during that time within the Liberties of London or Westminster where mony is taken

3d He shall have an Opera upon the same terms he had this year, every Season[1]

4d If Acting be forbid by the Government[2] or Lord Chamberlain for the time Being, or that Signor Nicolini shall not be able by reason of Sicknesse &c to perform the agreement on his part then an abatement to be made in proportion to the time of such cessation or non performance

5th He shall be obliged to perform three new parts every year if required, but he shall have the liberty of Choosing his parts.

6th I will pay him £150 for a fair Score with the words & parts of an Opera to be by him fitted for the English stage every Season, if such Opera's shall be approved of

7 He shall Receive every year 800 Guineas by six payments. 1st payment being 300. Guineas upon the 10th day of December. 2d payment being 100. Guineas upon the 10th of January. 3d payment being 100. upon the 10th of ffebruary. 4th payment being 100. upon the 10th of March. 5th payment being 100. upon ye 10th April, last payment upon the 10th of May being 100. Guineas.

8. he shall not be obliged to attend the businesse of the house between the first day of June and the last day of October in any of the three years.

Copy-text: MS in Broadley, p. vii (Swiney holograph). A clipping from a dealer's catalogue pasted in with the MS offers it for sale at £1 10s. This document may have been part of lot 199 in the 1876 sale catalogue. It was definitely part of 704 in the 1905 sale catalogue.

Comment: Nicolini first performed in England during the 1708–9 season. This is a proposal for a further three-year contract on lavish terms. (Swiney may have given a copy to Coke for his information because the terms were extraordinary.) Nicolini agreed to stay in England, but by May 1710 he was protesting what he regarded as breach of contract by Swiney.[3] See documents

83, 84, and 85 below. Later that month Swiney took him to court over this dispute.

1. I.e., a benefit performance.
2. For example, during a period of official mourning, as happened in the fall of 1708.
3. According to later testimony by Swiney, Nicolini signed a contract substantially identical to this proposal on 2 May 1709 (PRO C6/555/27). Swiney gives Nicolini's salary as £860, although in document 85 the singer claims 800 guineas, which is £840. Swiney also states that Nicolini was to have a benefit on a day of his own choice in March, paying the "usual charges." Nicolini had agreed that an abatement of his salary would be made if he were sick, but he required full payment if an official silencing interrupted the opera after the tenth day of any month.

75. Letter by Margarita de l'Epine [Missing]

(May 1709)

Known only from the 1876 sale catalogue (no. 194): "Margarita de l'Epine, famous Singer, wife of Pepusch, etc. A.L.s. in Italian, May, 1709, 20 lines entirely autograph and signed in full, *fine and very rare*. No letter of this admirable singer has ever appeared in a public sale."

76. Sir John Stanley to Coke about the Silencing of Drury Lane

(Tuesday [7 June or 6 September 1709?])
[Cover] Sir John Stanley about the play house in Covent Garden[1]
northend ˙ 2 a clock
Tuesday

Dear Vice
This serves only to inform you that I have taken all possible care to prevent their playing to day, & am going to town to follow ye blow, of which you shall have a further account to night. I receivd to day a letter from my Lord Chamberlain with ye inclosd to you whereby I find him resolv'd to hold it out to ye last I am Dear Vice

Yours most constantly
J STANLEY

Dame & I are some peoples
most humble servants.

    * *northend*: pencil annotations suggest that readers have tried to interpret this as "nov the ——— 2 a clock." Northend was Stanley's out-of-town residence.

    Copy-text: HTC Coke 34 (Stanley holograph). For nineteenth-century transcriptions see Winston, p. 70, and Drexel MS, fol. 131.

    Comment: This note almost undoubtedly refers either (a) to the Lord Chamberlain's silencing of Drury Lane in June 1709, or (b) to the renewal of that order the following 6 September. For the Lord Chamberlain's order of 6 June see the introduction to this season. Drury Lane advertised *Epsom-Wells* for Tuesday, 7 June, but the performance was stopped. For a highly colored anecdote of Rich's discomfiture before his gleeful actors see Cibber, *Apology*, II, 71–73. For the circumstances in which Stanley personally stopped an advertised performance on 6 September see the introduction to the Season of 1709–1710.

    A pencil annotation on this document tentatively ties it to an order of 25 January 1720, but this may be dismissed as a red herring.

1. I.e., Drury Lane.

SEASON OF

1709–1710

At the start of the season of 1709–10 the Haymarket was the only show in town. Two nights a week it normally mounted Italian operas; the other four it put on plays. The two genres could not exist happily together, however, and so this fulfillment of Vanbrugh's original vision proved of short duration.

During the preceding spring and summer Swiney, basking in the prospect of a profitable monopoly, had moved to consolidate his position by signing up actors at lavish salaries and concluding a partnership agreement with three senior actors—Wilks, Cibber, and Doggett. (For a summary of this agreement see document 79.) Two problems must have been obvious: ever since the Union of 1708 there had been a surplus of actors available; and more pressingly, to act plays only four nights a week would provide no more than two-thirds of the support heretofore enjoyed by the acting company. Swiney first tried to gain flexibility by making a grab for the vacant Drury Lane theatre. On 11 August he advertised in the *Daily Courant*, asking that "All persons who have any concern or property in the shares of rent of Drury Lane Playhouse" meet with him the following Tuesday to hear "very advantageous proposals relating to the said house." This ploy failed, and the best Swiney could do was offer operas on a day other than Saturday—a concession which cannot have gone far to appease actors deprived of two nights' employment every week. Nonetheless, over the summer Swiney carried out extensive improvements and renovations of the Haymarket, and invested enough money to provide the actors a necessary minimum of scenery and costumes—for of course what they had been using remained the property of Rich.

Probably very few people understood that the Lord Chamberlain had no intention of rescinding his suspension order of 6 June 1709. Numerous suspensions had been ordered in the preceding decades, and as a rule they were lifted within a day or two—as soon as the cause of offence had been removed or due apology made. The remaining Drury Lane actors petitioned for permission to reopen on 10 June, and again 20 June and 5 July. The Lord Chamberlain's only concession was an order of 8 July, formally granting permission for actors to perform at the Haymarket four days a week.[1] Shortly after that the actors gave up on the Lord Chamberlain and petitioned the Queen directly.[2] No response is recorded.

On 6 September the Drury Lane Company attempted to reopen, advertising *The Recruiting Officer* for that day. The *Post Boy* for 13–15 September reports that "On Tuesday the 7th [sic] instant in Drury-Lane, when the Players were just going to act, but were, by Order from their Superiors, stopp'd from farther Proceeding; so that they were, to their great Mortification, forced to dismiss their publick Auditors."[3] According to an investigation conducted following a petition to the Queen, Sir John Stanley wrote the Drury Lane performers a letter dated 6 September flatly forbidding them to perform until further notice.[4] This naturally bred distress and protest. (For one view of the situation in mid-September see Collier's letter to Booth, printed as the interdocument immediately following this introduction.) Charles Killigrew petitioned the Queen, pointing out that his right in the playhouse was part of his marriage settlement on his wife, rendered valueless by the stoppage of acting. Sometime during September or early October a large group of people with "right in the patents," including Rich and Collier, protested directly to the Queen against the highhandedness of the Lord Chamberlain.[5] This protest ultimately produced an order in Council (18 February 1710) for an investigation, and a report was issued on 8 October 1711 tending to uphold the petitioners in law—but by then a great deal of water had gone under the bridge.

In October 1709 the vacant Drury Lane playhouse must have been a tantalizing temptation to unemployed actors and to would-be theatrical entrepreneurs. The opportunity was duly exploited by William Collier, a lawyer, Tory MP, and courtier who had been a minor shareholder at Drury Lane. In September he had professed absolute loyalty to Rich and his fellow patentees, but when he saw his chance he took it. To the utter consternation of Swiney (see documents 78 and 80) Collier wangled a license to act at Drury Lane (granted 19 November); got a lease by promising to pay £4 instead of £3 per day; and at the head of the actors to whom he proposed to give employment he broke into the theatre on 22 November and turned Rich out of it. Rich had prudently removed most of the "stock" beforehand, but as of December 1709 London again had a second acting company—and one perfectly free to act six nights a week.[6] Collier's venture did not thrive. His actors bickered, and they fiercely resented Aaron Hill, put in by Collier as manager. The celebrated actors' riot of June 1710 was the inevitable result (see document 86), after which Drury Lane again fell vacant.

Meanwhile at the Haymarket affairs were only marginally better. The singers bitterly resented the presence of the actors (see document 85), and the actors cannot have been any happier. When Drury Lane reopened the Lord Chamberlain may have allowed Swiney to cut the fat salaries he had agreed to the previous summer, but even so the season proved unprofitable. Barker reports a small loss on the season as a whole, and we can see some clear signs of trouble.[7] As early as December 1709 Swiney imported a Dutch contortionist named Higgons as an entr'acte feature (commented upon with horror by Addison in the *Tatler*). In March Swiney tried to dragoon Nicolini, Valentini, and Margarita de l'Epine into performing entr'actes for plays— without success. (See the second interdocument between documents 82 and 83.) And in April the Haymarket resorted to advertising the attendance of "the Four INDIAN KINGS" lately arrived in London.[8] Little wonder that at the end of the season Swiney and his partners were squabbling over their depleted treasury. Rich had been forced out—but neither acting company nor opera company had benefited.

We should note that Charles Talbot, Duke of Shrewsbury, replaced "Bugg" Kent as Lord Chamberlain in April 1710, though the change had no immediately visible effect on the theatres.

1. PRO LC 5/154, p. 446.
2. A copy is preserved in British Library Add. MS 20,726, fol. 20. The earlier actor petitions are enumerated in this one but appear not to have survived.
3. *The London Stage*, Part 2, I, 198–99.
4. Add. MS 20,726, fols. 24–34, esp. 29v.
5. Copies of both petitions are preserved in Add. MS 20,726, fols. 22–23.
6. For details see Barker, *Mr Cibber*, pp. 82–94.
7. See Cibber, *Apology*, II, 87–91.
8. For an account of the visiting American Indians, see Richmond P. Bond, *Queen Anne's American Kings* (Oxford: Clarendon Press, 1952).

INTERDOCUMENT.
Collier to Booth about the Silencing of Drury Lane

September 13th, 1709:

Sir

Yours I received and am as much surprized at the late order sent[1] as you can bee, I thought that matters had been soe settled that you wou'd have met with no other Interruption from playing then to have one taken upp & then to bee bailed in order to try the validity of the Lord Chamberlains order against the Patents; I must doe Sir John Stanley that justice that he did not consent we should play, but if wee did it was agreed as is above & that was all we desired & that was the Lord Chamberlains own method, & as I apprehended the only way to satisfie every Body but it's pretty plaine that his Lordships methods are not regarded and it is very difficult to knowe who to obey there is a secrett in this affair which time will bring to light, in the meane time, I cannot see we have anything to doe but to Petition the Queen in our names and sett forth the whole matter which when rightly stated I am of Opinion her Majesty will readily doe us Justice who are soe very much injur'd and Oppressed against reason Justice and all the knowne Lawes of the Land: my affaires will not permitt me to come to Town till next month but whatever Mr Rich Mr Goodall Mr Metcalfe & the rest of the Gentlemen concern'd shall think fitt to doe I will consent too for Sir Tho: Skipwith & my selfe for matters are carried now soe high, that I think it impracticable to sue for favour by any other method than the rules of Westminster Hall, only first to Petition the Queen that her Majesty will be pleased to try our Right under her Ancestours Patent and that she will countenance Us in such manner as the Kings and Queens of England have always done, and not suffer her Subjects to bee injured & Oppressed by any private person put in Authority under her tis the undoubted right of the Subject to bee heard before he is condemn'd but we have Execution passed and Executed upon us without any Legall Tryall or Sentence given: I would have the matter Carryed on in the strictest manner it can bee, and since we are to receive no favour, not to give any, nor to spare any one of what Quality or Distinction soever that offer to make an ill use of the Crowns power: I am sorry that any one should suffer for being firme to their own Engagements & Undertakeings [2] especially your selfe for my part I will doe all I can to protect you & contribute in proportion to keep you and the rest that stand by the Patent in spight of any ones private interest. I hope the Queen will not by any meanes be perswaded to act in an Arbitrary way, it being what she alwayes has abhor'd, ever since her glorious and Auspicious Reigne: I am in no manner of paine, but we shall have justice done us, and ample satisfaction made for the Violence used in this affaire, If you write to me Let your Letter be left and my Clerke will send it to me my humble service to all freinds, and beleive me to be Sir

Your assured ffreind and
humble Servant
W. Collier

To Mr Barton Booth

  Copy-text: Scribal fair copy in British Library Add. MS 20,726, fols. 33–34.

1. Stanley's order of 6 September forbidding further performances at Drury Lane.
2. I.e., the actors who had signed binding contracts with Drury Lane.

77. Orchestra Roster

[Season of 1709–10?]

Clodio	15	
Corbet	15	1st Violins
Banister	15	
Pepusch	15	
Y. Babel	10	
Soyan	10	2d Violins
Roberts	8	
Plank	8	
Smith	8	Tenors
Armstrong	10	
Lully	15	Hautbois
Latour	11	
Babel: S:	15	
Pietro	15	Bassons
Cadet	10	
Saggione	15	Double base
Bolognese	30	Harpsicord
Haym	35	
Paisible	15	Violoncelli
Francisco	15	
Trumpet Gronon[1]	10	
	300	
	150	

Copy-text: HTC Coke 70.

Comment: From salaries and the people included we have tentatively as-signed this roster to the season of 1709–10. Compare document 73. The 21 performers here correspond precisely to the numbers of instrumentalists called for in that list—8 violins, 2 Tenors, and so forth. The reference to Plank is unique in this collection.

Comparison of this list to the roster of musicians under contract to the

Haymarket as of 24 December 1709 (PRO LC 5/155, p. 3) leads to some
questions. That list names Dieupart, Aylworth, Rogers, Desabaye, Sympson,
Kytes, Craigg, Walter, Lunican, and Davain, in addition to 18 of those
named here, but omits Plank, il Bolognese, and Gronon. Compare also document 81 below. As it stands, this list does not seem to represent the complete
opera orchestra. At least two hypothetical explanations seem possible. (1)
This list represents a concert orchestra, or the orchestra used on play nights
rather than for operas. (2) This was the normal opera orchestra, with other
performers filling in as necessary. Certainly the list in PRO LC 5/155, p. 3,
suggests that these were not the only musicians working at the Haymarket
this season.

1. John Baptist Granom, who sometimes grandly styled himself Giovanni Battista
Grano.

78. Swiney's Request for Confirmation of His Monopoly

[Cover] Mr Swiny   [November 1709]
[Direction] For The Right Honourable Mr Vice Chamberlain These.

Sir
    I have inclosed sent your Honour an abstract of the Articles of Part-
nership with Mr Wilks, Mr Dogget & Mr Cibber[1] which are founded upon
my Lord Chamberlain's order to me to Receive all her Majesty's sworn Comedians.[2] If that order is not observ'd I must Endeavour to preserve my self
from Ruin & have recourse to such Methods as shall be advised by the
ablest Lawyers in England for my security. I was with Mr Vanbrugh this
Morning who surprized me very much in telling me he found a great many
difficulty's to obtain an order to me for the security of those Actors and
other performers both in Opera's and Comedy's which are now Actually
Engag'd to me, I must therefore for my own sake resolve not to run my self
into any further Engagements for scenes cloaths &c nor perform Opera's
any more till I Receive such an order from my Lord.[3] When I do if there is
any Prospect left me of getting any thing by the Play-house I will go on if
there is not I hope it will be a justification of me if I Refuse. I am your
Honours most obedient

                                    most oblig'd and most humble servant
                                    OWEN SWINY

Copy-text: Harvard Theatre Collection TS992.31.D (37). Swiney holograph. For nineteenth-century transcriptions, see Winston, p. 40, and Drexel MS, fol. 63. This letter was probably part of lot 199 in the 1876 sale catalogue.

Comment: This is Swiney's dismayed reaction to the news that Collier was maneuvering to set up a rival acting company at Drury Lane. Swiney had believed that the Haymarket was to remain the sole venture authorized to employ actors. The key legality is contained in the phrase "Receive all her Majesty's sworn Comedians" (but see note 2 below). Once "received" in a London theatre, an actor could not legally work in any other without the Lord Chamberlain's acquiescence in the transfer—and this acquiescence Kent was evidently ready to provide for actors needed by Collier.

1. See document 79.
2. This implies that *all* of Rich's actors had moved to the Haymarket, which is at variance with Cibber's account. Cf. *Apology*, II, 77–78, 94, and casts in *The London Stage*, Part 2, I, 199–202.
3. I.e., the Lord Chamberlain.

79. Summary of Swiney's Agreement with Wilks, Doggett, and Cibber

[November 1709][1]

Mr Swiny having a Lease of the Play-house in the Hay-Market with an assignment of the Queen's License for Acting Plays &c from Mr Vanbrugh, upon My Lord Chamberlain's late order to him, to Receive all her Majesty's Sworn Comedians did Agree to Receive in as Partners with him Mr Wilks, Mr Dogget & Mr Cibber upon the following terms.

After all charges & Expences in carrying on the businesse of the Play-house being paid Mr Swiny is to Receive £300 per annum Mr Wilks £250 per annum with a benefit Play clear of all charges, Mr Dogget & Mr Cibber £200 per annum each with a benefit day clear of all charges, And then the clear profits are to be divided into two equal parts, one part to be paid to Mr Swiny and the other Part to the three sharing Actors, And in case of loss, one half is to be paid by Mr Swiny and the other half by the sharing Actors.

All affairs relating to the house to be carryed on by the Majority of the four sharers.[2]

Copy-text: MS in the Collection of William W. Appleton (Swiney holograph). For a nineteenth-century transcription see Winston, p. 42. This document was probably part of 199 in the 1876 sale catalogue.

Comment: These are the terms on which Swiney tried to merge with the acting company. Swiney provided a lease on a theatre and Vanbrugh's license from the Queen. Wilks received an extra £50 (as superintendent of rehearsals, we know from PRO LC 7/2, fol. 2). To put affairs in the hands of "the Majority of the four sharers" was a bit awkward—but in practice the three actors tended to stick together, the more so because "the Opera . . . was a constant Drawback upon their Gains," as Cibber was sourly to observe.[3] This partnership, so hopefully entered upon, was not destined to last long.

1. According to Barker, Mr Cibber, p. 79, the original agreement was made as early as 10 March 1709. It was certainly final by July, when the Drury Lane actors received official permission to work at the Haymarket.
2. Winston adds a note: "these 3 papers [documents 78, 79, 80] folded in one."
3. Apology, II, 87.

80. Swiney's Proposal for Sharers' Terms and Performers' Salaries at the Haymarket

[November 1709]

Sir[1]

I have been thinking of a Thousand ways to make this matter as easy to every body as it can be. For as it stands now it will be impossible for me to go on & consequently to receive any order from my Lord Chamberlain that will be so much to my prejudice; the vast hazards which are incidental to a Play house concern I woud rather leave off and must. Your Honour knows that the business in Drury Lane was formerly carried on by the Patentees and five sharing Actors who divided profitt and loss into two equal parts one part to be receved or paid by the five sharers and the other by the Patentees. Now I am willing to undertake the business with four Actors[2] in the same manner as they did which is more beneficial to the Actors by the fifth share being divided amongst the four, besides which each of the four sharers shall have a Benefit play paying £40 Charges which is a very great addition to each mans proportion, and which they never had before. If this is thought reasonable I am ready to receive my Lords orders as your Honour proposd with a list of the performers in opera & Comedy, with the salarys of each Comedian and the Benefit Plays fix'd to each name, My Lord and your Honour disered Mr Maynwaring[3] to tell me I should have no reason to complain and that matters should be made very easy to me before the Licence should be granted to the undertakers at Drury Lane,[4] If you dont think this a proper expedient I am willing to agree to any that shall be thought more reasonable by your honour who am

> Your most obligd most humble
> and most obedient servant
> OWEN SWINY

Copy-text: Winston, pp. 41–42. For another nineteenth-century transcription see Drexel MS, fol. 61. This letter was probably part of lot 199 in the 1876 sale catalogue.

Comment: Swiney here states the terms on which he is willing to acquiesce in the granting of a license to Collier for acting at Drury Lane. In essence, he wants a written list of performers definitely reserved to the Haymarket, and the Lord Chamberlain's authorization to reduce salaries originally set on the supposition that there would be no competition.

1. The recipient ("your Honour") is probably Coke, though Sir John Stanley is another possibility.
2. I.e., Wilks, Cibber, Doggett, and Anne Oldfield. Cibber tells us that "Swiny (who was then sole Director of the Opera only) had Permission to enter into a private Treaty with such of the united Actors in *Drury-Lane* as might be thought fit to head a Company. . . . The Actors chosen for this Charge were *Wilks, Dogget,* Mrs *Oldfield,* and Myself." Doggett objected to having a female manager, and Mrs Oldfield was given a substantial increase in salary and "a Benefit clear of all Charges" instead of a share in the management. See Cibber, *Apology,* II, 69–71.
3. Arthur Maynwaring (1668–1712) was party to these discussions, presumably on behalf of his mistress, Anne Oldfield.
4. A license was granted to Collier on 19 November 1709.

81. Proposed Performers and Regulations for the Haymarket

[Cover] Mr Swiney   [November 1709]

1st Whereas Mr Swiny has (upon the Lord Chamberlains order to Entertain the Actors) enterd into articles of Partnership with Mr Doggett Mr
Wilks & Mr Cibber for several years & hath also made contracts with several other actors to pay them great salarys supposing there was to be no
other Theatre Licencd by her Majesty His Lordship thinks fit (upon the
Queens granting a Licence for another company of Comedians) to dissolve
the contracts of such nature made with any Actor or Actress by Mr Swiny
and dos order and appoint him her Majestys Sworn Comedians (a List of
whose names are hereunto annexd) the yearly salarys affixd to each of their
names and that an entry be made of each actors name with his or her
Bargain in a Book in the Lord Chamberlains office and if acting is forbid by
order of the Government then an abatement to be made out of the Salarys
in proportion to the time of such Cessation.

2d Whereas several of the actors now entertaind in her Majesties Theatre
in the Hay Market have formerly been in articles with Mr Rich and have
been since persecuted by him for breach of em. His Lordship thinks fitt that
such articles be deliverd into the Lord Chamberlains office to be cancelld or
that the parties to whom the Licence is to be granted do give releases to
such Actors before the Licence is granted that there may be no Law suits
commencd against them afterward.

3d That the names of all the performers of which kind soever be inserted
in the Body of the Lord Chamberlains order to the Manager of the Hay
Market and that they nor any one of em be entertaind upon any pretence
whatsoever in any other Company without a discharge first had in writing
under the hand of the Manager of the Theatre in the Hay Market and
approvd off by my Lord Chamberlain.

a List of the actors with their respective Salarys

	£ per annum		
Mr Wilks	200	Mrs Barry	100
Mr Betterton	100	Mrs Oldfield	100
Mr Doggett	150	Mrs Betterton	25
Mr Cibber	150	Mrs Bucknell	80
Mr Estcourt	150	Mrs Cross	80
Mr Mills	100	Mrs Porter	80
Mr Johnson	100	Mrs Saunders	50

Mr Penkethman	100	Mrs Wilks[1]	30
Mr Bullock	80	Mrs Baker	30
Mr Thurmond	60	Mrs Mills	20
Mr Husband	60	Mrs Willis Junior	20
Mr Bowen	60	Mrs Robins	15
Mr Boman	40	Mrs Granger	15
Mr Bullock Junior	30	Miss Younger	10
Mr Cross	30		
Mr Thurmond Junior	25		

And whereas Benefit Plays have been a very great nuisance to the Town my Lord Chamberlain doth order that no actor have any shew of a Benefit play except the undermentiond who are allowd it in consideration of their particular merit and Industry sometime before the last day in april yearly paying £40 charges—

Mr Betterton	Mr Doggett
Mr Wilks	Mr Cibber
Mr Estcourt	Mrs Barry
	Mrs Oldfield

A List of the Singers & dances

Instrumental [*] Musick		
Signor Nicolini	Monsieur Dieupart	Mr Desaboye
Signor Valentini	Signor Haym	Mr Cadett
Mr Leveridge	Mr Poptry[†][2]	Mr Armstrong
Mr Laurence	Signor Clodio	Mr Sympson
Mr Ramenden	Mr Banister	Mr Kyber[3]
Mrs Tofts[4]	Mr Presible	Mr Cross
Mrs Margaritta	Mr Lully	Mr Walters
Baroness	Mr Corbet	Mr Lunican
Mrs Lindsay	Mr Ayleworth	Mr Roberts
Monsieur Cherrier[5]	Mr Sajony	Mr Smith
Miss Santlaw[6]	Mr Francisco	Mr Latour
	Mr Babel Senior	
	Mr Pietro	
	Mr Roger	
	Mr Babel Junior	
	Mr Soyan	

[*] *Instrumental*: MS reads *Instumental*.
[†] *Poptry*: reading doubtful.

Copy-text: Winston, pp. 38–40. For another nineteenth-century transcription see Drexel MS, fols. 71–72. This document was probably part of lot
199 in the 1876 sale catalogue.

Comment: In form, this document resembles an order issued by the Lord
Chamberlain on 24 December 1709. From the third point, however, and the
endorsement "Mr Swiney" in the usual fashion of Coke's office (according to
Winston), we would guess that this is a draft submitted by Swiney to the authorities for their consideration. In document 80 he had asked for such an
order in return for his acceptance of the loss of his monopoly.

What the Lord Chamberlain actually ordered (PRO LC 5/155, p. 3) was
somewhat more limited. He issued a list of performers (almost identical to
this one) together with the following injunction.

I do strictly Order and Require You the said performers to remain under ye direction
of You the Manager or Mangers of the Queens Theatre in the Hay Market and I do
hereby declare that they shall not have leave upon any Terms whatsoever to be
Entertain'd in any other Company without a discharge in writing under the hands of
the Said Manager or Managers and Approv'd by me provided their contracts are
made good by you the said Manager or Managers of the said Theatre.

Probably the Lord Chamberlain did not want to decree salaries or benefit
rights, but he was willing to guarantee Swiney the services of his principal
performers. There is, at any rate, no evidence that the Lord Chamberlain
issued an order in the terms of the present document.

The Lord Chamberlain's list contains all of the actors and actresses named
here save Mrs Betterton (whose salary was strictly a courtesy—she had been
inactive for some time) and adds Mr Ryan (a fresh import from Ireland) and
Mrs Powell (probably an accidental omission from this list). Among singers it
adds Mlle Girardo (Isabella Girardeau) who joined the company in mid-
season. Musicians present some small discrepancies and puzzles. The Lord
Chamberlain's list adds Pepusch, Craigg, and Davain while omitting "Poptry"
and Cross.

The presence of Tofts and Cherrier in both lists is surprising: neither was
active with the Haymarket company at this time. Possibly Swiney was indi-
cating his claim to their services if and when they became available.

The salary reductions are fewer and smaller than we might expect. Of the
fourteen actors and actresses for whom we possess comparable figures, six are
down for the same salary they agreed on the previous summer. Wilks, Cibber,
and Doggett are each cut £50, while Mrs Oldfield is cut 50 percent to £100.
Mrs Baker and Mrs Willis (senior) are dropped from £40 to £30.

1. "Mrs Wilks" is almost certainly an error for "Mrs Willis" (senior).
2. Both Winston and the Drexel MS transcriber seem to have had trouble with this name. It could be a very mangled form of "Pepusch" (present in the Lord Chamberlain's list, but missing here), or it could be someone who served the orchestra only briefly. William Popeley is a likely possibility.
3. I.e., "Kytes" in the Lord Chamberlain's list, "Kaite" in document 73.
4. Mrs Tofts remained off the stage after May 1709.
5. Cherrier is believed to have left England in May 1708.
6. Omitted in the Lord Chamberlain's list, probably deliberately, since she was allowed to perform at Drury Lane this season.

82. Note from Stanley to Coke about Collier

[Fall of 1709?]
Cockpit Thursday *

Sir

I have given Collier my Lord Bindons[1] memoriall, who is to waite on you to receive your directions about his brief to morrow morning, & have writt to Mr Killegrew[2] to give you an account of ye operis saturday morning as you directed

I go to morrow to northend to plant, & shall be ready to receive your commands saturday night being

Most faithfully
Yours
J STANLEY

I send you a letter to signe for a preacher who is to come into waiting before Lord Chamberlain comes to town

* *Thursday*: "friday" was written and canceled, and "Thurday" [sic] written beneath it.

Copy-text: HTC Coke 36 (Stanley holograph). For a nineteenth-century transcription see Winston, p. 84.

Comment: This appears to be an interoffice memo telling Coke that Stanley has made arrangements requested by Coke. The postscript concerns one of the Vice Chamberlain's nontheatrical duties.

1. Henry Howard, later sixth Earl of Suffolk (1670–1718), created Baron Chester-
ford and Earl of Bindon in 1706. He was known as Lord Bindon until 10 December
1709, when he succeeded his father as Earl of Suffolk. That date is a probable *terminus
ad quem* for this document. The "memoriall" may have been connected with Collier's
takeover of Drury Lane.
2. Presumably Charles Killigrew, Master of the Revels 1677–1725.

INTERDOCUMENT.
Stanley to Collier about the Terms of His License

Cockpitt 19th November 1709

Sir

My Lord Chamberlain has directed me to acquaint you in consideration of your
having surrenderd all your Interest and Claim to the Pattents granted to Mr Killigrew and Sir Wm Davenant and submission to her Majestys authority her Majesty is
graciously pleas'd to permitt you to act Comedy and Tragedy in the Theatre in Drury
Lane the First Play not to be Acted before Wednesday next being the 23d instant
and I am farther to acquaint you that her Majestys Lycence impowering you accordingly is preparing and will be speedily sent you.

And you are strictly required by his Lordship not to suffer Mr Rich or any other
Person claiming under the abovesaid Pattents to be any ways concern'd in the Management of the Company of Comedians under your direction.

You are also hereby requir'd to observe all such Regulations as have been made for
the better Government of her Majestys Theatre more particularly her Majestys
Order forbidding any Person to come behind the scens or stand upon the stage. I am

Sir Your most humble servant
J STANLEY

To Mr Collier

Copy-text: PRO LC 7/3, fol. 33, scribal fair copy.

INTERDOCUMENT.
Nicolini's Refusal to Perform Entr'actes

(17 March 1710)

It has been Publish'd in Yesterdays *Daily Courant*, and last Night in her Majesty's
Theatre at the *Hay-Market*, that to Morrow (being *Saturday* the 18th of *March*) will
be presented there, A Comedy, with several Select Scenes of Musick, to be perform'd between the Acts by Cavalier Nicolini, Signior Valentini, and Signiora Mar-

garita; which sort of Performance the Said Cavalier Nicolini finding to be directly contrary to the Agreement made between him and Mr. Owen Swiny, and that the same wou'd prove a real Means to Vilifie and Prejudice the Opera. He doth hereby acquaint all Gentlemen and Ladies, that his Intention is strictly to observe the Tenor and Meaning of the said Agreement, that is to say, to Sing during the Winter Season only formal Operas, and to be always ready to please and serve them according to his Duty and usual Custom.

Copy-text: Photocopy in British Library, 1879.c.3, fol. 58.

Comment: The Haymarket advertised in the *Daily Courant* of 16 March "Select Scenes of Musick" sung by Nicolini, Valentini, and Margarita de l'Epine between the acts of *The Scornful Lady* on Saturday, 18 March. On 17 March the preceding handbill was published.

83. Nicolini to Swiney about Money Owed to Him

[Cover] May 10th 1710.   (10 May 1710)

                                                          le 10 May 1710

Copie
Monsieur
   Apres qu'on eut recité trois fois l'opera d Hidaspes, Je vous demanday les cent cinquante livres, qui m'etoient deües en vertu du contract passè entre nous, et m'ayant repondu que vous ne me vouliez payer sans avoir premierement en vos mains The fair score, and all the parts of the Opera, ce qui ne reflechissoit pas bien sur moy, Je vous le donnay dans les formes il y a environ quinze Jours, depuis lequel tems J'ay attendu Jusques à Mercredy passé, que vous ne m'aviez pas encore payé, pour n'avoir pas ajusté vos Comptes avec M:̣ White, comme on me rapporta de votre part Il y a justement aujourd'huy huit jours, et ne doutant nullement que vous ne puissiez, ou vouliez a present me satisfaire, comme la justice le requiert, Je vous prie de me les envoyer au plutost.
   On me doit encore ce jourd'huy cent guineés de mon payement selon mon contract, que J'espere que vous m'envoyerez aussy sans me faire Languir, comme vous avez fait dans les derniers payemens. La chicanne en pareille occasion ne nous seant bien ny à vous ny a moy, et souvenez vous que Je vous fis bons tous les tickets, qui furent presentez le jour de mon benefice selon le nombre, que vous m'en accusates, sans que jusques à pre-

sent vous me les ayez rendus, comme vous m'aviez promis, et comme il etoit
de raison.
Je suis
Monsieur

Copy-text: HTC Coke 66 (Nicolini's scribe).

Translation: "Sir, After we had performed the opera of Hidaspes three
times I asked you for the one hundred and fifty pounds which were my due by
virtue of the contract passed between us; and since you answered me that you
did not want to pay me without first having in your hands 'the fair score and
all the parts of the Opera,' which did not reflect well on me, I formally gave
you these some fifteen days ago, and have been waiting since then until last
Wednesday, at which date you still had not paid me, because of your settling
your accounts with Mr White as you informed me eight days ago today, and
since I have absolutely no doubt that you can or will now give me satisfaction, as justice requires, I pray you to send them to me at once.

"To this day I am still owed one hundred guineas of my payment according
to my contract, that I hope you will send me as well without making me lan-
guish in waiting as you have done in the last payments. Litigation about such
matters befits neither you nor me, and remember that I made good for you all
the tickets presented on the day of my benefit, according to the number that
you presented me, without your having reimbursed them to me so far, as you
had promised to do and as was reasonable. I am Sir"

Comment: Evidently a scribal copy of a letter of protest from Nicolini to
Swiney, sent to Coke for the record. See documents 84 and 85 following.
Pyrrhus and Demetrius had been performed as a benefit for Nicolini on 21
March. According to testimony by Swiney, two days after sending this letter
Nicolini refused to sing the title role in "the New Opera called Hydaspe at
the said Theatre" (PRO C6/555/27).

84. Nicolini's Complaint against Swiney

(18 May 1710)

[Cover] Sign⟨r⟩ Nicolini's Complaint of M⟨r⟩ Swiny
        May 18th 1710

le 18⟨me⟩ May 1710

Monsieur
    Suivant vos commendemens J'e ay l'honneur de Vous envoyer le memoire
en question de ce qui se passe entre monsieur Suÿni et moy, avec les articles

de l'accord qui à ete fait entre lui et moy. Je vous supplie de votre Protection, et sur tout pour me delivrer d'un esclavage inquiet et honteux, qu' on
ne scauroit non plus s'immaginer ailleurs hors de l'Angleterra, et d'eux per-
suadé que Je serai toujours avec tout la sincerite et respect que Je dois—
Monsieur

> Votre tres humble, et tres obbeissant
> serviteur
> CHEVALIER NICOLINO GRIMALDI

Copy-text: MS in Broadley, p. vii (Nicolini holograph? unique sample in
this collection). This letter is item 183 in the 1876 sale catalogue. It is 692 in
the 1905 sale catalogue. An unidentified dealer's catalogue clipping is pasted
under the document. It states no price, but mentions that the letter is quoted
in Grove.

Translation: "Sir, Following your instructions I am honored to send you the
memoir about what is happening between Mr Swiney and myself, as well as
the articles of the agreement that was made between him and me. I beg you
for your protection, and particularly to deliver me from a disturbing and
shameful enslavement which one would not imagine outside England; and be
convinced that I shall always be with all the sincerity and respect I owe you—
Sir, Your very humble and obedient servant."

Comment: This is evidently a cover letter for document 85.

85. Nicolini's Claims against Swiney

[18 May 1710]
Memoire
Les pretensions du Chevalier Grimaldi contre Swiny ne sont autres que
celles qui sont renfermeés dans la Copie de lettre que le Chevalier luy a
ecrit par ordre de My Lord Chambellan, à la quelle Swiny ne fit aucune
reponce, et ce ne fut que deux jours apres que le Chevalier la luy envoya
demander par son valet, selon la direction que luy en avoit donné My Lord,
Qu'Il repondit en presence de My Lords Portland, et Burlington,[1] que si le
Chevalier pretendoit quelque chose de luy, il devoit la luy demander par la
loy, disant qu'il avoit d'autres pretentions contre le Chevalier.
Le Swiny doit rabbattre quatorze ou quinze livres sterlings qui ont eté
employeés inutilement à divers ouvrages de menuiserie fait à l'Amphi-

theatre, sur les sommes qui restent düez au Chevalier Nicolino, qui comme on voit sont de cent cinquante livres pour l'opera d'Idaspes qu'il a mis au Theatre, et cent guineés pour son dernier payement echu le 10 du present mois de May, qui est le reste de huit cens guineés qui luy doivent etre payeés annuellement par contract Swiny a un billet du Chevalier fait à condition que lorsqu'il le luy payera; les dites menuiseries qui n'ont servy a rien, et les Comptes des ouvrages susdits luy seront remis en mains.

Pour ce qui est des billets de benefice dont il est parlé dans la cy jointe lettre, et dont le Chevalier avoit tenu compte plusieurs semaines auparavant à Swiny à raison de demie guineé piece, et qui se montent à £190:05^s:6^d. Le Chevalier les a receus le soir du 12 du present Mois.

Au surplus ce que demande le Chevalier Nicolino est que (considerant que les disgraces, les incommodites les mortifications, et affronts qu'il a receus, même jusqu'a avoir eté malade pendant presque tout le cours dela saison passeé n'ont ete causés que par le depit que les Comediens, et Swiny avoient dele voir si attaché a l'opera et de le voir rendre par la d'agreables services à la noblesse, et qu'ils avoient dessein de faire tomber les Operas, comme tout le monde la pu visiblement voir) le Contract qui est entre luy et Swiny pour deux anneés à venir soit entierement rompu de maniere qu'il soit libre, et degagé d'une tirannie, et esclavage si facheuse, et qu'il puisse en toutte tranquillité d'esprit servir la noblesse dela quelle seule il veut dependre.

Le Chevalier espere, que cette demande ne sera pas seulement trouvée juste par le grand discernem.^{t} de My Lord Chambellan, et de Monsr Le Vice Chambel: Cook, mais même qu'elle sera ecouté favorablement et appuyeé de leurs autorité, et justice incorruptible. Il est bon de faire reflexion, que le contract du Chevalier pour les trois années 1709:10:11 à etè passé en May 1709 entre luy seul, et Swiny de la mème maniere qu'avoit eté fait le precedent[2] qui fut si bien dans les formes executé

Il y a au Theatre trois autres Maitres, tous trois Comediens, qui se sont associez depuis L'hyver passé avec Swiny, comme compagnons, Directeurs, et arbitres tant des comedies que des Operas, et des Musiciens; leur interest, et leur but est de detruire les Operas, et de faire insulte à ceux qui s'opposent à leur dessein, la raison veu donc que le Chevalier qui est toujours prest à rendre service à la noblesse ne soit pas exposé a l'insolence, aux cabales, et à la malice de ces nouveaux Directeurs, qui veulent luy donner tant de degousts, qu'il cesse de soutenir les Operas, ou qu'il se resoude * quitter l'Angleterre.

* *resoude*: *à* may well have been cropped from the MS at this point.

Copy-text: HTC Coke 67 (Nicolini's scribe).

Translation: "Memorandum. The claims of Chevalier Grimaldi against Swiney are no other than the ones expressed in the copy of the letter that the Chevalier wrote him by order of My Lord Chamberlain, and which Swiney did not answer; and it was not until two days after the Chevalier sent his footman for an answer as advised by my Lord, that Swiney answered in the presence of My Lords Portland and Burlington that if the Chevalier was claiming something from him, he would have to ask for it in court, adding that he had other claims against the Chevalier.

"Swiney must deduct fourteen or fifteen pounds sterling which have been uselessly spent on various pieces of carpentry built in the Amphitheatre, out of the amounts still owed to Chevalier Nicolino; these amounts, as one can see, are one hundred and fifty pounds for the opera *Hydaspes* that he staged and one hundred guineas for his last payment which was due on the 10th of the present month of May and is the remnant of eight hundred guineas which must be paid to him each year by contract. Swiney has a note from the Chevalier making the condition that when he is paid the carpentry pieces which were of no use and the bills for the abovementioned pieces will be handed to him.

"As for the benefit tickets which are mentioned in the enclosed letter and for which the Chevalier had credited Swiney several weeks earlier at a half-guinea apiece, the total of which amounts to £190 5s.6d., the Chevalier received them the evening of the 12th of this month.

"In addition, what Chevalier Nicolino is asking is that (considering the disgraces, discomforts, mortifications, and insults that he was subjected to, to the point even of making him ill for almost the whole duration of the last season, caused solely by the resentment by the comedians and Swiney at the sight of his attachment to the opera and the sight of his thus rendering pleasant services to the nobility, when their sole design was to destroy operas, as everybody has been able clearly to see) the contract existing between him and Swiney for the two coming years be entirely broken so that he may be free and delivered from such a deplorable tyranny and bondage; and so that he may, with full peace of mind, serve the nobility on whom alone he wants to be dependent.

"The Chevalier hopes that this claim will not only be thought a just one by the great discernment of my Lord Chamberlain and the Vice-Chamberlain Coke, but also that it will be favorably listened to and supported by their authority and incorruptible justice. It is fitting to remember that the Chevalier's contract for the three years 1709, 1710, 1711, has been drawn in May

1709 between him alone and Swiney in the same way as the former one, which was carried out so well in its form, had been made.

"There are in the theatre three other masters, all three comedians, who have become Swiney's associates since last winter as companions, directors, and referees of comedies as well as operas and musicians; their interest and their purpose is to destroy the operas and to insult those who oppose their design; reason therefore commands that the Chevalier, who is always ready to be of service to the nobility, would not be exposed to the insolence, intrigues, and malice of these new directors who want to get him so disgusted that he will cease to support the opera or bring himself to leave England."

Comment: For an account of the terms of Nicolini's contract, see document 74 above. On 22 May 1710 Swiney entered a bill of complaint against Nicolini in Chancery. We do not know whether the Lord Chamberlain intervened, but the dispute was apparently settled out of court and Nicolini remained with the opera company for the next two seasons.

1. Henry Bentinck, Earl, later first Duke, of Portland (1682–1726), was one of the original subscribers to the Haymarket theatre project (as Viscount Woodstock). He was also one of the original subscribers to the Royal Academy of Music in 1719. Richard Boyle (1695–1753) had succeeded his father as Earl of Burlington in 1704. He appears to have begun early cultivating the tastes which made him a great patron of the arts.

2. I.e., the contract for 1708–9.

86. Aaron Hill to Collier about the Actors' Riot at Drury Lane

(5 June 1710)

[Cover] Mr Hill to Mr Collier about the Players
[Direction] To William Collier Esquire at Windsor. These

Sir

Next to the very great Pleasure I conceive in your Conversation, The Honour of hearing from you gave me ye greatest satisfaction in The world; and I shou'd think it an extraordinary Happiness cou'd I see windsor, while your being in it, gives that agreable Place a double Relish; your Lady informd me, she expected you in Town last saturday, or To day at farthest, The Expectation * I was thence in, of seeing you; was ye Cause of my silence.

Sir, you may remember, before you left London, I had taken away ye useless Power of ye seven managers;[1] That unexpected Blow was a great surprize to 'em; resented warmly by all. But Mr Bickerstaff and Mr Keene appear'd most publickly disgusted, All ye other Actors, in general, were pleas'd beyond Expression, & ever since ye managers lost their Power, have shown a double Life, & Industry in their Application to Business.

I made Mr Pack Manager of Rehearsals, who, after a day or two, threw up ye Concern; then I offer'd it to Booth who with an Insolence, peculiar to his Nature, refus'd it, unless They might, all seven, be restor'd to their management.

I perceiv'd They had form'd a Resolution of holding together, as They call'd it; and, upon This, oblig'd my Brother to take upon him ye Care of Rehearsals, which, for some days, went on with a tolerable Quiet, till ye Night before you left London, a Little affair call'd me into Essex for a day or Two; where ye News reach'd me, that They were all in an uproar, at being forfeited; that They had flung up Their Parts, refus'd to act, threaten'd to take ye Cloaths out of ye House, &c: I came up to Town immediately; found all This true, with This Addition, That Bickerstaff had beaten a poor Fellow[2] blind, without any other Provocation, than reproving him for abusing me most scurrilously, that he had told Baggs[3] he wou'd push my Brother off ye stage by ye shoulders & in short; that he had, with Keene endeavour'd to disorder, & distract ye whole Company.

These, & many Insolencies more, which I blush to remember, & was confounded to see, obliged me to suspend Mr Bickerstaff & Mr Keene, to ye former of whome I writt a Letter, containing ye Reasons for my Proceedings, & Friendly Advice, not to be misled by villains, who made him but ye Cat's Paw to their designs; Instead of taking This as he shou'd have done, he forcd ye Printer to put his Name in ye Bills, told me he neither Valued you, me, nor any man alive, that himself was his own master, & he wou'd come behind ye scenes, & see who durst hinder him.

Leigh, with an Impudence unhear'd of, exceeded all This, and told me in publick defyance, that he wou'd not only be a manager when I was none, but wou'd go down & act with Pinkethman,[4] in spite of my Lord Chamberlain, or me either.

Booth, with a Thousand Raskally Invectives against yourself & me, told me publickly, at ye same Time, that Mr Bickerstaff shou'd act that night, & Mr Keene ye next, were it but in Contradiction to me; that I might take my way, & They wou'd take Theirs, & see who wou'd come by ye worst of it.

These Proceedings; & several anonymous Letters which inform'd me of designs upon ye House, ye Cloaths, &c, oblig'd me to send an order to stockdale,[5] not to open ye Doors that night, (last Fryday)[6] till I sent him a

Guard of Constables to keep ye Peace & protect him from being insulted in
his Duty. accordingly he shut up ye doors, & about 4 a Clock I found Mr
Baggs, (till then I cou'd not) come to ye office, I went in to direct him
about ye Constables, & while my Brother & I stood talking with him, we
heard Booth, Powel, Keene, & several others, breaking open ye great Doors
within; (It seems Mrs Bradshaw had let 'em in thro' a private way, from her
Lodgings) I made Mr Baggs open ye office window, & while I was calling, to
know what They were at, The Doors were† beaten open, & a Crowd, with
Booth at their Head, burst into ye office upon me, with drawn swords in
their Hands; with much ado I got out into ye open Passage had drawn my
sword, & while surrounded by a Crowd, some to prevent, & some to encrease ye Tumult, Powell had shorten'd his sword to stab me in ye Back,
and has cut a Gentlemans Hand through,‡ who prevented ye Thrust, Leigh
in ye mean Time, while my Brother was held, struck him a dangerous Blow
on ye Head, with a stick, from behind. This was done in ye open Face of ye
day, amongst Numbers of men & women, who came to see ye Play.

As soon as I cou'd, I left 'em; & went directly to st. James's, in Hopes I
might have met mr vice Chamberlain, but miss'd him there, & at Ken-
sington twice since. From st James's I went that Night, to your House, to
know how I might direct, waited on your Lady to ye Play, but when I wou'd
have gone behind ye scenes, found ye proper doorkeepers dismiss'd, & orders given, that neither my Brother, nor myself, nor any that belong'd to
me shou'd have admission there. Bickerstaff, that night, acted, & They
gave out Tomorrow,⁷ for ye last Time of acting, till next season, contrary to
ye pressing Desire of ye honest young Company, who are all confounded at
their Proceedings, & stark mad to go on without em.

Mr Rich happen'd to pass by in ye first Tumult,⁸ & was huzza'd along ye
Passage, had his Hands kiss'd, & was saluted by mr Leigh—God bless you,
Master, see here! we are at work for you. I give you but a tenth Part of ye
History of These worthy Gentlemen's Proceedings. The Cloaths that are
not gone already, are to be sent away tomorrow night, & mr Rich is to be
offer'd Possession of ye House, if he thinks fit to take it.

Now Sir, if such villanies as These must go unpunish'd farewel all Hopes
of order in a Playhouse. I know not which way best to proceed; After Bur-
glary & Felony & violent Possession, I can hope no Effects from ye Authority you gave me; And to go amongst 'em is in vain, since murder, one way
or other, must ensue, & that will ruin ye House instead of correcting it. In
short Sir unless Booth, Powel, & Leigh, are taken immediatly into Custody,
& silenc'd, your Interest in ye Playhouse will, from This Time forward, be
worth not one shilling, nor can any Authority appear among 'em, without
Ridicule, after such a Precedent as This has escap'd Correction. Tis already

ye Talk, & amazement of ye other Company, & ye whole Town; and as I have brought all This Trouble & Hatred on myself out of pure Justice to ye Friendship you are pleas'd to admit me to, I must entreat you to lose no time in getting ye 3 above nam'd, confin'd, & silenc'd, & an order pass'd against any of ye Company's going to Greenwich,[9] As for Bickerstaff & Keene They will presently be easy when Their Inflamers are made such necessary Examples. Till This be done, we can do nothing; But if we break This Barr, The House shall be a House indeed. I shall impatiently wait ye Honour of a Line, to

> Sir your most faithful and
> obedient humble servant
> A: HILL

London, June ye 5th 1710.

* *Expectation*: MS reads "Expectatation."
† *were*: reading doubtful.
‡ *through*: MS reads "thro'."

Copy-text: Aaron Hill holograph in the collection of Mary Hyde. For nineteenth-century transcriptions see Winston, pp. 24–29, and Drexel MS, fol. 79 and two unnumbered folios following. This letter is item 188 in the 1876 sale catalogue.

Comment: This celebrated letter was the basis for Percy Fitzgerald's oft-cited account of the Drury Lane riot.[10] The short-term result of the riot was an order from the Lord Chamberlain to Collier dated 14 June 1710.

Whereas Complaint has been made to me that five of the Actors belonging to her Majestys Company of Comedians under your Management vizt George Powell Barton Booth Jonathan Bickerstaff Theophilus Keen and ffrancis Lee [Leigh] did not only refuse to Obey ye Orders of Mr Hill who is appointed by you to take care of the said Company, but that they did also lately in a riotous manner break open the Doors of the Play house, beating and Abusing the Said Mr Hill and with their Swords drawn threatning his life and have also committed Severall other insolencys and disorders These are Therefore to charge and Require you imediately to dismis and remove the said Powell from the Service of her Majesty's Company he having been formerly guilty of the like offences and that you Suspend Barton Booth Theophilus Keen Jonathan Bickerstaff and ffrancis Lee from further Acting. (PRO LC 5/155, p. 11)

All five of the principal offenders were acting again at Drury Lane in the following fall—but in the company operated by Swiney, Wilks, Cibber, and Doggett. For the negotiations which put the opera in the hands of Collier and Hill see the introduction to the Season of 1710–1711. The riot effectively demolished Collier's venture at Drury Lane, and not until John Rich opened the third Lincoln's Inn Fields theatre in December 1714 was there again to be a second acting company in London during the regular season.

1. Early in the one season of Collier's Drury Lane enterprise seven of the actors were given "managerial" status. Exactly when Hill took over as Collier's deputy we do not know, but evidently he revoked that status and tried to induce first Pack, then Booth, to accept responsibility for superintending rehearsals before importing his brother.

2. Identity unknown.

3. Zachary Baggs, long-time Treasurer for Rich, who served this company in the same capacity.

4. William Penkethman operated a summer theatre down the river at Greenwich. His company opened 15 June and played three times a week until September.

5. Evidently a house servant. Affidavits from a George Stockdale are mentioned in British Library Add. MS 20,726, fols. 24–32.

6. I.e., Friday 2 June. The rebellious company put on Charles Shadwell's *The Fair Quaker of Deal* as scheduled.

7. I.e., Tuesday 6 June, which was indeed the last Drury Lane performance of the season.

8. For confirmation of the suggestion that Christopher Rich helped foment this riot, see *Tatler*, no. 193.

9. Powell and Leigh did in fact perform at Greenwich that summer.

10. *A New History*, I, 309–13. See also Dorothy Brewster, *Aaron Hill* (New York: Columbia Univ. Press, 1913), pp. 83–86.

SEASON OF

1710–1711

In September 1710 the organization of the London theatre was very much up in the air. Would there be two acting companies? Would operas and plays continue to be offered by an uncomfortable double company at the Haymarket? What rights did Collier's license carry after the fragmentation of his company caused by the riot in June? Swiney's letter of 23 September makes plain just how uncertain matters were. Aside from three performances at the beginning of October the theatres remained dark until 4 November, when the acting company started to perform at the Haymarket on a temporary basis.

The compromise which was worked out reflects at least three significant factors. (1) Singers and actors had both disliked the confinement of a double company to a single theatre in 1709–10. Consequently operas and plays were again divided. (2) The shareholders of Drury Lane were eager to have it rented profitably to someone (see document 88), and as it was the better house for plays, the actors were happy to return there. (3) Collier was determined to hang onto something in the reshuffle—and so he wound up with the opera.

These rearrangements required some rather drastic juggling. Swiney and his actor-partners (Wilks, Cibber, and Doggett) gave up both opera and the Haymarket to Collier (who retained Aaron Hill as manager)—a change which in essence made Collier a subtenant of Vanbrugh's tenant Swiney at the Haymarket. Vanbrugh agreed to this willingly enough, since payment on the same terms was guaranteed (document 92). The two acting companies were reunited at Drury Lane under a license granted to Swiney and the three actors (document 90). This arrangement, however, made Swiney more or less redundant. The actors had turned to him willingly enough in the spring of 1709, when they wanted to get away from Rich and only Swiney had another license and another theatre. But back at Drury Lane with a joint license the actors promptly claimed that the original terms of partnership were no longer

147

binding (see document 100). According to Swiney, the three actor-managers then began to loot the company treasury (document 101), and by the middle of the season the instability of the new arrangement was evident. The actors wanted to force Swiney out, or at least to make him an inactive partner. Swiney took the argument to court in January 1711, and in May a settlement was reached out of court: the 1709 partnership was formally canceled, Swiney was guaranteed £600 per annum, and the accumulated financial tangle was submitted to arbitration.[1]

Meanwhile at the Haymarket Collier's opera company was foundering financially (no doubt the reason so many box-office reports are preserved for this season). By March the opera was seriously behind with its bills, running up debts which carried over into the following season. No major change was to occur in the theatrical establishment until April 1712 (when Swiney and Collier traded places), but insiders must have known that the compromise threshed out in November 1710 was no more than a temporary expedient.

1. Relevant Chancery documents are cited by Barker, Mr Cibber, pp. 86–87.

87. Swiney to Coke about the Proposed Reorganization of 1710

[Cover] Mr Collier   (23 September 1710)
        September 23d 1710

Sir
    I have seen Mr Wilks & Mr Dogget who were with Mr Collier this Morning, Mr Shrman[1] who was formrly concern'd for several of the Renters of Drury Lane house was with 'em, who says that a great many of the Renters are out of town but that he can get possession of the house when he pleases & can maintain it for a year, & that he will procure a Lease from the Majority of the Renters between this & Christmass, how he will be able to do this, I can't tell or if he does whether it will be good since all persons concern'd in this intricate affair dont consent, besides this Lease is but for 7: or 8. years to come,[2] but they say they are to renew with the Duke of Bedford assoon as his Grace comes to town. I do not see any othr Method of bringing the Proprietors of that house to make a Lease but by giving liberty to the Actors to perform at the Hay-market till they do. If the diversions are kept separate I believe that will answer My Lord Chamberlains intentions, it is better to settle matters so now, that they may not be in disorder soon again, And Ime sure nothing can make both Entertainments

lasting but by putting the businesse of the Comedys into the Actors Management paying a Consideration, & My being obliged to pay Mr Collier
£500 per annum provided no other Company be set up against me, then Ill
venture to take the Management of the Opera's upon My self, if this
Method is not approv'd by My Lord Chamberlain Ime ready to surrender
My Interest in the Hay-market for the like Interest in Drury-Lane with the
Actors. Ime

> Your Honours Most obliged Most
> humble & Most obedient
> servant
> Owen Swiny

September 23d 1710.

Copy-text: Swiney holograph in Broadley, p. 33. For nineteenth-century
transcriptions see Winston, pp. 96–97, and Drexel MS, fol. 81. This letter
was probably part of lot 199 in the 1876 sale catalogue.

Comment: Swiney offers two proposals here, both presupposing that Drury
Lane can be made available for an acting company. (1) He will run the opera
at the Haymarket, collecting a percentage of what the actors make at Drury
Lane, and paying Collier £500 per annum in return for his not using his license. (2) He will give up the opera (presumably to Collier) and keep his
share in the acting company. The latter was more or less what finally
happened.

1. John Sherman bought or inherited part of Thomas Shepey's share in the rent of
Drury Lane Theatre sometime before 30 June 1702, when he was named in a suit by
Charles Killigrew and others as one of several "who all claime or pretend to have or
claime some of the said Thirty sixth parts or shares in the said Theatre and in the said
rent of three pounds per diem." Along with Rich and Skipwith, they were refusing to
vacate the theatre, although their lease on the building had expired. See PRO
C10/261/51. We have found no further reference to Sherman, but he had apparently
made good his claim to rent on Drury Lane.
2. The ground on which Drury Lane stood was owned by Wriothesley Russell, Duke
of Bedford (1680–1711), who had leased it to Christopher Rich on 6 July 1710. Rich
was no doubt one of those expected not to consent to the proposed arrangements. See
the *Survey of London* (London: Athlone Press, 1970), vol. XXXV, 31–32.

88. Petition for the Reopening of Drury Lane

[late September 1710?]

To the Right honourable Duke of Shrewsbury
Lord Chamberlain of her Majestys Household
Humbly sheweth
The humble Petition of GB

Whereas your Petitioner is one of the Proprieters of the Theatre Royal
Drury Lane amongst others hath had extraordinary great losses by the Lying
still of the Actors there, even almost to the utter destruction of some of
them and cannot make use of the House at present without ye Scenes &
Clothes which doth belong and are in the possession of Christopher Rich
Esquire now the said Christopher Rich is willing to quit the said Scenes and
Cloathes into the possession of your Petitioner provided your Grace woud
graciously please to grant a Warrant to your Petitioner that the Company
there belonging or may belong to the said Theatre Royall may have leave to
act under your Petitioner which would be a means to keep several poore
People concernd in the Play house to be preservd from utter destruction.
     And your Graces Petitioner shall Ever pray &c.

Petition of Proprietors * of Play House

* *Proprietors*: reading doubtful.

Copy-text: Winston, p. 37. For another nineteenth-century transcription
see Drexel MS, fol. 122.

Comment: This petition is evidently to be dated between the closing of
Collier's company in June 1710 and the reopening of a united acting company at Drury Lane under Swiney, Wilks, Cibber, and Doggett in November
1710. It cannot refer to the summer of 1709 (when Rich was silenced):
Shrewsbury did not reassume the post of Lord Chamberlain until April 1710.
     The identity of "G.B." is undeterminable on present evidence. The tran-
scriber of NYPL Drexel MS 1986 specifies "*George Bright*." We can find no
record of a Drury Lane proprietor with that name. Possibly the transcriber
filled in a name with appropriate initials, but if the actor George Bright is
meant (see document 6), this seems extremely farfetched. At any rate, by
this time Rich was evidently discouraged enough to be willing to give up his
stock of scenes and costumes (no doubt for a consideration) to someone else.
Despite the plea in the actors' behalf we may suppose that the petitioner's
primary motive was getting some rent out of Drury Lane again.

89. Orchestra Roster

[Season of 1710–11?]
The List of the Performer's, of the Opera in the Hay-Marcket Last Year,

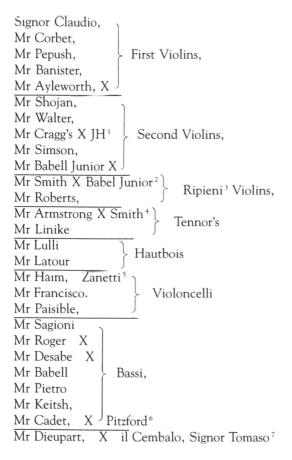

Signor Claudio,
Mr Corbet,
Mr Pepush, ⎫ First Violins,
Mr Banister,
Mr Ayleworth, X ⎭

Mr Shojan,
Mr Walter,
Mr Cragg's X JH[1] ⎫ Second Violins,
Mr Simson,
Mr Babell Junior X ⎭

Mr Smith X Babel Junior[2] ⎫ Ripieni[3] Violins,
Mr Roberts, ⎭

Mr Armstrong X Smith[4] ⎫ Tennor's
Mr Linike ⎭

Mr Lulli ⎫ Hautbois
Mr Latour ⎭

Mr Haim, Zanetti[5] ⎫
Mr Francisco. ⎬ Violoncelli
Mr Paisible, ⎭

Mr Sagioni
Mr Roger   X
Mr Desabe   X
Mr Babell ⎬ Bassi,
Mr Pietro
Mr Keitsh,
Mr Cadet,   X ⎭ Pitzford[6]

Mr Dieupart,   X   il Cembalo, Signor Tomaso[7]

Copy-text: HTC Coke 43 (Hand D with additions in another hand).

Comment: This appears to be a list of the Haymarket orchestra of 1709–10 with tentative changes for the new season entered later in a lighter ink (cf. document 81 and Nicoll, *History*, II, 278–79). All "X" marks are in the lighter ink. For other orchestra rosters probably associated with this season see documents 95 and 96. Pitzford and Zanetti seem first to have worked with the orchestra this season. Dieupart, Desabeye, Cadet, Armstrong, and Craig seem to have dropped out. Haym, Ayleworth, and Roger, though marked for exclusion here, seem to have been performing as of December 1710 (see document 96). Babel Junior and Smith were apparently shifted to different instruments from those in document 81.

1. "JH" (entered later): identity uncertain.
2. Correction in lighter ink, in another hand.
3. "Reinforcing" or "supplementary."
4. Correction in lighter ink, in another hand.
5. Correction in lighter ink, in another hand.
6. Correction in lighter ink, in another hand.
7. Correction in lighter ink, in another hand.

90. License to Swiney, Wilks, Cibber, and Doggett

(6 November 1710)

Anne R

Whereas we have thought fit for the good Government of the Stage, and the better Entertainment of the Town and encouragement of The Undertakers that only one Company of Comedians shall be hereafter allow'd and Established by our Royal License under the Direction of the Chamberlain of our Household for the Time being—

And Whereas Owen Swiny Gent Mr Robert Wilks Mr Thomas Dogget and Mr Colley Cibber have been Represented to us by reason of their Long experience and other Qualifications as fit Persons to be Undertakers and to have the management of our Said Company— we therefore reposing Especial trust and Confidence in you, The Said Owen Swiny Thomas Dogget Robert Wilks and Colley Cibber do * give and Grant unto them full Power & authority to form Constitute and Establish for us a Company of Comedians with full and free License to act and represent in any Convenient place during our Pleasure and no Longer all Comedies, Tragedies, and other Theatrical performances (musical entertainments excepted) subject for such rules and orders for their good Government Therein, as they shall receive from Time to time from the Chamberlain of our Household—

And we † do hereby further Revoke & make Void all former Liscenses and Powers Granted by us to any Person for that Purpose— Given at our Court at Hampton Court this 6th day of November 1710 in ye ninth year of our Reign.

By her Majesty's Command
SHREWSBURY,

Copy of the Liscense
Mr Colliers Name is in the Room of Mr Swinys [1]
Indorsed A Copy of the Queens Liscence to Drury Lane Play House

    * *do*: MS reads "to."
    † *we*: MS reads "they."

Copy-text: Winston, pp. 64–65. (Substantially identical to the order in PRO LC 5/155, p. 44, partially printed by Nicoll, II, 275–76.)

Comment: This license grants authority to Swiney, Wilks, Cibber, and Doggett without distinction among them—which was to cause immediate problems (see document 100). For restrictions imposed by the Lord Chamberlain not specified in this license see document 91.

1. The meaning of this comment is not clear. Conceivably this note was added in April 1712 to instruct a clerk to draw up a revised license for Collier, Wilks, Cibber, and Doggett, using the original of the document as his guide.

91. Wilks, Doggett, and Cibber Accept the Queen's License

[Cover] Mr Wilks Doggett and Cibber   (16 November 1710)

Sir
    We are willing to accept of her Majesties Licence, and to Act on such days in the Hay-market, as his Grace the Lord Chamberlain shall appoint: Wee hope our Ready Submission will intitle Us to his Grace's Favour, in case we are not able to support the Company, under the loss of Saturday: We are
        Sir

Your Honours most Humble & most obedient servants
ROB: WILKS   THO. DOGGETT
C: CIBBER

Thursday November
ye 16th 1710.

Copy-text: Harvard Theatre Collection TS 953.10F, Augustin Daly, *Woffington*, Vol. II, unnumbered folio following p. 104 of text in this extra-illustrated volume (Wilks holograph?). For nineteenth-century transcriptions see Winston, p. 5, and Drexel MS, fol. 83. This letter is item 213 in the 1876 sale catalogue.

Comment: There are several features of interest in this note. Ten days after the granting of a license by the Lord Chamberlain the three actors (*not* joined by Swiney) indicate their reluctant willingness to operate an acting company at the Haymarket "on such days" as the Lord Chamberlain allows. The recipient was probably Coke. Obviously the actors did not want to share quarters with the opera, and they were extremely unhappy about the prospect of being denied Saturday performances. As things worked out, the acting company opened on Monday the twentieth at Drury Lane under Swiney, Wilks, Cibber, and Doggett. The Lord Chamberlain allowed them to perform Saturdays, although he insisted that they keep Drury Lane dark on Wednesdays to give the opera at the Haymarket an uncontested night each week.

92. Swiney's Obligations to Vanbrugh and His Agreement with Collier

[Cover] November 16th 1710   (16 November 1710)

Mr Vanbrugh is to have £700 per annum, & the year Ends on the Tenth of May next. I desire to be secured that I may receive the £700 out of the receipts of the opera's. And Ten shillings each week for ye house keeper.[1]

Mr Collier or what other person shall have a power to Act Opera's shall have the use of All the opera cloaths, books scenes and other Materials belonging to the opera's which I am now possessd of, with the liberty to perform opera's two days in every week, And the cloaths scenes scores of opera's and all other Materials which shall be by him or them added to the stock this year are to be delivered to Mr Swiny into Mr Vanbrugh's original stock of cloaths and as his property. Mr Collier or any other person being concern'd as the undertaker this year declaring that they have no right to such additional stock, but that such Materials as shall be added are as a Consideration for the wearing out damage and use of the present stock.

The Wardrobe keepers to be servants to Mr Swiny but to be paid by the undertakers of ye opera's.

November 16th 1710.

OWEN SWINY

Copy-text: Swiney holograph in Broadley, p. 33. For nineteenth-century transcriptions see Winston, p. 69, and Drexel MS, fol. 85. This letter was probably part of lot 199 in the 1876 sale catalogue.

Comment: Swiney here states the terms (probably for Coke's benefit) on which he can sublet the opera concern to William Collier. He asks that he be guaranteed out of Collier's receipts the £700 he owes Vanbrugh each year, and notes that his own agreement with Vanbrugh about scenery, scores, and so forth, is binding on Collier: all additions to the "stock" become Vanbrugh's property.

1. Evidently Swiney wanted to pay the housekeeper directly, even though the money was to come from Collier. Compare the arrangement with wardrobe keepers specified below in the document, in which they remain Swiney's "servants" but are to be paid directly by Collier.

93. Armstrong to Nicolini about a Rehearsal

[Cover] November 17th 1710.   (17 November 1710)
[Direction] To Signor Cavaliere Nicolini Grimaldi att ye Princes
         head In St Martins Lane

Sir
    I understand a Messenger left word at my Lodging this day to come to Practice the Opera, to Night, but I must desire You to provide another being I once gave my Word I wou'd not Play except our Old Master Mr Du Parr was in also, It is not that I think my self a better performer than Others Or that I have less need of Mony then any Other that makes me do this, but it is a Principle of honesty, which Obliges every well meaning Man to stand as much upon his word as his bond, I shall be ready to serve You on any other Occasion, and wish You all Prosperity & success and Remain
                         Sir
                         Your most humble
                         Servant to Command
November 17   W: ARMSTRONG
1710

Copy-text: MS in the Hoblitzelle Theatre Collection, University of Texas (Armstrong holograph). This letter was no. 169 in the 1876 sale catalogue; it was no. 688 in the 1905 sale catalogue.

Comment: Almost nothing is known of Armstrong save from the Coke papers: see the *Biographical Dictionary*, I, 100. The first opera performance of the season was to take place Wednesday, 22 November. Dieupart was presumably left out of the opera orchestra either because Nicolini wished to exclude him or as part of a shake-up mandated by Collier and Hill when they took over the opera that month.

94. Box-Office Reports for the Opera

(22 November–2 December 1710)

[Cover] Opera Novmber 22d 1710.*

1710	Hydaspes		
November 22d[1]		£ s d	
	Pitt 178	44:10:0	
	Gallery 206	25:15:0	
	Upper Ditto 20	1:10:0	
	Boxes	55:10:0	
	Stage	25:18:0	
	Within the Railes[2]	19:5:0	
	Latter account[3]	0:15:0	
		£173: 3:0	
November 25th	Hydaspes		
	Pitt	42: 0:0	
	Gallery	14: 2:6	
	Upper Ditto	0:18:0	
	Boxes	50: 8:0	
	Within the Railes	18: 2:0	
	Stage	20:16:3	
	Latter account	0:16:6	
		£147: 3:3	
		Hydaspes[†]	
1710	Hydaspes		
November 29th		£ s d	
	Pitt 215	53:15:0	
	Gallery 152	19: 0:0	
	Upper Ditto 27	2: 0:6	
	Boxes	49: 2:0	

Within the Railes
    & Side   16:14:6
Stage   16: 0:0
Latter account   --------

                  £1ɔ6:12:0
         Hydaspes

December 2d

Pitt 190   47:10:0
Gallery 85   10:12:6
Upper Ditto 15   1: 2:6
Boxes   43:12:0
Within the Railes
    & Side Box   8:17:3
Stage Boxes   14:16:3
Latter account   1:19:0

                 £128:09:6

* *1710*: written in a different ink, possibly in a different hand, from the rest of the cover endorsement.

† *Hydaspes*: catchword.

Copy-text: HTC Coke 61 (Hand C). There is a summary in Winston, pp. 93–94.

Comment: Delivery of box-office reports to Coke at the start of this season suggests that the authorities were keeping an eye on the new opera management.

1. Opening night of the 1710–11 opera season.
2. Part of the pit was sometimes railed off to make extra boxes of a sort.
3. This phrase probably signifies what had been known in the late seventeenth century as "after money."

95. Haymarket Orchestra "Last Opera Night"

[late November 1710?]

The List of the Performer's of the Opera, in the Hay-Marcket, Last Opera
Night,

Signor Claudio,
Mr Corbet,   } first Violins,
Mr Pepush
Mr Banister

Mr Shojan,
Mr Walter,   } Second Violins,
Mr Igl,[1]
Mr Simson,

Mr Babel Junior   } Ripieni Violins,
Mr Roberts,

Mr Linike   } Tennor's
Mr Smith,

Mr Lulli   } Hautbois
Mr La Tour

Signor Zanetti.
Mr Haim,   } Violoncelli
Mr Francisco,
Mr Paisible

Mr Sagioni
Mr Babell
Mr Keitsh   } Bassi
Mr Pietro
Mr Pitshford

Signor Tomaso[2] il Cembalo,

Copy-text: HTC Coke 44 (Hand D).

Comment: We have assigned this roster to the early part of the season of 1710–11 because of the presence of Zanetti, Pitshford, and "Tomaso" (changes made in document 89). As in that list Babel Junior is identified as a "Ripieni Violin." "Igl" here replaces Craig (canceled in document 89).

1. Probably Henry Eccles. See the *Biographical Dictionary*, V, 3–4.
2. I.e., Tomaso Gabrielli, otherwise known as "Il Bolognese."

96. Haymarket Orchestra List and Two Sample Box-Office Reports

[Cover] November 22d 1710   (December 1710)

	Thomaso √	Harpsicord
	Heyam √ }	
	Pilotti }	Violoncelli
	Sagione √	D. Base
	Paisible √	
	Francisco √	
	Roger √	Violoncello
	Pitchtord √	
	Babel √	
	Pietro √ }	Bassons
	Creitch[1] √	
	Clodio √	
	Corbett √	
	Banister √ }	1st Violins
	Papusch √	
	Ailsworth √	

persons excluded

	sh			
D.B.—Simpson	10	2 Violin	Sojan √	
C. Gall:-Echel[2]	10	a Violin	Walther[3] √ }	2d Violin
Cadett	10	Basson *	Babel √	
Desabeye	10	Violoncello	Roberts √	

2:0:0

Mr Hill complains that
Nicolini when he had apointed
ye Practice att ye Chocolate
house which was taken for
that purpose he sent to them

Smith √ }	Tenorers[†]	
Lunican √		
Lully √ }	Hautbois	
Latour √		
Davin	Trumpett	

to come to his house & ye other Musicians take exceptions att coming to him. Mr Hill desires it may be att a Neutrol place & proposes to take ye Room in York buildings not taking ye Cloaths they would provide for him.

ye Charge each night
16:08:00
Heyam & Pilotti to play every night and to take their places att ye Harpiscord by Turns.

An Account[4] of what Moneys has been receivd at ye Operas in ye Queens Theatre in ye hay-Markett for 2 days and are as followeth Vizt 1710 November 22d At hydaspes—

	Number	
Pitt	178	44:10:0
Gallery	206	25:15:0
Upper ditto	20	1:10:0
Boxes	138[5]	55:10:0
Stage		25:18:0
Within ye Railes & Side Boxes		19: 5:0
Latter Account		0:15:0
		173: 3:0

December 9th   At Pyrrhus—

	Number	
Pitt	210	52:10:0
Gallery	103	12:17:6
Upper Ditto	11	0:16:6
Boxes	137[6]	55: 4:0
Stage		27: 8:6
Within ye Railes & Side Boxes		17:10:9
Latter Account		0:19:6
		167: 6:9 5:16:03[7]

44-10-0 [Hydaspes, Pit]
18-00-0 [difference; rightly 8-0-0]
52-10-0 [Pyrrhus, Pit]

25-15-0 [Hydaspes, Gallery]
12-17-6 [Pyrrhus, Gallery]
12-17-6 [difference]

1-10-0 [Hydaspes, Upper Gallery]
0-16-6 [Pyrrhus, Upper Gallery]
0-13-6 [difference]

55-10-0 [Hydaspes, Boxes]
55-04-0 [Pyrrhus, Boxes]
00-06-0 [difference]

25-18-0 [*Hydaspes*, Stage]
 1-10-6 [difference]
27-08-6 [*Pyrrhus*, Stage]

00-15-0 [*Hydaspes*, Latter Account]
 0-04-6 [difference]
00-19-6 [*Pyrrhus*, Latter Account]

19- 5-0 [*Hydaspes*, Railes]
17-10-9 [*Pyrrhus*, Railes]
 1-14-3 [difference]

Opera
ye Pitt with rails should hold 268 of which within
ye Rails 51

* *Basson*: "Bases" was written and canceled below this word.
† *Tenorers*: "Hautboy" was written and smudged or erased above this word.

Copy-text: HTC Coke 63 (Hand E with extensive additions in Hand A). Hill's complaint against Nicolini is transcribed by Winston, p. 94.

Comment: This paper came to the Lord Chamberlain's office as two box-office reports. With the addition of a current orchestra roster, a note about a squabble over rehearsal arrangements, and calculations, it is a memorandum. The four musicians "excluded" may well represent an attempt to cut the cost of the orchestra by £2 each night. Written on the back of one of the sheets of this document is a list of itemized taxes unrelated to the theatre which we have not transcribed.

1. I.e., Kytch.
2. "Gall:-Echel" may well be another form of "Igl" (cf. document 95).
3. The name Smith is canceled between Walter and Babel.
4. "An Account" through the total "167:6:9" constitutes the report written in Hand E. The rest of the document was written around this report in Hand A.
5. An indecipherable calculation follows "138." By these figures we can deduce that occupants of boxes paid approximately 8 shillings each, on the average.
6. An indecipherable set of squiggles precedes "137"—evidently part of the calculation by which £55.4.0 is determined.
7. This figure represents the difference in receipts between the two nights. It seems to have been obtained, clumsily, from the following worksheet rather than by just subtracting the total for *Pyrrhus* from that for *Hydaspes*.

97. Box-Office Reports for the Haymarket

(December 1710)

December 6th	Pyrrhus & Demetrius	£ s d
Pitt 191		47:15:0
Gallery 85		10:12:6
Upper Ditto 15		1:02:6
Boxes		42: 0:0
Within the Railes & Side Box		9:17:0
Stage Boxes		12: 4:0
Latter Account		: 7:6
		£123:18:6¹

9th	Ditto	
Pitt 210		52:10:0
Gallery 103		12:17:6
Upper Ditto 11		0:16:6
Boxes		55: 4:0
Within the Railes		7:19:0
Side Boxes		9:11:9
Stage Box		27: 8:6
Latter account		:19:6
		£167: 6:9

Verte [i.e., Turn]

1710		
December 13th²	Pyrrhus &c:	£ s d
Pitt 157		39: 5:0
Gallery 125		15:12:6
Upper Ditto 10		15:0
Boxes		48: 5:0
Within the Railes		4: 7:0
Side Boxes		6:18:9
Stage Boxes		14:17:3
Latter account		1:11:0
		£131:11:6

December 16th   Ditto
  Pitt 179   44:15:0
  Gallery 88   11: 0:0
  Upper Ditto 13   19:6
  Boxes   45: 1:6
  Within the Railes   5:11:0
  Side Boxes   7: 0:6
  Stage Boxes   8:11:3
  Latter account   1: 2:6
                       £124: 1:3

December 20th   Ditto
  Pitt 214   53:10:0
  Gallery 124   15:10:0
  Upper Ditto 14   1: 1:0
  Within the Railes   7: 1:0
  Boxes   49:19:0
  Side Boxes   5:18:3
  Stage Boxes   18: 4:9
  Latter account   2: 6:0
                       £153:10:0

December 27th   Hydaspes
  Pitt 189   47: 5:0
  Gallery 184   23: 0:0
  Upper Ditto 70   5: 5:0
  Boxes   48:13:0
  Within the Railes   4: 0:0
  Side Boxes   14:19:3
  Side Boxes[3]   3:15:0
  Latter account   0:17:0
                       £147:14:3

Copy-text: HTC Coke 62 (Hand C). There is a summary in Winston, pp. 93–94.

1. *The London Stage*, following Winston, reports £128.18.6.
2. An exact duplicate of the report for this night was sent to Coke separately. See HTC 64, written in an unidentified hand. The "Direction" reads, "To The Honour-

able Thos: Cock Esquire Vice Chamberlain to her Majesty / These." The cover endorsement, in Hand A, reads, "Pyrrhus December ye 13th 1710 / 131:11:6." *The London Stage* figure of £131.12.6 is a typographical error.

3. Evidently an error for "Stage Boxes."

98. Salaries and Receipts at the Haymarket

(November and December 1710)

The Opera begun ye		Paid	
22d November Hydaspes	173:03:0	Nicolini X	322:10:0
25th Ditto	147:03:3	Valentini X	107:10:
29 Ditto	157:10:0	Cieca & Husband[1]	215:00:0
2d [December] Ditto	128:07:0	Pillotti & Husband[2]	215:00:0
6 Pyrrhus	128:18:6	Isabella[3]	86:00:0
9 Ditto	167:06:9		946:00:0
12[4] Ditto	131:11:6		
16 Ditto	124: 1:3	10 Nights * ye Musick	
20 Hydaspes	153: 0:0	& £19 a night	190:00:0
	1311: 3:3[5]	Rent of ye House Ditto	
22 Hydaspes[6]		att £12 10 a night	125:00:0
ye D of O:[7]	21:10:0	Incidents att	
		about £20 a night	200:00:0
			1461:00:0

Singers Anual Charge	
Nicolini	860:00:00
Valentini	537:10:00
Cieca & Husband	700:00:00
Pillotti & Husband	500:00:00
Isabella	300:00:00
Baronessa	200:00:00
	3197:10:00[8]

* *Nights*: MS reads "Nighs."

Copy-text: HTC Coke 2 (Hand A). For nineteenth-century transcriptions see Winston, pp. 93–94, and Drexel MS, fol. 87.

Comment: These figures show that Collier and Hill found themselves in almost exactly the position occupied by Vanbrugh three seasons earlier—routine expenditures were barely covered by receipts, leaving nothing for new productions and special expenses, let alone profits.

1. Little is known about Signora Cieca and her husband. This was their only recorded season in London.
2. Elizabetta Pilotta Schiavonetti.
3. Isabella Girardeau.
4. The correct date is 13 December.
5. The correct total is £1311.1.3.
6. No figure is entered for 22 December. A performance was advertised (see *The London Stage*, Part 2, I, 239), but there is no box-office report for this date in document 97.
7. Identity uncertain; possibly the Duke of Ormonde. This entry concerns payment for a special box.
8. The correct total is £3097.10.0.

99. Box-Office Reports for the Haymarket

[Cover] 1710   (December 1710–January 1711)
[Direction] To The Honourable Thomas Cook Esquire / These[1]

December 20[2]		Pyrrhus	
214 Pitt			53:10:0
124 Gallery			15:10:0
14 Upper ditto			1: 1:0
Within ye Railes			7: 1:0
Boxes { Lovelace	20: 0:0 }		
White	15: 3:0 }		49:19:0
Halstead	14:16:0 }		
Side Boxes per Maintain[3]			5:18:3
Stage { Collier	8: 1:3 }		18: 4:9
Haughton	10: 3:6 }		
Latter Account			2: 6:0
			153:10:0

December 30th	Hydaspes			
1710		£	s	d
Pitt		41:00:0		
Gallery		12: 5:0		
Upper ditto		1: 4:0		
Within ye Railes		4: 0:3		
Boxes		48: 9:0		
Side Boxes		3: 4:6		
Stage		2:19:0		
Latter Account		1: 1:6		
		£114: 3:3		

January 3d	Pyrrhus &c—			
1710				
Pitt		54: 5:0		
Gallery		12:15:0		
Upper ditto		1: 5:6		
Boxes		51:16:6		
Within ye Railes		6: 6:0		
Stage		04:15:0		
Side Boxes		16: 0:9		
Latter Account		2: 2:6		
		£149: 6:3		

Copy-text: HTC Coke 65 (Hand C). For a partial transcription see Winston, p. 91.

Comment: No further box-office reports are available for the Haymarket until March 1711, when the opera once again found itself in serious financial difficulties.

1. The remains of a red seal are evident on the cover sheet.
2. The same total (without the breakdown by boxkeepers) is reported for this date in document 96.
3. The meaning of this phrase is unknown to us, unless it is an early reference to John Maine or Mr Maitland, later LIF house servants.

100. Swiney's Complaint against Wilks, Cibber, and Doggett

[December 1710 or January 1711?]

Mr Swinys Case, humbly Offerd to ye Consideration of my Lord Chamberlain.

Mr Swiny took a Lease of the Theatre in ye Haymarket with ye Clothes Scenes and Utensills thereunto belonging for 14 years from Mr Vanbrugh with an assignment of his License from her Majesty for Acting plays Operas &ca for a Yearly Consideration payable to ye said Mr Vanbrugh.[1] Some time after[2] Mr Swiny took Mr Wilks Mr Dogget and Mr Cibber into partner ship with himselfe for the remainder of the said terme subject to the following Conditions, as may be seen more at large by the Indented Articles of Agreement Sign'd by them.

ffirst it is Agreed that they shall with Mr Swiny be Copartners not only in the profits and loss that may happen in ye Theatre in the Haymarket, but in any other play House they shall think fit to remove to, without engaging in any other Society of Players whatever

2dly that Mr Wilks Mr Dogget and Mr Cibber shall do their utmost by managing Acting &ca to support ye Company

3dly That Mr Swiny shall Employ his constant care & pains in governing &ca and has not nor shall make over any part of his Interest in the Lease or License, but with ye consent of his partners

4thly That Mr Wilks shall Attend and take care of all Rehearsalls

5ly That a plain and true Account shall be kept of all Receipts and disbursements, that Mr Swiny shall out of those Receipts in the first place, and preferrably to all other deductions or payments discharge ye Rent to Mr Vanbrugh due According to his Lease and Conditions with him. That he shall next discharge and satisfye all Agreements with performers and servants Expences in Cloths Scenes &ca which shall be Allow'd to him in passing his Accounts. That after all charges thus paid and clear'd Mr Swiny shall Receive £300 a Year out of the profits in consideration of his pains and care in the government &ca. That Mr Wilks Mr Dogget and Mr Cibber shall for their care in managing and for their Acting on ye Stage receive each £200 a year And Mr Wilks £50 more for Attending and taking care of Rehearsals. And after these payments made, the clear profits shall be divided into two equall parts, one of which to be detain'd by Mr Swiny and the other to be Equally divided between Mr Wilks Mr Dogget and Mr Cibber. The Losses if any to be allow'd for after the same proportion

6ly That Mr Wilks Mr Dogget and Mr Cibber shall have every year each of them a play Acted for their Benefit without any deduction for ye charges of ye House

7ly That if Mr Swiny dyes before the Expiration of the Lease His Salary of £300 a year shall cease, and his Executors be Entituled only to one 4th part of the clear profits, And lyable only to the same proportion of Loss. That if any of the other three dye their Salary and Share both shall cease but their widdow or children shall have a Benefit play paying £40 for the Charges of the House. That within six months after such decease an other Actor shall be chosen by the surviving partners to supply the vacancy

8ly That the government and Management shall be in ye Majority, Mr Swiny to have but one voice, and in Case of equality of voices to be determin'd by Lott. All Law suits to be at the Common Expence, ffarther writings to be signd if Necessary for the strengthning these Articles, & a penalty of £2000 for non performance

But the Queen having since thought fit to divide ye Operas from the Comedys. And in Order to it, to grant distinct Licenses, Mr Swiny's partners complaining they had not that power in Managing which they conceiv'd themselves entituled to by their Agreement with him pray'd that their names might be inserted with his in the new License, which being done accordingly They now pretend they are by that means freed from all the former Contracts, That Mr Swiny is Entituled to Nothing more than one fourth part of the profits, and that they are no longer subject with him to make good the Engagements of Rent to Mr Vanbrugh. Tho' they at this very time have no other stock of Cloathes Scenes &ca but those Mr Swiny has furnish'd them with and is possest of by Vertue of his Lease from Mr Vanbrugh And which are all to Revert to Mr Vanbrugh at ye termination of the said Lease, with whatever is added in the mean time [3]

Mr Swiny therefore most humbly prays that my Lord Chamberlain will please by his Authority to Compell the said Mr Wilks Mr Dogget and Mr Cibber to proceed According to ye true tenure and meaning of the above Receited Contract, and that it may be enter'd in the Books of his Grace's Office, That by inserting their names in the License, there was nothing intended to Annull or Invalidate their former Agreements but only to give them an Equall power in the Management

Copy-text: HTC Coke 17 (scribal fair copy). For nineteenth-century transcriptions see Winston, pp. 71–75, and Drexel MS, fols. 64–65.

Comment: This is an unsigned fair copy of Swiney's plea to the Lord Chamberlain—probably sent to Coke by Swiney. On the ensuing litigation see the introduction to the documents of this season. The date is probably December 1710 or early January 1711: Swiney went to court 12 January.

1. Agreement made in May 1708.
2. Initially made in March 1709.
3. For later attempts by the actor-managers to avoid paying Vanbrugh for use of his theatre and stock see document 125, and the interdocument between documents 145 and 146, and PRO LC 7/3, fols. 130, 132, and 135.

101. Swiney to Stanley about Unauthorized Withdrawal of Company Funds by Wilks, Cibber, and Doggett

[ca. January 1711?]
[Direction] For The Honorable Sir John Stanley Bart. These*

Sir

Since I writ to you last, I went to look over the books of our office, where (to my great Surprize) I found that Mr Wilks Dogget & Cibber have taken out of the receipts of the house very near Eleeven hundred pounds, these proceedings if not immediately stopp'd must prove of the worst consequence to me, and I hope I shan't be thought ill of for preventing My Ruin, I am your Honour's most oblig'd & most

Obedient Servant
Owen Swiny.

* *These*: reading doubtful.

Copy-text: Swiney holograph bound into Folger Library PN2598 G3F5, copy 4 extra-illustrated vol. 3 of Percy Fitzgerald, *The Life of David Garrick*, grangerized by A. M. Broadley. For nineteenth-century transcriptions, see Winston, p. 53, and Drexel MS, fol. 62. This note is probably one of the items in lot 199 of the 1876 sale catalogue.

Comment: The preceding June the three actor-managers removed £350 from the company treasury after Swiney left London at the end of the season (see Barker, *Mr Cibber*, pp. 81–82), and an argument ensued. The actors were clearly trying to force Swiney out by any means which might prove effective. The sort of guerrilla warfare that was carried on in the spring of 1711 is evident in a letter from Swiney to Coke or Stanley dated 12 April, printed as an interdocument between documents 104 and 105.

102. Audience Threat to the Managers on behalf of Mrs Cross

[Cover] Play house   (15 March [1711])
     Mrs Crosse

To Mr Swiney Mr Cibber Mr Wilks and Mr Dogget These.

We cannot help taking notice of the injustice (to give it the mildest
name we can) which you have all this winter shown to Mrs Crosse, first in
refusing her not only to Act; but also the Advantages which she ought to
have by her Agreement with Mr Swiney; And then to Flatter the Towne
into a beleife that she her self had refused to play, when we are very well
assured that she has constantly attended, and that you have severall times
forbad her entrance even behind the Scenes. All these things put together
satisfie us that you doe it with a designe to defraud her of what is her due, as
well as to rob the Towne, of her performance which has not yet been dis-
agreable. We therefore being a great number of us who are pretty constant
at your house, thought fit to informe you, that since we pay for our diversion, hope that we may in some measure have the Liberty of interfering in
this Case; And are therefore resolved that no person whatsoever shall Act
in any play the part that Mrs Crosse has been used to Act, but that when
any such thing is attempted we will doe all that lies in our Power to put an
end to the play, And to disoblige all that shall Act in it, but perticularly
the person that shall play her part; Think upon this before Munday night
otherwise you may depend upon it, That Mr Doggetts benefitt will not be
very well treated. We should not think this Affaire so much concerned us
were we not satisfied, that you four, by contrivance betweene your selves
would evade the performance of her Articles on your parts and so deprive
her of her livelihood and performance on the Stage where she has been
bred up from a Child, and has as much or rather more pretence for a living
there then any of you.
    March 15th   Turne over.

We are Seventy Three of us who have perused this Paper and doe approve of it because we are satisfied it is just, and we doubt not but by
munday night to encrease our Party to neare as many more, if you are desir-
ous of it and will let us know it, on Saturday night * we will let you have a
list of all our names.¹ We give you this timely notice, because you should
not say, you did not know you disobliged us.

  * on Saturday night: phrase repeated and canceled.

Copy-text: Folger Y.c. 663 (2). Scribal fair copy. For nineteenth-century transcriptions see Winston, pp. 66–67, and Drexel MS, fol. 90. This item was offered as part of 174 in the 1876 sale catalogue, and as part of 690 in the 1905 sale catalogue.

Comment: Letitia Cross acted with the troupe (then at the Haymarket) in 1709–10. There is no record of her performing during 1710–11: indeed, she remained off the London stage until January 1715, when she reappeared as a member of John Rich's company at Lincoln's Inn Fields.

Monday 19 March 1711 was indeed a benefit for Doggett. The play in question was *She wou'd if she cou'd*, in which Mrs Cross had played Gatty as early as March 1705. On 21 December 1710 Mrs Santlow took the part, as she was evidently scheduled to in the present case. For the upshot of this abortive protest see document 103.

1. No such list has come down to us.

103. The Apology and Complaint of Letitia Cross

[Cover] Play house   (22 March 1711)
    Mrs Crosse
    March 22d 1711/10

Sir

    I designed to have done my self the honour of waiting upon you but heard you were out of Towne, I am informed that the manager's of ye Play house endeavour to perswade the towne that it was altogether by my management that such a letter was wrote to them, and that it was my Contrivance to engage so many Gentlemen to interest * themselves in my affaires. I confess there are few of my freinds that I have not told of ye injuries I have received from ye masters of the Play-house, and I am realey of ye opinion that few people would have suffer'd what I have done silently. but I was so far from incouraging the disturbance which was threatned in that letter, that I made it my bisness to write to all my freinds that I thought concerned in it, assuring them that should they persist in any such thing, instead of doing me a service it wou'd utterly ruin me with my Lord Chamberlain, and I have been informed by severall of them since, that was the only thing, prevented their designes, I hope therefore that their insinuation's will not lessen me in your opinion, when I assure you, that they are (like all their other dealing's with me) false and Groundless. I have inclosed a case of ye hardship's they have put upon me which I beg you to peruse,[1] and then I only beg your protection that they may be oblig'd to do me Justice according to my Articles, and it will be a very great obligation to Sir

Your most humble servant

ye 22 of March 1710/11

Let=Crosse

* *interest*: "themselfes" written and canceled after this word.

Copy-text: Folger Y.c. 663 (1). (Cross holograph? unique sample in this collection.) For nineteenth-century transcriptions see Winston, pp. 68–69, and Drexel MS, fol. 91. This item is part of 174 in the 1876 sale catalogue, and part of 690 in the 1905 sale catalogue.

Comment: This letter was evidently sent to Coke. Someone must have convinced Mrs Crosse that the proposed audience disruption threatened in document 102 would be counterproductive.

1. No such document is now to be found in the Coke papers or in the nineteenth-century transcriptions.

104. Haymarket Finances in the Spring of 1711

(March–May 1711)

Mr Collier's Receit

6 March:	18: 9:9	Mr Colliers has paid *	
10 ditto	27: 2:6	To Cieca ⌠ 180:00	
13 ditto	19: 8:3	⌡ 13:10	
17 ditto	107:12:-	193:10	
20 ditto	142:10:3	Isabella & ⎱	134:07:6
24 ditto	166: 2:6	Pilotta ⎰	
April the 7:	57: 3:9[1]	13 nights Musick ⎱	520:00:0[2]
the 14:	124:18:6	& Incidents ⎰	
the 18	80:19:5	Mr Heidegger	53:15:0
22[3]	70:13:6	Cassani	20:00:0
25:	129:10:3	aledare[4]	5:00:0
28:	99:11:3	Mrs Orm[+5]	16:00:0

May 2.   59:14:3   other Expences
                   £1103:16:2   about—   60:00:0
                                                             992:12:6[6]
                                   Isabella &
                                   Pilotta due
                                   ye 3d of May   134:07:6
                                                            1127:—:-[7]

            300 guineas
       ye 15th April a 100 guneas due
       ye 30th of April was ye last day he Sung[8]

   * *paid*: followed by a canceled word (now indecipherable).
   † *Orm*: reading doubtful; see note 5 below.

Copy-text: HTC Coke 1 (Hand A).

Comment: By March 1711 Collier's opera company was in deep financial
trouble. On 5 March the Lord Chamberlain sent an order to Collier noting
that despite large receipts many tradesmen's bills had not been paid and ordering him to send a list of his receipts to the Lord Chamberlain's office before disbursing any money (PRO LC 5/155, p. 75). This document presumably sums up the responses to that order. The period over which the singers
have been paid is not specified. Clearly this is not all that Collier owed his
singers: Nicolini and Valentini are omitted, unless the final three lines refer
to one of them.

1. There were no performances 26–31 March on account of Passion Week. Wednesday 4 April was a benefit for Nicolini. A performance on 11 April is likewise not
listed: it was a benefit for Valentini.
2. This figure is derived from a scratch calculation in the margin in which 40 is multiplied by 13.
3. Error for Saturday 21 April.
4. Otherwise unknown. The authors of the *Biographical Dictionary* read "Aledore" (I,
58). He or she was evidently a singer. Just conceivably this could be a mangled form of
Benedetto Baldassari, who performed with the company three nights in March and
April 1712 during a brief visit to England. However we have no evidence that he was
in England a year earlier.
5. This entry is carelessly written and run together. It can be read either as "Mrs
Orm" or "Mr Sorin." The only entry in *The London Stage* for a "Mrs Orm" (or Orme)
is as a beneficiary of a concert at Stationer's Hall on 27 May 1714. She was presumably

a singer. The dancer Sorin worked occasionally at the theatres for many years. Neither can otherwise be definitely associated with the Haymarket company this season.

6. The correct total is £1002.12.6.

7. The correct total is £1137.

8. The last three lines are written on p. [2v] of this document and appear to be an afterthought. The referent of "he" is probably either Nicolini or Valentini, but we cannot be sure which.

INTERDOCUMENT.

Swiney's Denial of Cheating Richard Cross

(12 April 1711)

Swiney to Coke(?)

Sir

The Person who made this Complaint against me is made use of as a Tool by my Partners to incense my Lord against me, and thô they very well know that what they alledge is a very false and scandalous reflection upon me, yet they hope it may have some effect with my Lord to my prejudice. But I hope (as the Petitioner Expected relief if my Lord shou'd think me in the wrong) that I may have satisfaction for the injury's offer'd me by their confederated Malice. Thô I can plainly demonstrate from his own Petition the untruths Contain'd in it, yet I have affixed an affidavit to prevent any further trouble to your Honour on this most insignificant affair. He Confesses the borrowing five pounds for which he gave me his Note, but he says I stop'd this mony out of his salary last year, And for the truth of what he says refers himselfe to the Play house book of Accounts now in my hands. This question will bring the truth out in spite of their artifice which is, how coud my particular debts be charg'd as paid in the accounts of the Play-house since Every body knows our businesse was in Partnership last year. but the case is this, Mr Wilks did desire that Mr Cross might have the liberty to dispose of some tickets which were to be taken at a Play that was given out for his benefit with this Condition that he shou'd be oblig'd to make up the Charge of the house out of his tickets, There was not above Twenty pounds in the house which made Mr Wilks desire (since it happend so very ill with Mr Cross) that we might be Contented with his paying into the office £5 out of his tickets, which he agreed shou'd be stop'd out of his Salary, but the remainder of his Salary that Season amounted to no more than £4-18s-0d which is charg'd by the Treasurer in the books of his office as paid for a deficiency of his benefit day and not in discharge of my debt as he most falsly alledges. I hope you'l Excuse the many troubles you have been put to on the Play house Account And think the many

Injurys offer'd me and which are now daily hatching against me by my Partners is the only reason that I have any Share in 'em. I am your Honour's

Most obedient & most humble Servant
April 12th 1711. Owen Swiny

Your Honour's direction for my answer bears date ye 26th of March, thô I did not receive it 'till this morning which is now almost three weeks, which makes me think they have done it design'dly to Expose me as neglecting my duty to my Lords order.

Copy-text: LC 7/3, fols. 124–25, holograph.

"Affadavit of Swiney":
Owen Swiny Gent Maketh Oath That he never was repaid ye sume of ffive pounds Nor any parte thereof by Mr Richard Crosse which this Deponent lent him upon a Note under his hand But that ye same is still due & remaines unpaid to this Deponent Nor was any parte of it Stopp'd out of the said Mr Crosse his Sallary By this Deponents Order or knowledge or has he any account thereof.

Owen Swiny
Jurat 12° April 1711 coram me Richard Bealing

Copy-text: LC 7/3, fol. 181.

Comment: These documents are a vivid illustration of the state of affairs between Swiney and his actor-partners by the spring of 1711.

105. Orders to Collier about Money in Connection with *Rinaldo*

[Cover] May ye 3d 1711 (3 May 1711)
Mr Hill & Collier

That Mr Collier pay back whatever he recievd out of ye subscription money over and above what was due att ye End of ye subscriptions to Mr Van brugh for Rent and the receits of ye gallery &ca over & above the said subscription money and Mr Hill to clear all the charges of ye six nights subscription
ye Receits of ye Gallery &ca

4th night—	18:09:09
5th—	27:02:06[1]
6th—	19:08:03
	65:00:06

Copy-text: HTC Coke 16 (Hand A). For nineteenth-century transcriptions see Winston, p. 37, and Drexel MS, fol. 92.

Comment: This note records an agreement connected with the tangled finances of the opera company. Handel's *Rinaldo* had received its premiere 24 February. The first six nights were by special subscription, though evidently the gallery was opened to the public for the fourth, fifth, and sixth nights. These figures show a large gallery attendance—probably between 180 and 260 people.
  Collier and Hill seem not to have been paying their bills (including the rent due to Vanbrugh). Coke here orders Collier to pay Vanbrugh surplus money from the subscriptions, plus the extra gallery income. What charges Hill was to take care of we can only guess, but see document 106.

1. The fourth and fifth nights were 6 and 10 March 1711. *The London Stage* incorrectly assigns these figures to the third and fourth nights.

106. Collier's Agreement with Lunican about Money Due for the Score of *Rinaldo*

(5 May 1711)

[Cover] Mr Colliers agreement about ye Lunicons payment * for ye
              Score of Rinaldo   May 5th 1711

May the 5th 1711

  Mr Collier agrees to pay to Mr Lunecan for the Copy of Rinaldo this day the sum of eight pound and three pound every day Rinaldo is playd till six and twenty pound are payd and he gives him leave to take the sayd Opera in his custody after† every day of acting it till the whole six and twenty pound are payd.

  * *payment*: reading doubtful (MS cropped).
  † *after*: MS reads "afer."

Copy-text: HTC Coke 22 (Heidegger holograph). For nineteenth-century transcriptions see Winston, p. 23, and Drexel MS, fol. 93.

Comment: *Rinaldo* (libretto by Rossi, music by Handel) received its premiere back on 24 February. Collier evidently failed to pay Lunican (a member of the orchestra) for providing a copy of the score, orchestral parts, and so forth. *Rinaldo* was performed three more times this season after the date of this letter, and nine times during 1711–12.

SEASON OF

1711–1712

U nstable and unsatisfactory though the arrangements of the previous
season had proved, they lasted until April 1712, at which time another reshuffle occurred among managers. Plays and operas remained
divided, with plays at Drury Lane and operas at the Haymarket. The upshot
of Swiney's extended litigation with the actor-managers had been a financial
settlement which removed him from an active role in return for a stipend of
£600 a year. This left Swiney shut out of management while Collier, foundering with the financially insecure opera, desired nothing more than a guaranteed income and complete freedom from responsibility. In April 1712 Swiney
was able to engineer a return to the Haymarket for himself, trading the silent
partnership at Drury Lane to Collier. We may presume that a number of possible schemes for reorganization were considered: the terms stated in document 107 appear to be one such trial balloon.

Most of the documents preserved from this season concern the financial
arrangements and problems of the opera: Collier had every reason to get out
from under if he could. Moreover Barker cites lawsuit testimony that Wilks,
Cibber, and Doggett considered Swiney a "troublesome person," and one
"they did not care to be concerned with." [1] But not until the final two months
of the season did the obvious exchange of places occur. On 17 April 1712 the
Lord Chamberlain issued a pair of licenses: one to Collier, Wilks, Cibber, and
Doggett, authorizing performance of plays at Drury Lane, the other to Swiney
authorizing performance of opera at the Haymarket. [2] For ancillary regulations
and agreements made at this time see the two interdocuments given between
documents 112 and 113. In light of Collier's dire financial straits in both this
season and the preceding one we should not be surprised that the settlement
of April 1712 was strictly transitory: Swiney was to go broke two months into
the next season.

1. Barker, *Mr Cibber*, p. 87.
2. PRO LC 5/155, pp. 157–58.

107. Proposal for an Agreement between Collier and Swiney

[Cover] Collier & Swiny   [Season of 1711–12]

Mr Collier and Mr Swiny to have a joint Licence for Opera & Comedy The Comedy to be farmd to Mr Wilks Mr Cibber & Mr Doggett for £600 a year and they to be ye sole Managers of Comedy—Mr Swiny & who he shall apoint his Deputy to be Managers of ye Opera in joint shares for Profitt & Loss.

Copy-text: HTC Coke 9 (Hand A). For nineteenth-century transcriptions see Winston, p. 36, and Drexel MS, fol. 135.

Comment: This note appears to be a proposal for an agreement which was never put in effect. The date is indeterminable on present evidence. Our best guess is that this scheme was considered at some point during the 1711–12 season—a period in which Collier and Swiney were casting about for some way to revamp the management arrangements which had worked to no one's satisfaction the previous season.

108. Haymarket Orchestra Roster and Salaries

[Season of 1711–12, referring to the Season of 1709–10?]

[Cover] Opera Musick Room

The Gentlemen in the Musick room receivd two years ago per opera night

	£ s		
Mr Dieupart	1:15:	Mr Paysible	15-
Mr Claudio	-:15:	Mr Smith	10:
Mr Bannister	-:15:	Mr Armstrong	10:
Mr Corbett	-:15:	Mr Roberts	10:
Mr Babel Senior	-:15:	Mr Liniken	10:
Mr Francisco	-:15:	Mr desabaye	10:
Mr Pietro	-:15:	Mr Davin	10:
Mr Latour	-:11:6		
Mr Rogers	-:11:6		
Mr Kytch	-:11:6		
Mr Bryan	-:11:6		
Mr Babel junior	-:10:-		

Mr Cadett	-:10:-
Mr Simpson	-:10:-
Mr Walter	-:10

Copy-text: HTC Coke 21 (hand labeled "Heidegger" by a modern hand; sample inconclusive).

Comment: This is a somewhat puzzling document. All of the musicians named except Bryan were part of the Haymarket orchestra as of the roster of 24 December 1709. Bryan appears nowhere else, so his presence is no help with the date.[1] The salaries are a little higher than those in the list for 1708–9 (document 73), and this list does not reflect the personnel changes made in 1710–11 (see document 89). We deduce that this list refers to the orchestra of 1709–10 from the perspective of 1711–12. Only twenty-two men are named, and the salary total (not given) would be only £14 6s.— which is very low. We would guess that this list gives only those musicians still with the orchestra in 1711–12. One possible explanation for this document is that it represents a protest by Swiney against salary inflation. Swiney returned to the Haymarket as manager late in the 1711–12 season after nearly two years away. He may be arguing that these were the salaries when he last managed there (i.e., in 1709–10).

1. The *Biographical Dictionary* (II, 379) dates this list "about 1713" and says that Bryan's 11/6 salary was "per week, presumably." But from other musicians in the list we can say definitely that it does not refer to a season later than 1709–10, and salaries in these lists give a per night, not a per week total. David Lasocki suggests that "Bryan" (otherwise unknown) may be a garbled version of "Shojan" (or Soyan, Shogon), a suggestion reinforced by his similar position in an orchestra list in document 73.

109. Collier to Coke about Subscription Arrangements for *Antiochus*

[Cover] Mr Collier   [9 December 1711]
[Direction] To The Right Honourable Thomas Coke Esquire[1]

Sir
    I have Inclosed sent you the paper which Mrs White Requires if you please to Lett my Lord Chamberlain peruse it and if his Grace will be pleased to signe it to Night I will Call for it when & where you please.

Tomorrow the Books² will be given out which she will not Take without the Order and I must be Necessitated to alter the prints & deliver them at the Office. I am Sir

　　　　　　　　　　　　　　　　your most Obedient humble Servant
Sunday *　　　　　　　　　　　　　WILLM COLLIER

* *Sunday*: part of the paper is cut away below this word. From the letters *ke* remaining we deduce that there was originally a "Direction" to Coke here as well as on the outside of the letter.

Copy-text: HTC Coke 35 (Collier holograph; figures on the cover in Hand A). For nineteenth-century transcriptions see Winston, p. 36, and Drexel MS, fol. 96.

Comment: For Collier's draft of the authorization to receive subscription money and Coke's response to this request see documents 110 and 111. Collier had left these matters dangerously late: the date on document 110 is 10 December, and *Antiochus* actually opened at the Haymarket on Wednesday, 12 December.

A chocolate house could serve as a convenient box office in a posh district, and White's had done so on previous occasions (cf. document 57). The tangled finances of the opera are probably the reason for Collier's having to get approval from the Lord Chamberlain's office for an otherwise routine arrangement. Collier's creditors were probably afraid that they would never see any of their money if it went directly to Collier (cf. document 111).

1. The following figures appear upside down above the "Direction."

```
    106        106
     10          9
   ————       ————
   1060       984 [sic]
```

As of 9 December the opera had given nine performances this season. We infer that Coke was making a rough calculation of its approximate income (at an average of £106 per night) before deciding whether Collier should be authorized to collect the subscription money from Mrs White or whether she should "receive ye money of ye subscription and pay it as my Lord Chamberlain directs" (see document 111). For an example of the Lord Chamberlain's intervention in related financial matters see document 112.

2. Collier was evidently going to deliver printed libretti to subscribers. The notice in the *Spectator* 7 December had said they would be available 11 and 12 December.

110. Collier's Draft of an Authorization to Mrs White

(10 December 1711)

[Cover] The order desir'd December 10th 1711

Mrs White
    You are hereby Impowred to Receave the Mony for the subscriptions from
the subscribers to the Opera Caled Antiochus and to pay the Same to Mr
Collier on his Order and for soe doing this shall be your Warrant Given
under my hand the 10° of December 1711

To Mrs White at her Chocolate house in St James Street

    Copy-text: HTC Coke 71 (Collier holograph). For nineteenth-century
transcriptions see Winston, p. 85, and Drexel MS, fol. 98.

    Comment: This appears to be the "order" requested by Collier and sub-
mitted by him in draft form with document 109. Note particularly that Collier wants Mrs White to be authorized to pay subscription money directly to
him on his demand: compare document 111.

111. Coke to Stanley (?) about Subscription Arrangements for *Antiochus*

[Cover] Mr Collier   [10 December 1711?]¹

Dear Sir
    I have spoke to my Lord Chamberlain about ye order Mr Collier desires
which I have enclosd you, and my Lord thinks it proper to have it made to
Mrs White to recieve ye money of ye subscription and pay it as my Lord
Chamberlain directs, of which I desire you to give Notice to Mr Collier for
him to come to take ye order. I am Dear Sir

Munday night.   Yours
                                                                T COKE

    Copy-text: HTC Coke 73 (Coke holograph). For nineteenth-century tran-
scriptions see Winston, p. 35, and Drexel MS, fol. 97.

Comment: This is evidently an office copy of a note written by Coke about Collier's request for an order authorizing Mrs White to receive subscription funds for *Antiochus*. The recipient is unspecified, but since he is evidently another official in the Lord Chamberlain's office, Sir John Stanley is a likely candidate. Note that the Lord Chamberlain has directed that Mrs White pay the money as he orders (e.g., to tradesmen), not to Collier (cf. document 110).

1. We have assigned this date on the presumption that this note is connected with documents 109 and 110.

112. Shrewsbury to Collier or Coke about Financial Problems at the Haymarket

[early January 1712?]

Wensday Morning

Sir

I have this Morning had another Petition from the Tradsmen belonging to the Play house[1] who as yet see themselves in no way of being payd the Debt owd them by Mr Hill,[2] and I doubt would yet be more clamarous if they should see part of the subscription[3] diverted before they are satisfyd: for which reason I desire you will not part with the 20 guyneas in your hands, nor give no promise of it to the Copist[4] till the matter has been further considerd. I am Sir

your most faithfull
humble Servant
SHREWSBURY

Copy-text: Winston, p. 47. For another nineteenth-century transcription see Drexel MS, fol. 80.

Comment: Date and recipient are uncertain. On the date we have followed the transcriber of the Drexel MS, who observes:

The Tradesmen who had credited the Opera, in 1710, advertised in December 1711, an intended general meeting to concert measures for petitioning the Lord Chamberlain, or commencing law suits against the Manager, who peremptorily refused payment, although the articles for which payment was then asked, were in constant use. In the *Postboy* Jan. 1.1712. is an advertisement[:] the Tradesmen Creditors to the Theatre in the Haymarket who furnished the several goods for the New Operas performed there last winter by subscription, paid by the Quality, now used at the Theatre are desired to meet at the Black Horse Ale house, against Charing Cross, On Wednesday Jan. 2. at four oClock of the afternoon, to consider of a method for the recovery of their Just Debts.

The transcriber identifies Coke as the recipient of the present letter, which is possible, though tone and content seem at least as appropriate to Collier.

1. I.e., the Haymarket.
2. Presumably debts contracted by Aaron Hill as opera manager for Collier in the 1710–11 season.
3. The subscription for *Antiochus*, which received its premiere 12 December 1711. Cf. documents 109–11.
4. I.e., copyist. According to document 106, Lunican, the copyist for *Rinaldo*, was to be paid £26 for that task.

INTERDOCUMENT.

The Lord Chamberlain's Regulations for Drury Lane and the Haymarket

(17 April 1712)

Whereas the Managers of the Opera and Comedy have Agreed upon the following Articles as Necessary for their better regulation. I do hereby Approve and confirm the Same vizt. The Undertakers and Manager of the Opera shall not be permitted to represent any Entertainment upon the Stage under his direction but Such as shall be Set to Musick. The Undertakers and Managers of the Comedy shall not be permitted to represent any Musicall Entertainment or to have any Dancing perform'd but by the Actors. The Managers of ye Opera and Comedy are permitted to perform as often and on what days they think fitt Wednesdays and ffrydays in Lent only excepted. That no play be Acted for the benefit of any Actor before ye first day of March nor more than one benefit play in one Week during the Season of performing Opera. That no benefit play for an Actor or the first day of a New play be on the same day the Opera is perform'd nor the third day of a New play except in the time of Lent and during ye time of Lent there is not to be Acted more than one New play.

Copy-text: PRO LC 5/155, p. 159.

Comment: The Lord Chamberlain issued these orders under the heading "Articles for regulating the Opera and Comedy."

INTERDOCUMENT.
The Lord Chamberlain's Order for an Opera Subsidy

(17 April 1712)

Whereas the Managers of her Majesties Company of Comedians have agreed for
the better Support of the expences of the Opera to pay to Mr Owen Swyney who by
her Majesties License is appointed Manager of the Opera the Sume of one hundred
pounds per Annum out of the receipts of the Comedy the said payments to Commence from the 1st day of June 1712 after which time the Money which they paid
by my Warrant dated the 20th of November 1711 towards the Rent of the Theatre
in the Hay Markett is to cease and have pray'd my Warrant thereupon.

I do hereby Approve and Confirm the said Agreement and do Order and direct
the Managers of her Majesties Company of Comedians to pay to Mr Owen Swyney
the Sume of One hundred pounds per Annum Acordingly towards defraying the
Expences of the Opera the first payment to become due the 10th May 1713 and I do
hereby direct that the payments by my Warrant of the 20th November 1711 are to
cease from, and after the 1st day of June next. Given under my hand this 17th day
of Aprill 1712 in the Eleventh year of her Majestys Reign.

SHREWSBURY

To the Managers of her
Majesties Company of Comedians

Copy-text: PRO LC 7/3, fol. 126.

Comment: The Lord Chamberlain issued this order under the heading "Mr
Swyney to receive £100 per Annum from the Managers of the Comedy" as part of
the reorganization worked out in April 1712.

113. Receipts Signed by Barbier and de l'Epine

(23 and 27 June 1712)

June 23 1712

Recevd by order of her Majesty from the Vice Chamberlain twenty Guineas

JANE BARBIER

June * 27 1712

Received by order of her Majesty twenty Guineas

MARGUERITE DE L'ÉPINE

* *June*: Winston reads "Jan" but this seems unlikely in light of the Barbier date and that of document 114. The Drexel MS transcriber reads "June."

Copy-text: Winston, p. 85, and Drexel MS, fol. 100. This document was part of lot 215 in the 1876 sale catalogue.

Comment: The occasion and significance of these receipts, like those in documents 114–16, remain grounds for speculation. Our best guess is that Shrewsbury ordered Coke to disburse small amounts of money (perhaps from subscriptions collected by Mrs White? cf. document 112) among specified singers and dancers.

114. Receipt Signed by "Pilotti"

[Cover] Pilotti & his wife   (23 June 1712)
      June 23d 1712,

A di 23 Giungo 1712 Londra

Confeso di auer Riceuto Per Ordine di Sua Maesta Quranta Gine

Io Giouanni Schiauonetto

Copy-text: HTC Coke 68 (Schiavonetti holograph). This document was part of lot 215 in the 1876 sale catalogue.

Translation: "On the day 23 June 1712, London. I, Giovanni Schiavo-netto, declare that I have received by order of Her Majesty forty guineas."

Comment: For discussion, see document 113. The singer Elisabetta Pilotti had married Schiavonetti, who evidently picked up the money due both of them via the Vice Chamberlain. Coke inaccurately used the singer's stage name to refer to her husband.

115. Receipts Signed by Musicians

[Cover] Keitsh,   Shogon,   (23 and 24 June 1712)
      Pietro,   Tomaso,
      Simson, Granon

Walther, Lynike
June 23th 1712

June ye 23d 1712

Received by order of her Majesty five guineas

J C KYTCH

June ye 24th 1712

Recievd by orders of her Majesty five guineas

JOHN SHOJAN

Recievd by order of her Majesty five guineas

PIETRO CHABOUD

Received by order of her Majesty four guineas

TOMASO GABRIELLI

Received by order of her Majesty four guineas

STRANGWAY'S SIMPSON

Received by order of her Majesty four guineas

JOHN GRANON

Received by order of her Majesty four guineas

JOHN WALTHER

Received by orders of her Majesty four guineas

D. LINIKE

Copy-text: HTC Coke 78 (Hand A and various signatures). This document was part of lot 215 in the 1876 sale catalogue.

Comment: For discussion, see document 113.

116. Receipts Signed by Armstrong and Dondell

[Cover] Amstrong & Dowdel [*sic*]   (24 June 1712)
June 24th 1712

June ye 24th 1712

Received by order of her Majesty two guineas

W ARMSTRONG

Received by order of her Majesty two guineas

SPRACKLING DONDELL

Copy-text: HTC Coke 79a (Hand A and two signatures). This document was part of lot 215 in the 1876 sale catalogue.

Comment: For discussion, see document 113.

SEASON OF

1712–1713

The generic division continued during the season of 1712–13, with plays offered exclusively at Drury Lane, operas at the Haymarket. The principal event of this season is Swiney's decamping to the Continent. "Colman's Opera Register" reports: "after these Two Nights [Handel's *Theseus*, 10 and 14 January] Mr Swiny Brakes & runs away & leaves ye Singers unpaid ye Scenes & Habits also unpaid for. The Singers were in Some confusion but at last concluded to go on with ye Opera's on their own accounts, & devide ye Gain amongst them."[1] Documents 122 and 123 concern the financial settlements worked out among the singers. Lack of animus against Swiney is somewhat surprising (he returned to England and a place in London society in 1735 under the name "Owen MacSwiney"), but most people probably realized that his insolvency was not his fault, and we do have some evidence that Swiney tried to deal with the situation in a businesslike way from the safety of the Continent.

Memorandum: The following paragraph was desir'd by Mr Swiney, in his Letter to Mr Vanbrugh dated the 12th of March 1714 from Leyden, to be entered in the Lord Chamberlains Office vizt.

And as to the Next Season, and so on for the three Years, or as long as he [Heidegger?] pleases farther—He shall have the entire Management of all Affairs, and my halfe of the profit shall be paid to the uses of the Tradesmen.

(PRO LC 7/2, fol. 10v)

And on 1 January 1715 Vanbrugh wrote himself a "Memorandum."

I have accepted of Mr Swinys Resignation of his Lease of the Playhouse as on the 10th of May last, to which time having settled the Account between us (with Mr. Sexton his Agent, he himself being in France) I paid him part of the Ballance, and Sign'd a note to him payable at Michaelmass next, of £125. for the remainder, which is in full, of All Accounts between him and me. The Surrender of his Lease is only by a Writing sent from France; the lease it self being lock'd up with things of his at Leyden as likewise a Mortgage he had upon the Playhouse for £1000. But I have his Receipts for the Whole Sum Written upon the Counterpart or annex'd to it.[2]

As a result of the managerial void left by Swiney, John Jacob Heidegger began to come into the prominence he was to enjoy in the London opera world for so many years.

Meanwhile at Drury Lane the Triumvirate management was settling down to steady, profitable operation. For the agreement signed between Collier and Wilks, Doggett, and Cibber on 6 December 1712, see the interdocument, dated about February 1714, between documents 131 and 132. Problems with Swiney as a partner during the previous two seasons seem to have led the actor-managers to work out a set of operating principles which in their essentials were to last into the 1730s. In a later lawsuit Doggett says they agreed

ffirst that your Orator should be the Treasurer and Cashier for keeping all and every sume and sumes of money ariseing from the acting . . .

Secondly that no sume exceeding forty Shillings should be expended without the unanimous Consent & agreement of every one of the said three Partners Wilkes your said Orator [Doggett] and the [said Cibber]

& thirdly that no bill should be Paid to any Person of whom your Orator and his said two Partners should buy [any] goods or whome they should Employ to do any work for them without the Consent of every one of them the said Wilkes your Orator and the said Cibber

and Fourthly that no Actors or Servants should be taken in or turned out of the service of the said Partners without the consent of every one of them.[3]

Doggett claims that this agreement was in effect from 17 April 1712 until January 1713, but he explains that "the Said Agreement being so short plain & easy & being also to be carryed into an immediate Execution it was not thought necessary by your Orator & his Said Partners to reduce the same into Writing." In their answer to Doggett's bill of complaint, Wilks and Cibber deny any formal agreement but admit that the managers functioned on the basis outlined by Doggett until he stopped participating in the daily business of the company. Bills and authorizations signed by all three Triumvirs (Booth replacing Doggett in late 1713) are a commonplace among manuscripts in theatre collections.

Because Drury Lane ran smoothly this season we have no documents directly relating to its actual operations. But in documents 120 and 121 we see the first signs of a ruckus which was to disrupt the theatre for the next two seasons. Barton Booth wanted to join the management and share in the profits—and if the Triumvirs did not wish to invite him in, he was quite prepared to use his connections among people of quality to force his way in. These letters are the beginnings of what became open civil war in November 1713.

1. Konrad Sasse, "Opera Register from 1712 to 1734 (Colman-Register)," *Händel-Jahrbuch*, 5 (1959), 199–223, quotation from p. 202.
2. Downes, *Vanbrugh*, p. 180.
3. PRO C11/6/44. Barker notes that this agreement is similar to the "Rules and Regulations for the Management" in LC 7/3, fols. 149–50 (*Mr Cibber*, pp. 88–89). However, we believe that document is slightly later: see document 131.

117. Performers at Concerts Given for the Duchess of Shrewsbury in Kensington

[Season of 1712–13?]

given att ye Duthess of Shrewsburys at Kensenton *

Pilotti and her husband	40
Isabella	40
Margarita	20
Barbier	20
Clodio	8
Papusch	8
Corbett	6
Soyan	5
Walters	4
Symson	4
Unican¹	4
Lully	8
Tomaso	4
Dowdell	2
Pietro	5
Keitch	5
Gronon	4
armstrong who plaid ye Musick before ye last but not this last,	2

189

Nicolini had by my Lord Chamberlain   <u>200</u>

In all <u>389</u>

[The verso (transcribed below) appears to be a scratch sheet for this list.]

Singers	Harpsicord
Nicolini	20 Tomaso |
Isabella	Double Base
Margarita	10 Dowdel |
Barbier	Base Viols
Pilotti	Paisible
Instrumentall Musick	Francisco
	Pilotti
Violins	Bassons
per[†] night	Babel
20 sh Clodio ||	12:6 Pietro ||
ditto Papusch ||	ditto Keitch ||
Banister[‡]	Trumpett
15 Corbett ||	10 Gronon ||
Young Babel	Armstrong plaid a tenor
12 Soyan ||	in the musick before this
10 Walters ||	but did not play in this.
10 Simpson ||	2sh[§] a Kettledrum &ca
Tenors	
8 Unican ||	
Hautboys	
20sh Lully ||	
Latour	

* *given . . . Kensenton:* originally written between the lines after the first entry in the document.

† *per:* reading doubtful.

‡ *Banister:* "Aylesworth" written and canceled immediately below this name.

§ *sh:* reading doubtful.

Copy-text: HTC Coke 6 (Hand A).

Comment: These lists evidently refer to private concerts given for the Lord Chamberlain's wife, the Duchess of Shrewsbury (née Adelaide Roffeni). Coke probably undertook to make the arrangements. The expense—some £95 for each of two performances—is steep, but this group represents many of the top singers and musicians in London, and these concerts were presumably very grand society affairs. The differences in the salaries stated recto and verso evidently reflect the difference between concert rates and regular nightly salaries at the Haymarket. We are unable to explain the single and double vertical lines by some of the names on the worksheet.

The date is conjectural. Shrewsbury held office between April 1710 and July 1715. Under "Dowdell" (and elsewhere) the *Biographical Dictionary* dates this document "about 1710," but the inclusion of Jane Barbier (who first performed in public on 14 November 1711) suggests a later date. For Barbier to be paid at the same rate as Margarita de l'Epine indicates that she was not an absolute beginner.

For commentary on the Duchess of Shrewsbury's artistic and musical interests see Dorothy H. Somerville, *The King of Hearts: Charles Talbot, Duke of Shrewsbury* (London: Allen & Unwin, 1962).

1. I.e., Lunican.

118. Receipt Signed by Coke

(25 October 1712)

[Recto]   Coke Oct 25 1712
             Sir pray pay this Bill to Mr
             Robt Hayward yours
                        JOHN BILLING
             Wittness
                        ROBT HAYWARD
[Verso]   October ye 25 1712
             Received of Mr John Billing the
             Summe of tenn pounds which I
             am to pay to Mr Robert
             Heyward on* order att London
                        T COKE
[On another piece of paper]
             Sir plese to pay to Mr Robt Hayward in
             allhollows Lane themps street upon the account
             of John Billing of Bath ten pounds
             £   s   d
             10:00:00

* *on*: MS appears to read "or."

Copy-text: HTC Coke 76 (Billing holograph with Hayward signature; Coke holograph; unidentified hand). This document was part of lot 215 in the 1876 sale catalogue.

119. Receipt signed by Loeillet

(15 December 1712)

Recievd December ye 15 1712 of Mr Cook vice chambarlane ye sume of eight ginnies

by me J: LOEILLET

Copy-text: HTC Coke 79 (Loeillet holograph?). This item was part of lot 215 in the 1876 sale catalogue.

Comment: The occasion for this payment is undeterminable. Coke may well have been paying Loeillet for private services.

120. Barton Booth to Lord Lansdowne about His Career

(16 December 1712)

[Cover] Mr Booth the player to my Lord Lansdown—
       December 16: 1712

Tuesday December 16th 1712.
My Lord.
   I cannot forbear Returning you my most humble thanks for your kind promise of assisting me, tho at the same time, I cannot but be concern'd at the trouble I give you.
   Let me humbly beg leave to give your Lordship some further light into this affair. a short History of my Misfortunes, since I first undertook this unhappy Business, I am now engag'd in, may prevail upon your Lordship's good Nature, and Generosity, to redress the oppression I now labour under with more dispatch, than, perhaps, might seem necessary to you, if you were unacquainted with my present Condition.

After having been six years at Westminster School, instead of going to either University to pursue my Studies, My folly led me to the profession, I now must stick to, while I live. As the World goes, Actors are very rarely preferr'd to any other Employment. I blush to own my Indiscretion: I was very Young; but since I have brought myself to a bad Market; I must make the best of it

I have been thirteen Years an Actor. five years in Lincoln's Inn fields under Mr Betterton; and during that time, I did not receive Communibus annis[1] thirty pounds by my salary: from thence I removd under Mr Vanbrugh, and Mr Congreve, to the playhouse in the Haymarket; where for four Years I far'd not much better than before: These Misfortunes threw me naturally behind hand in the World, and had I not married a Gentlewoman of some fortune, I must have perish'd. for the four remaining years I receiv'd my full pay, which amounted to one hundred and ten pounds per annum, or thereabout. I have had success in my Benefit plays for the four years past, but never yet was able to retrieve the Losses, I sustain'd before. I was always chearfull in my Misfortunes, and endeavourd, by much Industry, and application in my Business, to render my self acceptable to the town: still flattering my self with hopes, that one time, or other, Actors wou'd be encourag'd, as they were at the Restoration, and many years afterwards. Voluenda dies en attulit![2] but Mr Wilks, Mr dogget and Mr Cibber only enjoy the Benefit of this alteration in our Theatrical Government. These Gentlemen have been, and are in possession of what has already made 'em happy in their Circumstances. While I must act, and labour to divert the town for a bare subsistence only. this, my Lord, is hard upon me: Yet I have something to urge further, to satisfy your Lordship, that my Case is still worse. My present livelihood depends upon my Health: and even at this time I lye too much at the mercy of my Creditors.

Thus, my Lord, If I am not redress'd, I must be a sacrifice to my Equals. Mr Wilks, Mr Cibber, and Mr dogget must raise fortunes to themselves, and families, while I starve.

I know the Worth, and honour of the Vice-Chamberlain, but not being so well known to Him, as to your Lordship; I have humbly begg'd of You, to be my Patron, and Advocate to him; & I am well assurd, he has ever had a just, and true Regard for your Lordship.

I must beg leave to tell your Lordship, that You are an Honour, and an Ornament to dramatic Poetry in particular. The knowledge of that naturally inclin'd me to believe, your Lordship wou'd readily endeavour to help an Oppress'd Actor, who has had the good fortune to please the Town, and sometimes your Lordship, whose Judgement I wou'd willingly stand or fall by.

I never coud hope to be forgiven the freedom I have taken, were not your Lordship one of the best temperd Noblemen living.

I humbly beg that my Necessity, and the Justice of my Cause may prevail upon your Lordship to pardon my presumption of Writing to you.

I am, my Lord,
your Lordship's most obedient
& most humble Servant
B Booth

To the Right honourable
The Lord Lansdowne.

Copy-text: Booth holograph in the library of the Historical Society of Pennsylvania. For nineteenth-century transcriptions see Winston, pp. 6–9, Drexel MS, fol. 101, and Folger Y.c. 197(1)—the latter in the hand of George Lamb. This letter is item 172 in the 1876 sale catalogue. It is 689 in the 1905 sale catalogue.

Comment: In this letter we see Booth drumming up support for his claims to a share in the Drury Lane management and profits. Lansdowne must have responded favorably to this plea for intercession, since a week later Booth wrote him with further details and arguments to be employed (see document 121). Booth's efforts proved successful the following November: for discussion see the introduction to the Season of 1713–1714.

1. "In average years."
2. Booth appears to be quoting Vergil, *Aeneid*, IX, 7: "Behold, the day in its revolution has brought [this] spontaneously."

121. Booth to Lord Lansdowne about the License

(23 December 1712)

[Cover] Mr Booth the player to my Lord Lansdown December 23d 1712.

Tuesday December 23d 1712

My Lord.

I have presumd to inclose to your Lordship a Copy of the License.[1] There is no other Consideration mentiond' than that of their having had long Experience and being well Qualify'd for the Management: and They are to be subservient from time to time, to all orders they shall receive from the

Lord Chamberlain's office. The same power, that redeemd' the Managers from the oppressions of the patentees, and procurd' this License, may with the same Ease, and with Justice too, add another Actor to their Number, if he be as well qualify'd.

I own they have been much longer upon the Stage than I.[?] But by their shares for these two years past, Each of 'em has receiv'd more money, than I have by my Salary, since I was first an Actor. This, I am sure, is true, My Lord. I mention it to set aside their Plea of Seniority, if it shoud' be usd' as an argument against me, & to convince your Lordship, that it is reasonable, I shoud' be Encouragd' in my Turn.

I cannot hope to succeed in this affair, unless by your Lordship's Means. Your Lordship cannot want an opportunity of talking over the Whole Matter with his honour the Vice-Chamberlain, and I doubt not, but by your Persuasion & Interest with him, Your Lordship will prevail upon him to do me Justice. I hope to owe my Preservation to your Lordship's Intercession, and receive that Encouragement from the Vice-Chamberlain, I have labourd' to deserve in my Business. All, that an Unfortunate Man can owe to those, that Generously make him easy in his Circumstances, will be due from me, both to your Lordship, and the Vice-Chamberlain, which is more than I can Express.

I have often waited for admittance to your Lordship & humbly beg leave, that I may attend sometimes in Expectation of that honour. I am, my Lord,

> Your Lordship's most Obedient
> & most humble Servant
> B Booth:

Copy-text: Harvard Theatre Collection TS 953.10F, Augustin Daly, *Woffington*, Vol. I, between pp. 32 and 33 of text, fol. [169] of this extra-illustrated volume (Booth holograph; cover in an unidentified hand). Not copied by Winston or the transcriber of the Drexel MS. This letter is item 171 in the 1876 sale catalogue.

Comment: This letter is further to that of 16 December: compare document 120. Lansdowne evidently passed Booth's letters along to his friend Coke. If he added any written representations of his own they have not come down to us.

1. Presumably the license granted on 17 April 1712 to Wilks, Doggett, Cibber, and Collier. No such copy is now with the letter.
2. Cibber and Doggett joined the United Company in 1690; Wilks came to Rich's

company at Drury Lane from Dublin in late 1698 or 1699. Booth joined the Lincoln's Inn Fields Company in 1700.

122. Legal Opinion by Mr Baron Price Concerning Valentini's Financial Rights after Swiney Absconded

[ca. early February 1713]

Signore Valentino having informd Mr Baron Price of the tenure of his Articles signd by Mr Swiny and of the first payment made to him upon them and also of the manner of Mr Swinyes going off, & absenting him self from his Creditors, among which Signore Valentino is also one for one hundred guineas more, due for the second payment on his articles, some time before Mr Swiny absconded, twas his opinion that the said Mr Swiny is a Banckrupt, and his Creditors have their remedy against him as such, and whereas the new agreement made among the singers had no retrospection to Mr Swinys debts, made by him when in possession of the Theatre, therefore it * cannot in Justice be urged that the first payment made by Mr Swiny to Signore Valentino so long before he became Banckrupt, should be urged to hinder him, from coming in, as a divider of the proffitts now arising on their new settlement

* it: MS reads "in."

Copy-text: HTC Coke 55 (unidentified hand). For nineteenth-century transcriptions see Winston, pp. 63–64, and Drexel MS, fol. 136.

Comment: After Swiney absconded (ca. 15 January 1713) the singers agreed to continue performing on a cooperative basis: for discussion, see the introduction to this season. Valentini was evidently excluded from a preliminary form of this agreement because he had already received 100 guineas from Swiney. For the Lord Chamberlain's arbitration in the matter, see the following interdocument.

INTERDOCUMENT.
Coke's Directions to the Treasurer of the Opera at the Haymarket

(13 February 1713)

Whereas there remains in your hands the Sume of One hundred Sixty two pounds Nineteen Shillings being the clear receipt[1] of the Opera Since Mr Swiney left the House

I do hereby direct you to pay the Said Sume of One hundred Sixty two pounds Nineteen Shillings to the following persons in proportion to their Severall contracts made with Mr Swiney vizt. Signor Valeriano, Signor Valentini Signora Pilotta and her husband, Signora Margerita, Mrs Barbier, Mrs Manio, Mr Hendell, Mr Heideg-ger, which Method of payment you are to Observe in the clear receipts of the Opera which Shall hereafter come into your hands

But whereas Signor Valentini and Signora Pillotta have already receiv'd Some Money from Mr Swiney in part of their contract, you are not to pay them out of these receipts till ye rest are paid their contracts in proportion to what they have been paid. Given under my hand this 13th day of ffebruary 1712/13 in the Eleventh Year of her Majestys Reign

T COKE

Copy-text: PRO LC 7/3, fol. 129, scribal fair copy signed by Coke.

1. I.e., receipts over and above rent, servants' and hirelings' salaries, and incidentals.

123. Payments to Opera Personnel in 1712–1713

[Cover] Opera   [ca. late May 1713]

Signora Margarita has receivd
in the first division	£ 80
in the second	25:
her benefitt day[1]	76: 5: 8
remains due to her	218:14: 4
	£400:—

Mrs Barbier has receivd
in the first division	£ 60
in the second	18:15
her benefitt[2]	15:—
remains due to her	206: 5
	£300:—

Mr Hendel has receivd
in the first division	£ 86
in the second	26:17
his benefitt day[3]	73:10:11
remains due	243:12: 1
	£430:00

Signora * Manina receivd
   in the first division   £ 20:
   in the second   6: 5:
   remains due to her   73:15:
                            100:—

Signor Valerian [4] has receivd:
   in the first division: £129
   in the second   40: 6:
   his benefitt day [5]   73:19:
   remains due to him   401:15:
                       £645:00

Signora pilotti has receivd
   In the first division   £89: 5:
   in the second   27:14:
   from Mr Swinay   53:15:
   her benefitt day [6]   75: 7: 3
   remains due to her   255:18: 9
                      £500: 0 [7]

Signor Valentini has receivd
   of Mr Swinay   £107:10
   in the first division   86:—
   in the second   26:14
   his benefitt day [8]   75: 8: 5
   remains due to him   241:14: 7
                      £537:10:0 [9]

   Remains [10] due to
Valeriano   401-15-0
Pilotti   255-18-9
Valentini   241-14-7
Margarita   218-14-4
Barbier   206-05-0
Hendel   243-12-1
Manina   73-15-0
   Total Remaining due 1641-14-9

Received in Money
& Benefit days   1272-15-3
                             ─────────────
                              2914-10-0

my own 11 1/2 gsh †11

Has been paid to	in Money	Benifits	Total
Valeriano	169- 6-0	73-19-0	243: 5:0
Pilotti	170:14-0	75-07-3	246:01:3
Valentini	220:07-0	75-08-5	295:15:5 12
Margarita	105:00-0	76-05-8	181: 5:8
Barbier	78:15-0	15-00-0	93:15:0
Hendel	112:17-0	73-10-11	186:07:11
Manina	26:05:0	- - - -	26:05:0

                    883:04:0—389:11:03—1272:15:3 13
                    389:11:3
                    ─────────
                    1272:15:3

* *Signora*: reading of abbreviation doubtful.
† *gsh*: reading doubtful. The "g" is followed closely by what appears to be a superscript "sh."

Copy-text: HTC Coke 20 (Heidegger holograph). Because this document is not transcribed or summarized by Winston or by the transcriber of the Drexel MS, we are inclined to think that it may have been added to the collection by W. H. Cummings sometime before 1914, though it is certainly the sort of document which got sent to Coke.

Comment: This document lists the sums actually paid to opera personnel during 1712–13 and the amounts still owed them under the terms of their contracts with the departed Owen Swiney. The date must be later than 16 May 1713, since Handel's benefit occurred that day. The singers had then received less than half the money due them.

1. 25 April.
2. 9 May.
3. 16 May.
4. Given below as "Valeriano"—i.e., Cavaliero Valeriano Pellegrini.
5. 2 May.
6. 28 March.

7. The correct total is £502:0:0.

8. 11 April.

9. The correct total is £537:07:0.

10. From this word the rest of the document is in a different, unidentified hand.

11. The significance of this entry is unknown.

12. The writer miscalculated the amount of money Valentini had already received by three shillings. All subsequent totals based on this figure are three shillings high.

13. A set of scratch figures totaling money and benefits is omitted.

SEASON OF

1713–1714

Once again plays were offered at Drury Lane, operas at the Haymarket. This was, we should probably note, the last season in which a single London playhouse was ever to have a monopoly in legitimate drama. We have little information about the opera or its management. Document 134 is the sole opera item this season, which is in itself a good sign. Drury Lane enjoyed a solidly profitable year (see document 138) despite a management dispute which after many months of acrimony finally wound up in the courts. Most of the documents for this season concern this altercation.

The crisis was precipitated by Barton Booth. The previous fall, as we have seen, Booth was busily enlisting the aid of the influential Lord Lansdowne in his campaign to add himself to the privileged group of Drury Lane actor-managers. In April of 1713 Booth scored an immense personal triumph in Addison's *Cato*, and this doubtless added to his social and professional importance. Exactly how he wangled it we do not know, but on 11 November 1713 the Lord Chamberlain issued a new license for Drury Lane in which Booth's name was added to those of Collier, Wilks, Cibber, and Doggett.[1] The outraged actor-managers met to consider what to do, and could not agree.[2] Making Booth a partner involved selling him a one-fourth interest in the "stock" (scenery, costumes, and so forth) of the theatre. Wilks and Cibber set an exaggerated value on the stock (£5350); Doggett said flatly that he would not sell his own property. The Lord Chamberlain, annoyed, ordered Booth admitted to full partnership and set £600 as a reasonable price for a one-fourth interest. Doggett then walked out of the theatre (ca. 20 November). He maintained, however, that he was entitled to his full share of the Drury Lane profits, whether he acted and participated in the management or not. Cibber and Wilks ordered that nothing more be paid to him, whereupon Doggett protested violently to Coke and Shrewsbury. The argument raged all spring, finally making its way into the courts when Doggett sued his partners in De-

cember 1714. Wilks and Cibber filed a countersuit in March 1715, and the
whole business dragged on into 1716—largely because of the stalling tactics
adopted by Cibber. A compromise was almost but never quite achieved, and
in the end Doggett found himself excluded from the management and its
profits.

By the middle of the 1713–14 season Wilks and Cibber, unhappy at the
prospect of losing one-fourth of their income, cast about for ways of reducing
outgo and hit on the expedient of refusing to pay William Collier his £700
per annum and Vanbrugh the £100 owed to him each year for the use of the
old Haymarket "stock." (For part of Vanbrugh's protest, see document 125.)
How all this might have come out had Queen Anne lived another few years
one can only guess. But of course the accession of George I in August 1714
considerably altered the political circumstances. The members of the recon-
structed Triumvirate were quick to seize the chance to exclude Collier by inviting the influential Richard Steele to join them—a move which soon got
them a "patent" and ultimately got them into all sorts of new difficulties.

1. PRO LC 5/155, p. 261.
2. Our fullest source of information is Cibber's *Apology*, II, 130–33, 140–55. The
best analysis from all sources remains Barker, *Mr Cibber*, pp. 90–97. See also Loftis,
Steele at Drury Lane, pp. 33–34.

124. Booth to Coke(?) about the License and Rights to the Stock of Scenery and Costumes

(Wednesday [4 November 1713?])

Wednesday Morning

Honoured Sir
    Till the Licence is signd the Managers will delay the Agreement in Rela-
tion to the Cloaths &c— Tis above five Weeks since Her Majesty was
pleasd to give her Royal Assent to alter the License which advantageous
delay was obtain by Praying in their Petition, that they may have Satisfaction for their Cloaths &c, which (with most humble submission to your
honours Judgment) may be done by an Order, that one quarter part of my
share shall be Stopt, and remain in the hands of the Treasurer, till the
Terms about the Cloaths are settled, in order to pay my proportion. Therefore I most humbly beg, that your Honour woud be pleasd to have the
License signd, and sent to the Office upon the Conditions above, that I

may be no longer a Sufferer, having entirely submitted my self to your Honours Determination, which then may be made at your Leisure. I am Sir

> your most obedient & most
> dutiful Servant
> B Booth

Copy-text: Winston, pp. 5–6. For other nineteenth-century transcriptions see Drexel MS, fol. 121, and Folger MS Y.c. 197(2)—the latter in the hand of George Lamb. This letter is item 170 in the 1876 sale catalogue (where it is dated "1712").

Comment: This plaint must precede the issue of the license of 11 November 1713 (PRO LC 5/155, p. 261). For discussion of the argument over the stock, see the introduction for this season.

INTERDOCUMENT.
Wilks and Cibber's Valuation of Stock Belonging to Drury Lane

(12 November 1713)

To the Right Honourable Thomas Cooke Esquire Vice Chamberlaine of her Majesties Household &c.
The Humble Remonstrance of the Managers of the Theatre Royall

Sheweth That in Obedience to her Majestys Comands for Seperating the Opera from the Comedy the Managers did Surrender to Mr Collier all the Cloaths Scenes &c. belonging to the Operas In Consideration of which they were Assured of having her Majesties Sole Licence for Comedy And the said Managers do bona fide beleive that their Shares in the said Cloaths &c. So Surrender'd were in Value att least One thousand four hundred pounds

That to make an end of a Law suit wherein the Proportion of the said Managers property in the Cloaths &c. was disputed and to gett full Releases upon Mr Swinnys giving up all to the said Managers they paid him Down in ready mony as appears by his receipts three hundred fifty pounds

That Since they have had the Comedy Solely on the nearest Calculation they can make upon So Short Warning they beleive they Underate the Expence of Cloaths &tc three thousand Six hundred pounds Opera Cloaths Surrendred One thousand four hundred pounds paid Mr Swinny three hundred and fifty pounds Calculation Since the Managers had the Licence three thousand Six hundred pounds Totall five thousand three hundred and fifty pounds

The Managers therefore Humbly hope that if any part of this Account is Questioned they may have due time allowed them to produce their Vouchers

Theatre Royall November the Twelfth One thousand Seven hundred And thirteen

Copy-text: PRO C11/6/44.[1]

1. Doggett included a transcription of this document in a bill of complaint against Wilks, Cibber and others, PRO C11/6/44. He "left the said paper with his Clerke in this Honourable Court to the intent that the [said] Wilkes and Cibber may resort to and peruse the Same," and they acknowledged it in their answer to Doggett's complaint. We have therefore included the text, even though the location of the original document is not known.

125. Vanbrugh to Coke about His Rights in Drury Lane's Stock of Scenery and Costumes

(20 November 1713)

Castle Howard. November ye 20th 1713.
    I troubled you lately with a Letter relating to the Comedy Stock in Drury Lane.[1] I am since informed you have directed the Present managers to lay before you an Inventory of what was carryed from the Haymarket. I hope they will give you a right one; if they do, you will see, it was the Richest and compleatest Stock, that ever any Company had in England. Consisting of All that was in Lincolns Inn fields (for which I gave £500—). * All that was added to it upon the first opening the Haymarket house (which came to a very great Sum) and what was in a most profuse manner added farther, when Mr Swiny brought all the Chief Actors thither from Drury Lane and was Oblig'd to gratify them with whatever they would have. There was besides this (by neglect of those Mr Collier employ'd) a great part of the Opera Stock carryed off. So that, there can be no doubt left, of the Stock being far beyond what ever had been known before upon the Stage. And there was no pretences whatever from those Present Managers to a property in one ragg of it. I give you the trouble of what I now observe to you, doubting whether in Mr Swiny's Absence you may have that exact account in particular which I suppose he could give you. I have an entire Relyance on your Justice, from what I have already found, and for which I shall Always own my Self

Sir Your much oblig'd
And Obedient humble Servant
J. VANBRUGH.

* £500: Webb reads £900. Winston gives £500, which is correct: see document 6.

Copy-text: Vanbrugh, *Works*, IV, 57–58. Webb used "the original in the possession of Messrs. Tregaskis, of London" (p. xli, where it is misdated "29th November"). We do not know the present whereabouts of this letter, which is item 209 in the 1876 sale catalogue, where it is said to be addressed to Coke. Webb says that it is "To an unknown." For nineteenth-century transcriptions see Winston, pp. 56–57, and Drexel MS, fol. 107.

Comment: This letter is part of a lengthy effort by Vanbrugh to collect the £100 due to him by reversion from Swiney. For a full statement of the case, see the interdocuments for about February 1715 (between documents 145 and 146), and Vanbrugh's letters of 6 July, 13 August, and 27 December 1714 published by Rosenberg in "New Light on Vanbrugh."[2]

1. Date and contents unknown.
2. PRO LC 7/3, fols. 169–72, 130, 132, and 135.

126. Doggett to Coke Maintaining His Right to His Share in Drury Lane

(6 January 1714)

Sir

It is now seven or eight weeks since I deliver'd to you in wrighting as you commanded me such proposals as I did hope you wou'd think so reasonable that I shou'd have had your imediate order for my share, which I have bin keept out of ever since the new licence, the Managers * say by your direction, and mr Cibber has told me I must sue for it if I will have it. Sir my Lord Chamberlaine did tell me my propertie wou'd not be toucht and I had your owne word for it too and if after that I am forcet into† Westminster hall to trie whether it is or not and shall be oblige'd to ingage such persons in the dispute and to produce such papers as I am very well assur'd are not proper to be brought there from the office I hope it will not be imputed my fault if I can cume at my right no other way tho I had much rather Sir reseive it from your justice that I might have greater obligations to subscribing selfe Sir

your most obedient humble servant
THO. DOGGETT

London Jan ye 6th 1714

* *Managers*: reading doubtful.
† *into*: MS reads "int to."

Copy-text: Doggett holograph in the possession of Mary Hyde (R. B. Adam Collection). For nineteenth-century transcriptions see Winston, p. 19, and Drexel MS, fol. 108. This letter may well be item no. 175 in the 1876 sale catalogue, which item is dated "Jan. 26." For discussion see document 130.

Comment: This is the first in a long series of communications from Doggett. He did not act on his threat to take the matter to court until December 1714.

127. Affidavit of Wilks and Cibber [Missing]

(7 January 1714)

Known only from the 1876 sale catalogue (item 211): "Wilks and Colley Cibber's Affadavit. *Jan.* 7, 1714 Respecting Dogget's affair. Signed by Robt. Wilks, C. Cibber, and J. Medlycott, Witness. Very fine."

Comment: This could well be a response to Doggett's letter of 6 January (document 126). No such document with this date was copied by the nineteenth-century transcribers, which is surprising. If the sale catalogue date is entirely wrong this affidavit may be what is printed below as document 137. Winston gives "29 Jan 1714" as the date of this "oath" by Wilks and Cibber; the Drexel MS dates it "29 June 1714," which is evidently correct.

128. The Remonstrance of Wilks and Cibber Concerning Doggett

(16 January 1714)

[Cover] January 16th 1713 Cibber & Collier about the Play house

The Humble Remonstrance of Robert Wilks, & Colley Cibber of the Theatre Royall.

About six Weeks ago Mr Evans¹ inform'd the Managers, that Mr Doggett had agreed before Mr Vice Chamberlain to pay Mr Wilks and Mr Cibber their Proportion of what money he had in his hands till the Expiration of the Late Licence, and that he wou'd Comply with the New Licence, and go on Amicably.

But Mr Doggett has refus'd to pay any part of the said money, and has never join'd in any one thing relating to the Company, and has totally absented himself both as a Manager, and an Actor, ever since the present Licence was in force.

Mr Doggett Notwithstanding this has this very day, demanded in writing his share of Mr Wilks, before he proceeds to extremity, Adding that he will, to his Utmost, maintain his Right; Mr Doggett has likewise forbid the treasurer of the House, at his Peril, to pay any Bills &c. whatsoever without his consent in writing, yet he never comes near the House to consider of what is necessary to be done.

By such Mr Doggett's proceedings, Mr Wilks & Mr Cibber are left liable to suits at Law, for their having admitted Mr Booth to a share, as Mr Doggett pretends of his Property &c.

Mr Wilks and Mr Cibber therefore Humbly hope; That in Consideration of the Hazards they run, in having so readily Comply'd with the Measures proposd for Admitting Mr Booth as aforesaid, that Mr Doggett will not be protected and Enabl'd, by his Right in her Majesty's Licence, to Act so directly in opposition and Disobedience to it, and consequently to the Ruine and Detriment of the whole Company: And whether Mr Doggett ought to be Entituled to any proportion of the profits ariseing from Acting, since his so absenting himself, and Disobeying her Majesty's Commands, Is Humbly Submitted to the Consideration of the Right Honourable Mr Vice Chamberlain.

ROB WILKS
C CIBBER.

I attest the Remonstrance above written to be true

B Booth.

Copy-text: MS in a private collection (Wilks holograph? with additional note in Booth's hand).[2] For nineteenth-century transcriptions see Winston, pp. 10–11, and Drexel MS, fol. 110. This letter is 214 in the 1876 sale catalogue.

Comment: The date is taken from document 129. For the financial matters alluded to in the first two paragraphs, see the interdocument of 12 November 1713, between documents 124 and 125.

1. Probably John Evans, who was senior clerk in the Lord Chamberlain's office. See Chamberlayne, *Angliae Notitia*, p. 169.
2. The owner has asked that his anonymity be preserved.

129. Collier's Postscript to the Wilks-Cibber Remonstrance

(16 January 1714)

Honored Sir

I hope you will Imediatly Informe her Majesty of mr Doggets Disobedience and signe an Order for his being struck out of the Lycence that the busness of the House may goe on which will allways be under Difficulty's while he is in. I am your most obedient humble servant

WILLM COLLIER

Theatre Royall
January ye 16th 1713/14

Copy-text: MS in a private collection (Collier holograph). Collier's note is written at the bottom of the second page of the Wilks-Cibber "Remonstrance" (cf. document 128). For nineteenth-century transcriptions see Winston, p. 12, and Drexel MS, fol. 111. This note is physically part of document 128 and is described in 214 of the 1876 sale catalogue.

Comment: Wilks and Cibber had evidently not yet revealed their intention to rid themselves of Collier.

130. Letter by Doggett about Cibber [Missing; Ghost?]

(26 January 1714?)

Known only from the 1876 sale catalogue (item 175): "Doggett, famous actor, singer, and founder of Doggett's Badge. A.L.s. 2 pp. 4to. *Jan. 26, 1714,* respecting Cibber, etc. *fine and rare.*"

Comment: This may very well be a ghost. We are inclined to identify it with document 126 (Mary Hyde MS, dated 6 January 1714), though this cannot be absolutely proved. Four Doggett letters were offered for sale in 1876. Those of 23 February, 17 April, and 14 June (misdated 14 January in the sale catalogue) are duly transcribed by Winston and the Drexel MS writer. No letter of "26 January 1714" appears in those transcriptions, but both have a "6 January 1714" letter for which there is no original in the Harvard Coke papers and no sale catalogue entry. The likeliest explanation is a simple error in date in the 1876 sale catalogue. Its dates are so erratic as to be almost worthless in identifying documents.

131. Wilks, Cibber, and Booth about the Managers' Agreement

(5 February 1714)

To the Right Honourable Thomas Coke Esq. Vice Chamberlain of her Majestys Household at Windsor

Sir

The inclosd is what we judge absolutely necessary to be Sign'd by all the Managers for the better Government* of the Company; And Whereas the Words of her Majestys Licence subjects us to such orders as shall from time to time be sent us from the Lord Chamberlain for the time being: we therefore, Sir Humbly Beg for all our Securitys, that you will be pleasd to indorse the Inclos'd with your Approbation, and order to all the Managers to sign it:

> We are Sir your most obedient and
> most humble Servants
> ROB WILKS   C CIBBER   B BOOTH

February 5th 1713[/4]

* *Government*: Winston reads *Goverment*; we have followed the Drexel MS.

Copy-text: Winston, p. 12. For another nineteenth-century transcription see Drexel MS, fol. 112. This letter is item 212 in the 1876 sale catalogue.

Comment: No enclosure is transcribed by Winston or is now to be found in the Coke papers at Harvard. However, we would like to offer the hypothesis that this was the cover letter for the unsigned "Rules & Regulations for the Management of the Theatre" preserved in LC 7/3, fols. 149–50.

We the Managers of her Majesties Company of Comedians acting under her Majesties Royal licence at the Theatre in Drury lane Doe hereby agree for the Better

Regulation & Menagement of the said Company, and for the prevention of any Disputes that may arise among us the said Menagers in the Execution, or Conduct of our Respective Rights or Power Granted by the said Royal licence Doe agree, & Jointly [subscribe] our selves to the True, & Punctual observation of the Following Rules, & orders viz

1st That once a week at least, or oftner (if any two of them require it) There shall be a meeting of all the Menagers at the Office to consult, and order all matters relating to the Company.

2d That all orders shall be enter'd in a Book kept for that use by the Treasurer, & shall not be revok'd or Contradicted, without the Consent of all the Three Menagers.

3d That all orders be sign'd by all the three Menagers And that nothing be an Order, That has not all their three hands to confirm it; excepting any little Necessarys, that may be wanting not exceeding the value of twenty shillings, which any one of the said Menagers may from time to time direct to be bought, or Provided: And if any one of the said Menagers shall Refuse, or neglect to be present at the said Weekly meetings Then the other Menagers There present shall have full Power to order, and Direct all matters whatsoever relating to the Company, as if such absent Menager had there been Present.

4th That no new play be receiv'd, that is not approv'd by all the Menagers, nor any Play Reviv'd or the Parts of it cast without The approbation of all the Three under their hands.

5th That no Actor, Officer, or servant be discharg'd taken down, or rais'd without the consents, & hands of all the Three.

[6th] That all Tradesmens Bills be sign'd by all three and Paid every week if there be mon'y enough receiv'd & no mony shall be shar'd till all Debts, & Disburstments be Discharg'd.

[7th] That the Tresurer shall not pay or refuse to pay any mony Contrary to these orders upon Penalty of being Discharg'd.

These regulations expand on those asserted by Doggett to have been in effect (see the introduction to the Season of 1712–1713). The spelling is characteristic of Cibber; the hand is unidentified.

The cover letter appears to be asking that the Lord Chamberlain issue these rules or something similar as an official order for the regulation of the theatre. We have no evidence that Shrewsbury interfered in the daily operations to this extent. For Doggett's alternative proposal, see document 133 below.

INTERDOCUMENT.
Collier's Memorial to Shrewsbury

[ca. February 1714]

To his Grace the Duke of Shrewsbury Lord Chamberlain of her Majestys Household
   The Memoriall of Wm Collier humbly Represents

That In Consideration of the said William Collier his Delivering upp the possession
of the Theatre in the Haymarkett with all the scenes Cloaths etc to Mr Swinny the
said Willm Collier was Admitted into the Lycence and share of the said Mr Swinny
and Cloaths sceens etc of the Theatre in Drury Lane:
   That the said Mr Swinny had a Moity of the same at the Time of the Agreement
That in Consideration of the said Colliers not Interfeering or Medling with the
Management of the business of said Theatre the following Agreement was Entered
into

   This is to Certify that I Willm Collier of Hatton Garden Gentleman doe Hereby
agree to and with Mr Robert Wilks Thomas Dogget and Colly Cibber the present
Managers of the Theatre Royall in Drury Lane That the Remainder of the Lease
which I have of the said Theatre is and shall be for and to the use of the said
Dogget, Wilks, and Cibber and Whereas I have a Covenant from the Lessees of the
said Theatre to Renew the Lease thereof for the same Terme of yeares as they the
said Leasors shou'd or have Renew'd theire Time therein from the Duke of Bedford,
Now I doe here by promise to assigne over to the said Wilks, Dogget, and Cibber
the Whole Terme I shall have therein as soone as the Lessors shall Renew theire
Lease to me, Upon Condition they Wilks Dogget, & Cibber, pay me Eight Hundred
pounds per Annum for my share in her Majestys present Lycence, Granted to me
the said William Collier Joyntly with the said Wilks Dogget & Cibber, which said
Eight Hundred pounds per Annum is Lyable to the following Abatements Vizt the
said Wilks Dogget & Cibber are to have power to stopp out of the said £800 per
annum £100 per Annum to be paid to Mr Swiny for the support of operas according
to an Order of the present Lord Chamberlain: And when the said Order shall be
Revoaked by the Lord Chamberlain and the said £100 per Annum Likewise Ordered
to be paid to me in the same Manner as it was before to Mr Swiny, then the said
Wilks, Dogget & Cibber shall Obey such Order & pay the said £100 per Annum
Accordingly but not Otherwise and I the said Wm Collier will Indemnify the said
Wilks, Dogget & Cibber from any Demand Mr Swiny may or shall have uppon the
said Wilks, Dogget, & Cibber, for the said £100 per Annum and when Acting is
forbidd then A proportionable Abatement is further to be made out of the said £800
per Annum or in Case the said Lycence shall be Recaled or Destroyed then this

Agreement shall Cease & be of no Effect. In Wittness whereof I have set my hand this sixth day of December 1712.

Wm Collier

Wittness
   R Castleman
   Ed Jones

That her Majesty haveing bin pleased to Add Mr Booth to the Liccence Mr Cibber Wrote a Letter to me, that the Agreement was Void and that I should have no Mony paid me and Insists * that I have nothing to doe with nor any share in the Cloaths sceens etc.

That they have received of Mr Booth Six Hundred pounds for Cloaths sceens etc and Refuse to pay the said Willm Collier the halfe parte thereof or any Mony on account of the Lycence.

That Mr Swiny have left the Theatre in the Haymarket they Refuse to pay the 100 without your Graces Order.

That without your Graces Justice and Interpositon the said Willm Collier will be Deprived of the Benefit of the Lycence & Agreement after all his Expences for Cloaths sceens etc in the Haymarket by submitting his share in the pattent to her Majesty his Charge in Getting A Lease of the House in Drury Lane and possession.

All which is Humbly submitted to your Graces
Consideration by may it please your Grace
your Graces most Dutifull and Obedient
Humble Servant

Willm Collier

[Endorsed] Mr Colliers Memorial against Cibber & others relative
           to an agreement about his share in the Licence of
           the Theatres in the Haymarket & Drury Lane 6 December
           1712

* *Insists*: MS appears to read "Insiss."

Copy-text: PRO LC 7/3, fols. 127–28.

132. Doggett to Coke about the Dispute over His Share

(23 February [1714])

[Direction] To The Right Honourable Mr Coke Vice Chamberlain

Sir

Since her Majesties new Licence I have bin excluded from haveing any share or profitt of the Theatre and the Treasurer forbid to lett me see or to give me any account of the receites thereoff if the Managers have don this of theire own accord (as I doe presume) without any order from you, I hope Sir that you will think it reasonable to oblige them first to settle accounts with me and lett me reseive my share according to the intent of her Majesties Licence and I shall then be very ready to agree to such Articles as I doe not doubt but you will think reasonable and proper for the good and fair management of the Company

Sir
Your most obedient humble servant

February ye 23   Tho: Doggett

Copy-text: MS in the collection of William W. Appleton (Doggett holograph). For nineteenth-century transcriptions see Winston, p. 17, and Drexel MS, fol. 113. This letter is 177 in the 1876 sale catalogue.

Comment: Doggett suggests here that he will compromise after the other managers pay him his share for the past three months.

133. Doggett's Proposals for the Management of Drury Lane

[ca. February 1714]

Mr Doggetts proposals for Management of ye Playhouse

ye 1st point is that ye 4 Plaintiffs *1 do make their accounts with Mr Doggett and pay down ye money due to him and for his not having acted this winter Mr Doggett refers himself to allow what my Lord Chamberlain shall order.

1 That the Managers meet once a Week at† least to settle ye affairs of ye House accounts and Bills and pay the Bills of & no debts remain longer than a week for Cloaths or any thing else.

2 That noe person shall lay out any summe above 20 shillings without ye

consent of all the Managers and enter it into a Book to be kept on purpose
for that matter all orders are to be enterd in a minute Book ye Book at the
weekly meeting to be signd by the managers.

3 That ye cash be lodgd in ye Treasurers hands who shall give security to
the satisfaction of all the managers.

4 That if ye ballance at making up ye accounts be not sufficient at ye
weeks end to pay off the Debts they are to be satisfyed out of ye first money
that shall be recevd and no money is to be shared till those Debts are paid
off.

5 That if ye Treasurer shall goe beyond ye sum‡ enterd in the minute
Book and signd by ye managers it shall be in the power of any manager to
displace him.

6 That noe person be taken down or raisd in the Sallary taken in or
turnd out of ye company without ye consent of all ye managers.

7 That noe play be taken into ye house without being approvd of by ye
majority of ye managers and an agreement made with ye Authors and Enterd into ye minute Book.

8 That every Manager take a Week in his turn to attend ye House morning and Evening to overlook the Direction of ye House and see ye orders of
ye Managers as they are minuted down and signd by Them duely executed
by both actors and Servants.

9 That every Manager take at least six prentices which must not be under
15 years old.

10 That there be a Value set upon ye Cloaths Scenes &c of ye Stock by
ye Managers and if any of them shall have a mind to leave they shall receive their proportion of ye said valuation according to the usual manner of
sharing viz. his share shall be paid him till he has recevd ye summe agreed
on and then all his property shall go to ye use of ye House according to ye
direction of the Lord Chamberlain.

11 When any Manager shall die all right in ye shares and property without any consideration for it shall go to ye use of ye House according to the
direction of the Lord Chamberlain.

* *Plaintiffs*: MS appears to read "Pl."
† *at*: MS reads "a"; we have followed the Drexel MS.
‡ *sum*: Winston leaves a blank here; we have taken this reading from the
Drexel MS.

Copy-text: Winston, pp. 30–32. For another nineteenth-century transcription see Drexel MS, fol. 103 and unnumbered folio following. This document does not appear separately in the 1876 sale catalogue, but is item 717

in the 1905 sale catalogue. According to Cook, *Thomas Doggett*, p. 30, Doggett's holograph was in the possession of A. M. Broadley as of 1908.

Comment: These are evidently not the "proposals" delivered to Coke in writing about 12–19 November 1713 (mentioned in Doggett's letter of 6 January 1714—document 126). This document mentions Doggett's "not having acted this winter," but it seems to predate the greater acrimony of the late spring. At this point Doggett is apparently still willing to discuss a return to an active part in the management of Drury Lane.

1. I.e., Wilks, Cibber, Booth, and Collier.

134. Singers' Petition for Regulation of Benefits

(16 March 1714)
March the 16 1713[/4][1]

Sir

We underwritten beg the favour of you to regulate the order of our Benefit days which by contract are intirely left to your decision. And we promise to submitt ourselfs with all humility to the order you will be pleasd to give.

STEPH: BARBIER[2]
CATTERINA GALERETTI[3]
J C PEPUSCH for Mrs Margeritta
THO: ROBINSON
VALENTINO URBANI

Copy-text: Winston, p. 44. For another nineteenth-century transcription see Drexel MS, fol. 115. This document is item 210 in the 1876 sale catalogue; it is 711 in the 1905 sale catalogue.

Comment: The 1876 sale catalogue states that "the Document is written by Heidegger." Lacking the original document we cannot verify this assertion, but it is plausible enough.

1. From the singers who signed we deduce that the year is 1713/4 rather than 1713.
2. Stephen Barbier was presumably a male relative (a brother?) of Jane Barbier, on whose behalf he was evidently signing.
3. Catherina Galerati. The Drexel MS transcriber could not read this name and left it blank; the 1876 sale catalogue gives it as "Catterina Galevelli."

135. Doggett to Coke about the License Dispute

[Cover] petitioner Doggett.   (17 April 1714)

Sir

I have obayed all your Commands and from the assureance you was
pleased to give me that I shou'd have justice don me I was perswaded to
give you an account what mony I had in my hands and upon my doeing so I
had your promise that the managers shou'd be obliged in two dayes that is
to say on the Wendsday followeing to bring in theire account likewise and
clowse with me: but I beg leave to remonstrate to you that tis now neare six
weekes since and I have not bin able to obtaine any account nor any manor
of sattisfaction which I hope will excuse my takeing such methods as shall
be advised proper to cume at my right and as I have indevord to shew a just
regard Sir to all your commands and omitted nothing that I thought was
due from me to the office I hope my Lord Chamberlin and Sir John Stanley
will be sattisfied that what I doe is from nessesetie not choice.

Sir there was a paper deliverd to you under Mr Willks and Mr Cibbers
hands of an account of the vallue of the clothes and scenes * &c which I
beg you will please to lett me have which will very much oblige

Sir your most obedient humble servant
Tho: Doggett

April ye 17 1714

* *scenes*: MS reads "scnes."

Copy-text: Doggett holograph in the Pierpont Morgan Library (R–V Au-
tog. Misc. Dram.). For nineteenth-century transcriptions see Winston, pp.
20–21, and Drexel MS, fol. 116. This letter is item 178 in the 1876 sale
catalogue. According to Cook (*Thomas Doggett*, p. 30) this letter was in the
possession of A. M. Broadley in 1908.

Comment: By this time Doggett evidently realized that he would not easily
get his way. Here we see him asking for a copy of the stock valuation—probably a sign that he was ready to negotiate on the enforced sale.

136. Doggett's Request for a Settlement

Sir   (14 June 1714)

I am sorre that I am forcet upon giving you this trouble so soon as you are come to towne while I had the power of a Manager I always took * care to prevent your reciving any from the Play house but should have bin excluded from having any Vote there above this twelve month past and in november last the cash that was always loged in my hands till the end of the year to defray such Debts as should be forgott and left unpaid was taken from me and part of my share in the Cloaths & Scenes &c sold to Mr Booth by the direction of Mr Vice Chamberlain and the rest as I am informd is divided between Mr Wilks & Mr Cibber upon my complaining of those injuries Mr Vice Chamberlain was pleased to send for me and to promise me If I woud give an account what money I had then in my hands and perform such other conditions as he then proposd to me the other Managers shoud do the like and I shoud have my share. I did as he requird of me and have since obeyd all his commands but have not been able to obtain any maner of redress.

Sir I woud Petition his Grace the Duke of Shrewsbury but when I had the honour † to wait upon him last I found I had the misfortune to have fallen under his displeasure. I cannot tell for what but coud not have believed I shoud have found such effects of it. If it is his Graces pleasure that I shoud quit my business I hope he will be pleasd that I should receive a reasonable satisfaction for it without apealling from his Grace. Sir I hope before fryday you will please to lett me knowe what I am to expect for that I understand is the last day of acting this season ¹ and the managers will be gon out of towne to the end that they may give as much trouble and delay as they can to

Sir your most obedient humble Servant
THO: DOGGETT

June ² ye 14th 1714

* *took*: Winston reads "what"; we have followed the Drexel MS.
† *honour*: Winston reads "honoror"; we have followed the Drexel MS.

Copy-text: Winston, pp. 21–23. For another nineteenth-century transcription see Drexel MS, fol. 109. This letter was item 176 in the 1876 sale catalogue (misdated 14 January 1714). According to Cook (*Thomas Doggett*, p. 30) the holograph of this document was in the possession of A. M. Broadley in 1908. Cook prints a facsimile of the last sentence and signature: we have silently corrected accidentals from that source.

Comment: The recipient is not specified, but from internal evidence cannot be either Coke or Shrewsbury. Sir John Stanley is a plausible candidate. By this time Shrewsbury's patience with Doggett was evidently exhausted, and Doggett seems increasingly ready to accept a cash settlement.

1. Friday 18 June 1714 was the last day of the regular acting season (see document 138 below and *The London Stage*, Part 2, I, 325).
2. MS reads "Jun." Winston reads "January," as do the 1876 sale catalogue and Cook in *Thomas Doggett*. But the reading by the Drexel MS transcriber is correct, as the reference to the end of the 1713–14 season makes plain.

137. Wilks and Cibber on Oath against Doggett

(29 June 1714)

Rob Wilks & Colley Cibber jointly make oath &c that in November last they informd Thomas Doggett that they had receivd a new Licence for acting plays &c & offerd to shew it him but he turnd away & said he * would not directly or indirectly have any thing to do with it & has not tho repeatedly solicited never come forward as actor or Manager but has demanded one fourth share which when refused he asserted his right to one third but would take one fourth as composition.
29 June¹ 1714   ROB WILKS
                                                           C CIBBER

* *he*: supplied from the Drexel MS.

Copy-text: Winston, pp. 14–15. For another nineteenth-century transcription see Drexel MS, fol. 117. For discussion of an entry in the 1876 sale catalogue which might conceivably refer to this document see the Comment on document 127. Part of lot 716 in the 1905 sale catalogue may well be this item.

Comment: Winston adds a note, "The above is an Extract JW," and the Drexel MS transcriber likewise says "Extract." Since they give exactly the same text, and since the two transcriptions are independent, we deduce that the original in Coke's possession was merely this summary, not the complete deposition.

1. Winston reads "Jan," but in light of document 138 we have accepted the reading of the Drexel MS transcriber.

138. Statement of Drury Lane Profits from November 1713 to June 1714

(29 June 1714)

June 29 1714.
The clear profits since the new Licence
from November ye 23. 1713 to 18th June 1714   1520-9
inclusive
A Fourth part of which amounts to   380-2-3

Copy-text: Winston, p. 13. For another nineteenth-century transcription see Drexel MS, fol. 120.

Comment: These figures were presumably furnished by Wilks and Cibber. According to document 137 Doggett had offered to settle for a quarter of the profits. Whether this total includes or excludes money owed to Collier and Vanbrugh we have no way to determine.

139. Cibber to Shrewsbury about Doggett's Legal Threats

(30 June 1714)

May it please your Grace
The inclosed[1] is what I was yesterday directed by Mr Vice Chamberlain to lay before you relating to Mr Doggetts refusal to accept of her Majestys new Licence.
I therefore humbly beg your Graces Favour, and Protection for Mr Wilks & myself in our having admitted Mr Booth (as we were then commanded by Mr Vice Chamberlain) on Reasonable terms to a share, notwithstanding the several protests, menaces, & Declarations of Mr Doggett against our so

doing, and I most humbly entreat your Grace to peruse the Affidavit of Mr
Philips the Messenger² who is a person wholly unconcern'd.

I am my Lord Your Graces most
Obedient Servant
C Cibber

June ye 30th 1714

Copy-text: Winston, p. 13. For another nineteenth-century transcription
see Drexel MS, fol. 118. This document is item 173 in the 1876 sale
catalogue.

Comment: By now Cibber and Wilks were afraid that Doggett might sue
them successfully for having carried out the orders of the Lord Chamberlain's
office. Here we see Cibber specifically requesting "protection" on the grounds
that they had simply been following orders.

1. Winston says that "Inclosd with above was a note." The Drexel MS transcriber
specifies that it was the financial statement here printed as document 138.
2. See document 140.

140. The Deposition of Phillips and Booth against Doggett

(1 July 1714)

Griffantius Phillips one of her Majestys Messengers & Barton Booth severally make oath— And first the said G Phillips maketh oath that B Booth
on 27th November last did * demand of Mr T Doggett according to order
from Vice Chamberlain that † an appraiser might be admitted to value the
Cloaths scenes &c—which he refused to obey & that Doggett did 2 or 3
days before that time declare that he did not allow of the Authority of the
new License & that he would pay no obedience to the orders from the Lord
Chamberlains office unless he saw the seal of the office affixd to said order
& vice Chamberlains hand to the same & then he knew what to do in
vindication of his rights. Booth confirmd the above & that Doggett had
from the time of the new License absented himself from the Management as
Actor &c.

Sworn 1 July 1714

Griff. Phillips
B Booth

* *did*: added from the Drexel MS.
† *that*: added from the Drexel MS.

Copy-text: Winston, p. 14. For another nineteenth-century transcription see Drexel MS, fol. 120. This document does not appear in the 1876 sale catalogue, but it is item 713 in the 1905 sale catalogue.

Comment: The strategy of the Drury Lane managers was to prove formally that Doggett had voluntarily "deserted" his job as actor and manager and hence that he was no longer entitled to his share. Winston adds two notes: "Stampd with one shilling stamp," and "The above is an extract."

141. Coke to the Lord Chamberlain about Wilks and Cibber Stopping Doggett's Share

[Cover] Dogget   [Summer 1714]

That Mr Wilks and Mr Cybber having Assum'd to themselves to stop from Mr Dogget his share of the License, and of what Mr Booth payd for his share of the Cloths and scenes with out my consent, and have notwithstanding severall Orders from me directing they shou'd Account with Mr Dogget for his proportion of ye said shares, he paying them the Sume of Two hundred thirty one Pounds stopt by him before the granting of this License,¹ have still refus'd to do it. I therefore propose to your Grace to grant an Order to the said Mr Wilks and Mr Cybber to Account immediately with Mr Dogget for his share of ye profits of ye License from the date thereof, and for ye share of the money paid by Mr Booth for his property in the Cloths and Scenes, And that before the Season of Acting begins some Rules for the future Managment of the Play House be made and Agreed to by all the Managers, and to be enter'd * in your Grace's Office for them to govern themselves by.

* *enter'd*: word repeated.

Copy-text: HTC Coke 78 (scribal fair copy). For nineteenth-century transcriptions see Winston, p. 18, and Drexel MS, fol. "102."

Comment: Writer and recipient are readily deducible from the text. The date must be the summer of 1714, sometime between 18 June when the spring season ended and 21 September when the 1714–15 season began.

1. This is the "money I had then in my hands" to which Doggett refers in document 136.

142. Mills's Request for Consideration as a Manager

[Spring or Summer 1714]

Sir

I humbly beg pardon for thus presuming to trouble you, and leave to inform your Honour, that upon her Majestys commanding a new Licence therein nameing and adding Mr Booth, Mr Doggett left the Stage, has never acted since, and declard he never will again for any Consideration. Yet insists upon a proportion of the profits, notwithstanding he has quitted the Business, and woud encrease* his wealth at the expence of others Labour, and secure a good income under her Majestys Licence, when he has shewn the utmost contempt for her Authority, in not approving the said Licence, nor allowing Mr Booth for a Manager.

This is therefore most Humbly to desire your Honours favour and Interest; that (as I have been Eighteen years a Member of the Company¹ have constantly attended the Business of it and often assisted in the management) your Honour will be pleasd to recommend me to his Excellency the Duke of Shrewsbury (whom I purpose to Petition) as a fit person to succeed Mr Doggett in Her Majestys Licence.

And give me leave to acquaint your Honour that I have some reason to beleive I shall be acceptable to the other Managers, who think it a very great hardship, that any man should share the Profits who refuses to labour with them; for they are well satisfied that I shall always be ready to the utmost of my power, with Care and Industry to promote, and help Carry on the publick Diversion.

I humbly submit this to your honours consideration and when it comes to be examind, earnestly entreat your good offices, for him who is with great respect

> Sir your honours most humble
> and most obedient Servant
> to Command
> John Mills

* *encrease*: Winston reads *encrase*; we have adopted our reading from the Drexel MS.

Copy-text: Winston, pp. 15–16. For another nineteenth-century transcription see Drexel MS, fol. 119. This letter is item 192 in the 1876 sale
catalogue (where it is misdated "1712").

Comment: The recipient was probably Coke. The date is evidently spring
or summer 1714. Mills hoped to replace Doggett; why Wilks and Cibber
should want to replace Doggett after having Booth thrust upon them Mills
does not explain. We have no evidence that this request was ever given serious consideration.

1. Mills is first recorded with the Patent Company in the spring of 1695. "Eighteen
years" starting with the season of 1695–96 would put this letter at the end of the
1713–14 season.

SEASON OF

1714–1715

Thit last season from which we have Coke documents, the season of 1714–15, was marked by two events of great importance in the history of the theatre in eighteenth-century London—the reestablishment of a second acting company and a new patent grant to Richard Steele. Rather oddly, none of our documents concern the reopening of the Lincoln's Inn Fields theatre, planned by Christopher Rich and carried out after his death by his son John. Permission to reestablish a company on the authority of the patents granted by Charles II was given by George I, newly come to the throne after the death of Queen Anne in August 1714. Cibber tells us that Christopher Rich "prevail'd with Mr. *Craggs* the Younger (afterwards Secretary of State) to lay his Case before the King, which he did in so effectual a manner that (as Mr. *Craggs* himself told me) his Majesty was pleas'd to say upon it, 'That he remember'd when he had been in *England* before, in King *Charles* his Time, there had been two Theatres in *London*; and as the Patent seem'd to be a lawful Grant, he saw no Reason why Two Play-houses might not be continued.'"[1] Lincoln's Inn Fields duly reopened on 18 December 1714, employing many of the younger actors who had been at Drury Lane and thereby precipitating something of a crisis at that house.

The death of Queen Anne voided the license upon which Drury Lane had been operating. Wilks, Cibber, and Booth,. knowing that "the Pension of seven hundred a Year, which had been levied upon them for *Collier*, must still be paid to somebody," cast about for a good Whig with influential government connections to replace the Tory Collier. Not surprisingly, they hit on the notion of taking Richard Steele as a partner. "We therefore beg'd him to use his Interest for the Renewal of our License, and that he would do us the Honour of getting our Names to stand with His in the same Commission."[2] Steele succeeded without difficulty, and on 18 October 1714 a license was granted in the usual terms to Steele, Wilks, Cibber, Booth, *and Doggett*.[3] The Lord Chamberlain may have decided that a case *sub judice* should not be prejudiced by arbitrary intervention—or Steele may have felt that he could handle Doggett and settle the litigation by bringing him back into the theatre.[4]

Partly in response to the challenge from Lincoln's Inn Fields, partly as a means of trying to evade the irksome authority of the Lord Chamberlain, and partly just to give themselves "a more ample and durable Authority" (in Cibber's phrase) the Triumvirs enthusiastically encouraged Steele when he suggested that he could try to get a patent from George I. This he succeeded in doing with remarkable celerity. The "Attorney & Solicitor Generals Opinion upon Mr. Steeles' Petition" is dated 12 January 1715; the patent itself was drawn up on the 14th, and it passed the Great Seal on the 19th.[5] The patent was valid for Steele's life plus three years, and it stated specifically that Wilks, Cibber, and Booth "have Signed their Consent to the Petitioner's desire." Doggett had evidently not been consulted, and in document 144 we see Steele presenting him with a *fait accompli* and an invitation to return and cooperate. Doggett's predictably angry response is preserved in document 145.

Little is known about the finances and administration of the opera company at the Haymarket this season. Heidegger seems to have been centrally involved in the management, and he—or someone—assembled a strong company. But document 146 seems to imply that the venture was not a financial success.

Surveying the theatrical situation in London as of the spring of 1715 we can see developments which in at least three respects foreshadow future events. First, theatrical competition had been restored. For the first time since 1710 there were two acting companies, and for the first time since 1707 serious competition between solidly established companies was possible. Never again was London to dwindle to a single theatre. Second, the patent grant to Steele set up the situation which was to lead to the great ruckus of 1719–20 in which Newcastle asserted and enforced the power of the Lord Chamberlain to control patent theatres. And finally, the sagging finances of the opera company suggest that only a massive subsidy scheme would preserve Italian opera on this scale in London—subsidy which was provided by the foundation of the Royal Academy of Music in 1719.

1. *Apology*, II, 165–66.
2. Ibid., 162–63.
3. PRO LC 5/156, p. 31.
4. Steele had been friendly with Doggett. On 13 April 1713 he wrote to his wife: "Dear Prue I have met with Doggett and We shall fall into a discourse which will turn to account. I shall dine with Him at some Eating House. If you will be exactly at five at Button's We will go together to the Park or elsewhere" (*The Correspondence of*

Richard Steele, ed. Rae Blanchard [Oxford: Oxford Univ. Press, 1941], p. 285). This discussion may well have been connected with Lansdowne's project of putting Steele in charge of the theatre. See Loftis, *Steele at Drury Lane*, pp. 25–33.
5. For texts (printed from copies in LC 7/3) see Loftis, *Steele at Drury Lane*, pp. 243–45.

143. The Terms of Mrs Robinson's Agreement with Heidegger

[Cover] Mrs Robinson and Heidegger   [October 1714]
       Mrs Robinsons bargain was to sing for the summ of
       £500 not to have more

Mrs Robinson was agreed to sing in the Opera on these Conditions
    The Opera's were affirmd by Mr Heidegger could not begin till the New yeare for reasons he then gave. Mrs. Robinson to have 500 for singing in the Opera and a benefit day.
    This bargain to be of no force unless Cavalier Nicolino returnd to sing in the Opera.
    By Comand of Mr Vice Chamberlain (on his declaring the Opera's to begin next week.)[1] Mrs Robinson offers to begin then to sing, pretends no alteration as to the price of five hundred pounds & submitts [*] to that; but by reason the operas are to begin eleven weekes sooner then Mr Heidegger propos'd when the agreement was made, she onely requires to have her benefit without any charges what ever.[2]

    I made a bargain with Mr tho Robinson upon the 14 of July past in the presens of Her Grace the Dutchess of Shrewsbury as follows.
    Mrs Robinson Daughter[3] is to sing in the Operas under my Direction the following Season.
    I am to pay her the sum of five hundred pound and a benefitt day at the usual charges and in case I should be a gainer by the Operas I oblidge me self to make her a present of a gold Watch.

                                              J J HEIDEGGER

[*] *& submitts*: "but" written and canceled between these two words.

Copy-text: MS in Broadley, p. 43 (part in an unidentified hand, part in Heidegger's hand). For nineteenth-century transcriptions see Winston, p. 48, and Drexel MS, fol. 114. This document is item 186 in the 1876 sale

catalogue; it is 693 in the 1905 sale catalogue. A clipping from a dealer's catalogue found with the MS prices it £4 4s.

Comment: The substance of this agreement was recorded (unsigned) in
PRO LC 7/2, fol. 9. "Articles Concluded between Mr Thomas Robinson and
Mr Heidegger in the presens of her Grace the Dutchess of Shrewsbury: the 13
of July 1714. Mr Robinson promises that his daughter Anastasia Robinson
shall sing under the direction of Mr Heidegger in the operas during the following season (which is from the 1 of october to the last of June). Mr Heidegger promises to pay her the said Mrs Robinson the full sum of 500 pound and
a benefitt day at the usual charges. And in case he should be a gainer by the
Operas then he promises farther to give her a gold Watch." Nicolini did indeed return to London after an absence of several seasons, and the opera
opened nearly eleven weeks earlier than it had the previous season.

1. The first performance of the 1714–15 season took place 23 October.
2. The remainder of the document, overleaf, is written in Heidegger's own hand.
3. This should probably read either "Mrs Robinson" or "Mr Robinson's Daughter."

INTERDOCUMENT.
Wilks and Cibber to Stanley(?) about Their Dispute with Doggett

(3 November 1714)

Sir
Upon our Receiving Mr Vice Chamberlains Orders to Agree with Mr Booth, as a
Sharer, according to Her Majesty's last Licence Mr Doggett always resolutely protested, that he wou'd never admit him: Upon which Account Mr Booth was, severall days, delay'd; till Mr Vice Chamberlain told Us, that it wou'd be Highly
Resented, And that he wou'd Acquaint her Majesty, who was Obstinate in order to
their being struck out of the Licence: And he likewise promis'd Us protection, if we
wou'd Agree with Mr Booth, without Mr Doggett, which we imediatly did: *But* Mr
Doggett Absolutely refus'd to look upon the Licence and protested, that he wou'd
not Act under it, nor Acknowledge it, nor be concern'd with it; And to this day he
has made his words good, by voluntarily withdrawing himself from the Company,
both as an *Actor*, or *Manager*: And of this we have made *Oath* before A Master in
Chancery, and the Affidavit was presented to his Grace the Lord Chamberlain last
Summer; To which we Beg Leave to refer: And, if requir'd, we can produce severall
Gentlemen to witness, That we have from time to time *intreated* Mr Doggett to
come, and take his equal Share with Us in the pains, and profits of the Stage, but
never cou'd prevail: And, farther, upon our receiving His Majesty's present Licence,

Mr Doggett still refus'd to come near Us, and was pleas'd to say, he thought it not a fair Question to ask him (vizt) whether he wou'd come, or no; of which Mr *Steele* was witness.

As for the pretended terms, on which Mr Doggett (as he says) was willing to Act, they were so Clogg'd with Single *Negatives*, as made him, in effect, Sole Master of the Company: But, upon our having amended them, by making the power, the Safety, and the Credit of us all equal (which Mr Vice Chamberlain seem'd to approve) we never yet heard, that Mr Doggett was ready to consent to them, when so amended.

We Utterly deny, our having contracted any Debts whatsoever; nor did we ever pay any one Bill, while Mr Doggett remain'd with Us, that is not Actually, and severally allow'd, sign'd, and consented to, under his own hand writing, which we can produce.

Tis True, Sir, that we made Mr Doggett Cashier, for our own conveniency; And for the same reason, we presume, had a right to recal that Trust; which however, we never did, till the New Licence oblig'd Us to *New Date* our Accounts from Mr Booths Admittance, and then, it was, Sure, high time to clear our old ones, and demand our Shares, which Mr Doggett (in apparent breach of his trust) refus'd to give Us: Notwithstanding all which we are still willing to admit him to an equal Share, from the day he thinks fit to begin to *play*.

Now, Sir, we beg leave to observe, That no Actor, for above these Twenty Years, has ever received Redress, of any pretended Grievance, while they refus'd to do their business, of which Mrs *Bracegirdle* was a Noted Instance, when she left the stage.

'Tis out of dispute, that the publick diversion has Suffer'd incredibly for want of Mr Doggett's Acting; And as we do not desire, our Selves, to make the Licence a Sinecure, we hope it was not design'd one for him.

We therefore Humbly pray, that his Grace will be pleas'd to order Mr Doggett to Act his Usual parts on the Stage; and upon his obedience to such order, we shall gladly admit him to an equal share of profit, power and property, from that time: We are

> Sir Your most obedient &
> most Humble Servants
> Rob Wilks
> C Cibber.

November ye 3d 1714

Copy-text: PRO LC 7/3, fols. 133–34.

144. Steele to Doggett about the Patent Grant

(19 January 1715)

St. James's Street.
January 19. 1714[/5]

Sir

I am obliged to go out of Town tomorrow morning to my election:[1] therefore must acquaint you this way, that our licence is turned into Letters Patent in my name.

Due care is taken to leave a way open for you to come amongst us with Credit and advantage. This, I thought due to your merit though indeed your perseverance in estranging yourself from our interests, would have tempted any man, that had less respect for you, than I have, to have ceased to be your advocate on many occasions, during the course of our affair, wherein there are so many jarring interests concerned. The patent, Mr Castleman,[2] will shew you, and you will give me great pleasure at my return to town, if you will give me leave to call myself your partner who am, very sincerely,

Sir, Your most obedient humble servant,
RICHARD STEELE.

[Endorsed] To Doggett

Copy-text: Drexel MS, fol. 138. This letter was apparently not known to Winston, and it is not listed in the 1876 sale catalogue. The Drexel MS transcriber does not state his source (and the letter is not in the Blanchard edition of Steele's *Correspondence*), but since the rest of his documents are genuine and accurate we have no reason to doubt the legitimacy of this one.

Comment: For Doggett's angry response to this diplomatic gesture see document 145.

1. Steele was standing for Parliament in Burroughbridge, Yorkshire.
2. Richard Castleman, treasurer of Drury Lane from 1711 to 1739.

145. The Case of Thomas Doggett

[late January 1715]

Her late Majesty—for valuable considerations was pleased to grant unto him, in conjunction with others, Her licence to form, establish, and regulate a Company of Comedians for Her service; which said licence was renewed by His present Majesty—, since his happy accession to the Throne, and in like manner granted, during His Majesty's royal pleasure, unto Mr Dogget; and to Mr Richard Steele, Colley Cibber, Robert Wilks, and Barton Booth.

Notwithstanding which, the said Mr Steele on false suggestions, and without the knowledge or consent of Mr Dogget hath since obtained the said licence to be converted into Letters Patents to himself alone for the forming and establishing a Company of Comedians for His Majesty's Service, during the natural life of him, the said Mr Steele, and for three years after his death; and in order to his obtaining such letters patents, he, the said Mr Steele, together with the said Wilkes, Cibber and Booth, consented, upon some previous agreement made amongst themselves; to surrender His Majesty's said licence, without ever consulting or making Mr Dogget in the least acquainted therewith, who knew nothing thereof, till Mr Steele was gone out of Town to his election, who then sent him the letter wherein he pretends to have left a way open, for Mr Doggett, to come in amongst them.[1]

The way it seems proposed for that purpose, is, an assignment of the said Patent, from Mr Steele to the rest of the proprietors, claiming by the said Licence; but Mr Dogget can neither obtain a copy of the said assignment to advise upon, in which there are some clauses he cannot comply with; nor can he have so much as a sight of the agreements made betwixt Mr Steele and the other said persons aforementioned, for the surrender of the said licence so very much to the prejudice of Mr Dogget, as that by this contrivance he is not only clandestinely deprived of what was his real property, but also of several considerable sums of money, laid out and expended by him, for Cloaths, scenes, and other necessaries for that undertaking; nor hath he been able to obtain any account or share of his part of the profits, since November last, was twelve months.

And it is still the more grievous to him, for that this his misfortune is, by some persons imagined to be a mark of His Majesty's displeasure toward him, thus to be set aside after all the Zeal he hath ever shewed to testifie his profoundest duty and affection to his most sacred Majesty—and the Protestant succession, in His most illustrious Royal family.

Mr Dogget doth therefore hope His Majesty, will be graciously pleased to give such orders herein, as to His Royal Wisdom and Justice shall seem meet; so as that Mr Doggets right and interest in the premises may be preserved to him, in as full and ample manner, as he should have enjoyed the same, by His Majesty's Royal Licence aforementioned, without any other restrictions, limitations, or Conditions, than are therein contained.

Copy-text: Drexel MS, fols. 139–40. No source is stated, and this document is not referred to by Winston or listed in the 1876 sale catalogue.

Comment: The title of this document was supplied by the transcriber of the Drexel MS.

This protest was of no avail. Doggett, who in December had started a suit in Chancery against the actor-managers and others, complained further on 27 January 1715, including the new patent as a grievance (PRO C11/6/44). For some account of the ultimate outcome of the dispute with Doggett and the patent grant to Steele, see Barker, *Mr Cibber*, pp. 92–98, 102–3, and Loftis, *Steele at Drury Lane*, pp. 35–41.

1. See document 144.

INTERDOCUMENT.
Vanbrugh's Claim for Rent on the Drury Lane Stock

[ca. February 1715]

[About February 1715 Vanbrugh made yet another attempt to collect the money due to him for rent of the stock. (Cf. document 125.) There was probably some sort of cover note, now lost. What Vanbrugh provided for the Lord Chamberlain's consideration was (A) a memo setting forth the history of his agreement with Swiney;[1] (B) a copy of Shrewsbury's own order of 14 January 1714/5 directing the managers of Drury Lane to pay the rent; (C) a copy of Cibber's blunt refusal, dated 22 January 1714 (i.e., 1714/5); (D) lengthy quotations from letters by Owen Swiney detailing his understanding of the agreement.]

[A. History of Vanbrugh's Agreement with Swiney]

In the Year 1707, Mr Swiny took a Lease from me of the Playhouse in the Haymarket for 14 years, where the Rent to be paid is expressed to be for the Stock of Cloaths Scenes &c: as well as for the house. And it is agreed, that at the Expiration of the said Lease, the said Stock shall be delivered up to me in good Condition, and not be lessened or Embezzled, it being declared that the property of it remains entirely & absolutely in me.

Mr Swiny afterwards tooke into Partnership with him Mr Wilks Mr Cibber and Mr Dogget on the Terms and foundation of his Lease from me, which they were all well acquainted with.

At length they removed from the Haymarkett to Drury Lane and the Opera came to the Haymarkett under Mr Collier, But Mr Swiny and his Partners thought it adviseable enough however to keep the Lease; since by that means they had a Compleat Stock of Cloaths Scenes &c to Act with, which to have bought new, would have Cost a vast Summe of money.

So they tooke the Stock that related to plays along with them from the Haymarkett, Leaving the Opera Stock to Mr Collier.

But they Agreed (in consideration of that Stock they tooke with them) to allow Mr Collier £200 a year towards the Rent and paid it accordingly.

At last Mr Swiny and Mr Collier chang'd, Mr Swiny taking the Opera and Mr Collier the Comedy, and then Mr Collier got an Order from my Lord Chamberlain That there should be but one hundred pounds a year allowd from Drury Lane for the use of the Stock, and that £100 was paid, till at last Mr Wilks Cibber and Dogget getting clear of both Mr Swiny and Collier, resolvd to try if they cou'd not shake off this Allowance for the Stock which remaind in their Possession, and so refusd to pay it, saying the Stock was theirs.

The simple Question on this matter is, which way they came to have any property in this Stock, they never having any pretence whatever in this whole matter, but what they derived from their Partnership with Mr Swiny, and that was on the terms he stood bound to me by his Lease.

J Vanbrugh

[B.] "Copy of an Order from the Lord Chamberlain to the Managers of Drury Lane Play house to pay the £100 per Annum."

Whereas by my Warrant of the 17th of Aprill 1712, I did direct the Managers of His Majesties Company of Comedians to pay unto Mr Owen Swiny the Sume of one hundred pounds per (Annum) towards defraying the Expence of the Opera.

And the said Mr Swiny having desired that the said Sume of one hundred pounds may be paid to Sir John Vanbrugh.

I do hereby Order and direct, the Managers of his Majesties Company of Comedians to pay unto the said Sir John Vanbrugh the said Summe of one hundred pounds per Annum till farther Order.

Given under my hand this 14th day of January 1714, and in the first year of his Majesties Reigne.[2]

Shrewsbury

To the Managers of his Majesties
Company of Comedians in Drury Lane

[C.] "Copy of the Managers Answer to me, upon sending them my Lord Chamberlains Order."

Sir

When we had first the Honour of Her Majesties Licence, Sir John Stanley perswaded us to do something in favour of the Opera, in consideration of our being the Sole Company then permitted to Act, And we hoping it would recommend us to the Court did Spontaniously pay severall hundred pounds to the Opera, But when our licence was broke into by the Addition of Mr Booths name, we thought our selves no longer under that obligation and have never paid it since nor received any Order about it till now, which at this time seems as reasonable to be sent to the other Company³ as to ours, Especially since the best part of theirs are made up of our Actors, whom we cannot get an Order to oblige them to return to us—And farther neither the late Licence nor his Majesties Letters Patents (by virtue of which we now Act) nor any agreement whatsoever obliges us to continue such payments.

This Sir is what I am directed to acquaint you with. I am

Sir Your most humble Servant

January 22d 1714. C CIBBER.

[D. Swiney's Understanding of the Agreement with Vanbrugh]

In a letter from Mr Swiny in March last, he writes thus

—The Managers of Drury Lane house, were oblig'd every year, to deliver up an Inventory of the Stock of Cloaths &c And they were to deliver them up on the 10th of May which shou'd happen in the last year of the Term of your Lease to me; So that 'tis impossible but my Lord Chamberlain will be so just, to have it declar'd in his Office, That the right and Title of that Stock, after the Expiration of the said time, is in you. If you'll look back to my Agreement with Them, which was lodged in the office, it will plainly appear, so that I hope you will settle the matter, without much trouble.

In an other Letter, he writes Thus.

It is absolutely necessary, that a Paper be entered in my Lord Chamberlains office, with his approbation, Signifying your own Tytle to her Majesties Licence after the expiration of my Lease; And whereas for the better regulation of the Stage, the Opera and Comedy are under different Directors, and the Stock of Cloaths which are now used in the Theatre in Drury Lane, with all the other utensils belonging to the said house, are your Property, Therefore my Lord dos direct, That all the Stock of Cloaths, Scenes and other Utensils, which now are in their Possession, or which shall hereafter be by them added to the said Stock during the Term of your Lease to me, shal at the Expiration of the said Lease, be by them delivered to you, in the same condition they generally are kept, for the use of the said Theatre. And that the said Managers shall not dispose, of any of the said Stock nor let them run to decay. And that they be obliged, once in every year, to deliver in (at your Request) an Inventory of their entire Stock of Cloaths, into my Lords office. You'll get the Paper drawn out more fully than I have done, and I don't doubt, but Sir John Stanley will get it done immediately it being what was agreed to, before him by the Managers, for Dogget wou'd have nothing to do with me, and desired that such a Paper might be made to you.

In a Letter dated the 25th of October last he writes Thus.

—When the £100 per annum was ordered to be paid me, it was for the Same Consideration that Mr Collier was allow'd £200. per annum which was in considera-tion of the Stock of Cloaths sent to Drury Lane house; But when I came to read the Order for the £100 per annum which was sign'd by my Lord Chamberlain, I found that no mention was made, of the reason of paying it. Upon which I told Sir John Stanley it was necessary that it shou'd be alter'd; and that it shou'd be entered in the Books of my Lord Chamberlains Office, that at the Expiration of my Lease the Cloaths shou'd be deliver'd back to me with all the Stock belonging to Drury Lane Upon which, Dogget declared, He wou'd have nothing farther to do with me, And that he wou'd not have any prospect of dispute, tho' at the end of nine years; Upon which it was Agreed before Sir John Stanley, That Releases shou'd be drawn be-tween us, And that it shou'd be entered in the Books of my Lord Chamberlains Office, That the Right and Property of the Cloaths, were in you, and shou'd be delivered back to you, by the Managers of Drury Lane House, at the Expiration of my Lease.

My Sudden departure for France, hindred me from Seeing it done, And upon my Return the hurry of my affairs was so great, that I never thought of it.

No doubt of it, Sir John Stanley cannot forget this, and that upon your laying this matter before him, he will do you Justice.

Copy-text: PRO LC 7/3, fols. 169–72.

1. Printed by Rosenberg in "New Light on Vanbrugh" without date but in a context that implies 1713 or early 1714. Entered by Kerry Downes under 1713 (*Vanbrugh*, p. 270). Nicoll cites a penciled date of "? Feb. 1715" (*History*, II, 284), which seems to us highly plausible.
2. I.e., 1714/5—George I came to the throne in August 1714.
3. John Rich's company at Lincoln's Inn Fields, which had opened in December 1714, to the vast annoyance of the managers at Drury Lane.

146. Heidegger's Account of the Subscription Money

[June 1715?]

[Cover] Heidegger's account of subscription money.

payd to Mr Long	G150			
to Mr Potter	72			
to Mr Hendel	50			
to Signor Nicolini	50			
to Signore Pilotti	50			
for the instruments	50			
to Signor Bolatri¹	38			
	460			
to Signora Galerati	50			
to Signor Angel *	37			
	547	Mr Hendel	50	
Galerati 41-12-6			761	
Charges of ye H² 100			50	
Potter for S.³	73	214-12-6	In all	811
		761-12-6		

* *Angel*: reading doubtful. This name might be Kogel or Vogel. We suspect that Angelo Zanoni is meant, though he is not known to have had a part in *Amadis*.

Copy-text: HTC Coke 19 (Heidegger holograph).

Comment: From the singers given this document can be assigned to the season of 1714–15 with some confidence. The only opera for which there was definitely a subscription this season was *Amadis* (*Amadigi di Gaula*; music by Handel, text probably by Heidegger), which received its premiere on 25 May 1715. Consequently we have tentatively assigned this document to June 1715. There are, however, some problems. Nicolini and Pilotti definitely took part in that production, but so did Mrs Robinson and Diana Vico, who are not named here. Galerati might have sung Organda, or she might have replaced Anastasia Robinson, who fell sick after the first performance.⁴ Long and Potter are not otherwise known to us. Why Handel and Galerati were paid twice we do not know. Cummings published the first part of this document (through the £460 subtotal), misreading "Bolatri" as "Valentini," and dating the document 1711, which is impossible.

1. Filippo Balatri (Salatri, Baletti).
2. "H" presumably stands for "House."
3. "S." may be an abbreviation for "Scores," or for "Scenes" if this refers to the scene painter (John?) Potter.
4. Deutsch, *Handel*, pp. 67–68.

Documents Not Assignable to

Particular Seasons

The seven documents following (one of them a song, one a scratch sheet, two missing) cannot be dated precisely enough to put them in chronological position in the main text.

147. Note by Kent about a Private Concert to be Given by Mrs Tofts

[1706–9?]

I approve very well of the scheeme you have sent me I have only added the first song of Mrs Tofts (Freedom) & I think none of the songs should be without ye Instruments. Therefore I have also added them where you had left them out.

I have returnd your paper to you again and am

Sir your most obedient
servant
KENT

Tuesday 3 Oclock

Copy-text: Winston, p. 34. For another nineteenth-century transcription see Drexel MS, fol. 130. This letter is item 189 in the 1876 sale catalogue.

Comment: Coke had evidently set up a private concert for Lord Chamberlain Kent. The date could be any time between December 1706, when Coke took office, and May 1709, when Mrs Tofts suffered a nervous breakdown and ceased to perform. Mollie Sands notes that in the Tofts entry in

Grove, Julian Marshall "says 'she also sang at the concerts at Court,' but gives no dates or authority."[1] Marshall owned some of the Coke papers in the 1890s, and we presume that this letter was part of his authority.

We have not been able to identify the song Kent wanted Mrs Tofts to sing.

1. "Mrs. Tofts," p. 103.

148. A Song ("Whether Oh Love")

[1706–15?]

Whether oh Love willt thou lead a poor Swain? to what Desarts at Land & what Gulphs in the Main? But follow I must let what will be the pain, for oh Love by resisting, what what doe I gain! True to my vows must I be, & my Passion retein, tho I bear it in vain, tho I dye, tho I dye by Disdain.

Cold as a Stone fair Aminta is grown:
Her Dislike she express'd in so scornfull a tone
at a time when I hop'd She my greifs wou'd bemoan
that I fear now I never can make her my owne.
Yet must I doat on the Nymph by whose Eyes I'm undon,
& adore her alone,
& adore & adore her alone.

Copy-text: HTC Coke 41 (with music).

Comment: The presence of this song among the Coke papers is probably accounted for by Coke's having arranged private concerts for himself (documents 1–3), and perhaps for his superiors (document 117).

149. Letter by Margarita de l'Epine [Missing]

[1706–15]

Known from the 1876 sale catalogue (item 195): "Very fine and curious A.L.s. in French, 1714, respecting some quarrel about a song. *Excessively rare.*" This description is repeated verbatim as 700 of the 1905 sale catalogue.

Comment: Since 1714 is the sale catalogue's guess on most undated items, and since it is usually wrong, we cannot treat this suggestion as having any real weight.

150. The Case of William Smith, Oboist

[Cover] Smiths ye Hautbois case   [1706–13]

The case of William Smith Hautboy.

That in or about Christmas last Colonell Harrison[1] desired the said Smith to furnish him with a Sett of Hautboys & was by Positive agreement with him to have five Guineas for each man he should so procure for ye said Colonell.

That with much Trouble Paines & Industry to ye Intire Neglect of all his other business by which his Family was to be maintain'd, the said Smith did Procure and bring severall Men to the said Colonell for his Approbation some of which the Colonell dislikeing, the said Smith brought others from time to time & at last accomadated the said Colonell to his Intire Satisfaction.

That after the said Colonell was so accomadated to his intire Satisfaction & being very Willing to have the said hautboys improved by the said Smith desired him to teach them which he did for Five Months during all which time he constantly attended them to his great Trouble & Expence, which was he to be paid for the Teaching alone would come to Thirty Guineas at the common Rate of Teacheing by an Indifferent Master besidess the Twenty Five Guineas according to agreement for the Men so Procured.

That ye said Smith being fully Satisfyed with the benefitt and Improvement the said Hautboys had made under the same Smiths care acquainted the said Colonell therewith who ordered him still to continue his further * Care & Paines in Instructing them & he should be fully Satisfyed for so doeing.

Now the time drawing near for ye Colonell going beyond Sea ye said Smith being willing to be Satisfyed for his Trouble as aforesaid thought it Proper to Waite on the Colonell which he many times did before he could have the Honour of seeing him which when he did see him he order'd the said Smith to go to his Captain for that he had order'd him to Satisfye him to whome the said Smith accordingly did go a great many times & was by him told that he had not any orders from the said Colonell to pay him any money.

Whereas ye said Smith being somewhat concerned went again severall times to the said Colonell he ye said Colonell expecting every day to be order'd out of England at last the said Smith mett with the said Colonell by whome he was told that he had nothing more to say to him haveing ordered his Money. But the said Smith applying again to the Captain & finding no orders at all relateing to his said money being informed that ye said Colonell would certainly be gon beyond Sea in Two or Three days at farthest, Went to his Attorney desireing him to write in a Civill Manner to him which he did accordingly but receiving no answer he Proceeded against him according to Law.

Now the said Smith Intirely hindring all his other business was obliged to borrow severall Summes of Money to support his Family which he Promised to pay in a very short time Intirely depending on the Punctuall Payment of the Colonell money to make good his said Promisses touching the money so lent to the said Smith who haveing a great ffamily & being much Pressed for ye Money so by him Borrowed.

Was under an absolute necessity of takeing the Measures he did with ye said Colonell, but if he mett with any rude or unmannerly treatment from the Bayliffs employed twas without any orders from the said Smith he haveing given strict directions to Treat the Colonell with all Possible[†] Civility & good Manners and to give the Colonell a further Proof thereof notwithstanding his agreement as aforesaid condescended to take and accept from the said Colonell Twenty Pounds which[2] according to agreement and Common rate of Teacheing came to Fifty five Guineas, and the said Smith was also obliged to pay his Attorney's bill for charges at Law which amount to the Sume of Six Pounds so that he had but Fourteen Pounds Instead of Fifty five Guineas.

Now the said Smith is heartily Sorry for the Proceedings aforesaid and is ready to ask the said Colonell Pardon in any manner as Your Honour shall think fitting.

[*] *further*: MS reads "furthe."
[†] *Possible*: MS reads "Possibly."

Copy-text: HTC Coke 33 (scribal fair copy). For nineteenth-century transcriptions see Winston, pp. 61–63, and Drexel MS, following the insert after fol. 151.

Comment: Why this document came to Coke we do not know. Colonel Harrison apparently complained to the Lord Chamberlain's office when Smith, a member of the Haymarket orchestra, sued him. This response from

Smith is analogous to the effort by Swiney to explain his fight with Lord
Tunbridge (see documents 11 and 12). The date could come anywhere between the time Coke took office in 1706 and the Treaty of Utrecht in 1713.

1. Presumably Colonel Thomas Harrison of the First Foot Guards, later commander
of the Sixth Regiment of Foot. He became a lieutenant colonel in 1705, and brevet
colonel in 1707, and served as adjutant-general in Spain beginning in 1708. An active campaigner, he was in and out of London constantly during these years.
2. Some words were probably dropped by the copyist at this point.

151. Proclamation Declaring Unlicensed Theatres a Public Nuisance

[Cover] Stage / Cortiselli [1]   [1706–14]

Whereas the Laws already in being have not been sufficient to restrain
the Prophaneness and Impiety of the Stage which of late years have so
greatly prevail'd, that Plays which ought to be not only an innocent but
Instructive Diversion, by the abuses of the Stage sometimes prove Incen-
tives of Vice and Immorality to the dishonour of Almighty God and the
Scandal of Christianity, For the better Remedy whereof Be it Enacted by
the Queens most Excellent Majesty &ca That all Comon and publick Players who use the Acting of Tragedies, Comedies, Opera's or other Plays or
Interludes in any Comon and publick Playhouses or upon any Comon and
publick Theatre or Stage within the Citys of London or Westminster or
elswhere within this Realm shall be under and subject to such Government
Regulations and Orders as her Majesty her heirs and Successors shall from
time to time think meet And that no person or persons shall presume to
Act in any such publick Plays or Opera's without Due Licence first had from
her Majesty her Heirs or Successors.

And be it farther Enacted by the authority aforesaid, That all and every
Playhouse or Playhouses Theatre or place where Plays or Interludes be
openly and comonly Represented, which shall not be Licensed by her Majesty her heirs or Successors shall be deem'd and is hereby declar'd to be a
publick and Comon Nusance. And all and every person or persons not
having such License as aforesaid who shall publickly practise the Acting in
any Tragedy, Comedy Opera or other Play or Interlude upon any Comon
Stage or Theatre within this Realm shall be subject and lyable to such
Punishments as the Law inflicts upon Vagrants and Vagabonds.

Copy-text: HTC Coke 32 (scribal fair copy). For nineteenth-century transcriptions see Winston, pp. 57–59, and Drexel MS, fol. 133.

Comment: This document is in the form of a proclamation to be issued by the Lord Chamberlain's office. So far as we are aware, this particular proclamation was never promulgated. Possibly it was a draft offered for the Lord Chamberlain's use by one of the reforming societies which harassed the theatres in these years. The reference to Queen Anne does place the document in her reign, and Coke took office in 1706, but we cannot narrow down the date any further than that. The real object of the attack is evidently strolling companies and fair performers.

1. All that we know of "Cortiselli" (if it is indeed the same one) is that Cassani stayed at "the house of Mr Corticelli" in England sometime during 1708. See document 72. We have no idea what connects him to this draft proclamation.

152. Scratch Sheet

[ca. 1708?]

ye Musick is £17:10:00
10
5:00:00
170:00:00
175:00:00[1]

900 guineys	
500	7:10
700	7
300	3:10
500	49
200	52:10[2]

Copy-text: HTC Coke 30 (Hand A).

Comment: We cannot definitely associate this scratch sheet with any other document. The column on the left probably refers to salaries of leading singers. For an orchestra salary total of £17 12s. see document 62 (7 April 1708). What the third calculation concerns we have no idea.

1. In this calculation what is evidently the nightly salary total for the orchestra is multiplied by ten.

2. In this calculation £7 is evidently subtracted from £7 10s., the remaining 10s. then being added to the newly entered figure of £3.

153. Two Letters by the Duke of Shrewsbury Concerning Mrs Saggione [Missing]

[1710–15?]

Known from the 1876 sale catalogue (item 200): "Saggione, celebrated Singer, two holograph papers relative to. Shrewsbury (Duke of) A.L.s." Item 705 in the 1905 sale catalogue probably refers to one of these papers: "Shrewsbury (Duke of) A.L.s. 1 p. 8 vo, *n.d.*"

Comment: These letters probably concerned private concerts (see document 117). Especially in the off-season singers were glad to get private engagements. In the Drexel MS (fol. 47) there is a copy of a letter from Anne, Countess of Sunderland, to Thomas Stephens, Secretary to Charles, Earl of Sunderland, dated "August 1708?": "If you could find out any way of knowing whether Mr. Sagioni and his wife would not come down to Althorp the 22 of this Month for a week, I should by [*sic*] mighty glad to have 'em, provided they would not be above dining with the servants, or by themselves, and that I could know what they would expect me to give 'em, for if they will say what I please, I can't tell what to do; nor I don't think any singing will make amends to me, for dining and supping with 'em every day, but if I could have 'em without that trouble, it would be a great pleasure."

Appendix
Index

Appendix

List of Documents and Interdocuments

Index

257

—*Rinaldo*, xxiii, 175–77, 184

—*Theseus*, 189

Harris, Mrs (house servant), 87

Harrison, Thomas, Col.: Smith's complaint against, 241–43

HTC Coke MS, xiv, xxix–xxxviii

Harvey, Francis, xxxii

Haughton, Mr (house servant), 165

Haym, Nicolino Francesco (musician; *also* Nicola or Nicolas Haim, Hayams, Heyams), xxxiii, xxxiv, 18, 63; in Haymarket orchestra, 33–34, 38–39, 133, 158, 159; letter about Cassani's debts, 114–15; letters to Coke, 2–3, 3–4, 56–59, 80–81, 114–15; said to have written "A Critical Discourse on Opera and Music in England," xxi; salary, 31, 38–39, 68, 77, 78, 118, 127; Vanbrugh plans to make a sharer, 99

—*Camilla* (English libretto by Swiney, music by Bononcini), xxii, xxiv, 3, 9, 11, 18, 27; the Baroness in, 57; Cassani in, 80–81, 91–92; de l'Epine in, 3; Nicolini in, 116; singers refuse to perform, 30; subscription and receipts from, 9, 11, 83, 90–92; Mrs Tofts' clothes for, 46; wigs for, 94

—*Pyrrhus and Demetrius* (English libretto by Swiney, music by Scarlatti and others), 18, 81–82, 138; charges of, 68; Haym's terms for, 56–59; opens, 116; preliminary cast for, 63–4; receipts for, 160–61, 162–63, 164, 165–66

Haymarket Theatre (*also* Queen's Theatre) actors at, xviii–xix, xxiv, 5, 11, 27, 51–52, 52–53, 123–25, 132–33; administration, xviii–xxiv, xxvii, 7, 27–28, 106–7, 132–35, 147–48, 157, 178, 189–91, 213–14, 227; Coke's directions to treasurer, 198–99; dancers at, 64, 68, 70, 75, 79, 88, 95, 97, 101–3, 133; finances, xxii–xxiv, 1, 6, 27–28, 30, 40–42, 50–51, 67–71, 72–73, 75, 76–77, 78–79, 88–89, 91, 93, 94, 109–10, 112–13, 130–31, 132–33, 148, 164, 172–73, 181, 183, 186, 189, 199–200, 237; house charges, 40–42, 69, 75, 77, 94, 97–98, 164, 172–73; house servants, xli–xlii, 69, 75, 77, 86–88, 97;

as London's only theatre, 123, 128–29; opened by Vanbrugh, xviii, xxi–xxii, 1; orchestra, 27, 30–32, 32–34; 38–39, 40–42, 67–69, 75, 77, 78–79, 97–98, 118–19, 127, 133–35, 151, 158, 159–60, 172, 179–80; proposed royal subsidy for opera at, 83–84, 85; proposed union with Drury Lane, xviii, 1, 5, 10–11; receipts, 27, 73–74, 89, 90–91, 156–57, 160–61, 162–63, 164, 165–66, 172–73, 175; scenes and costumes, xviii, 14, 16, 40, 64–65, 75, 77, 93, 94, 96, 97, 116, 206, 233–36; singers, xxii–xxiv, 27, 28, 38–39, 40–42, 50–51, 67–68, 75, 76–77, 78–79, 88, 97, 132–33, 164, 172–73, 217; Swiney's management of, xviii, xix, xx, xxiii, 6, 7, 11–12, 28, 82–83, 106–7, 116, 123, 147–48, 189–90, 233–36; tradesmen's bills for, 92–93, 183–84. *See also* Genre separation in the London theatres

Hayward, Robert: witnesses document, 193–94

Heidegger, John Jacob (impressario; *also* John James), xx, xxxi, xxxii, xxxiii, xxxiv, 40, 89, 98, 172, 180, 199, 217; account of subscription money for *Amadis*, 237–38; agreement with Ramondon and Dieupart, 34–35, 39–40, 47–49; Anastasia Robinson's terms with, 228–29; and dancers' bill, 35–36, 47–49; manages Haymarket, 227; prominence of, 190

—*Thomyris*, xxii, 54–55, 78, 97–98; performances, 27, 29, 56–59, 73; subscription and receipts from, 11, 16–18, 83, 90–92; terms for, 16–18, 18–19, 98; Mrs Tofts' clothes for, 46; Valentini's bill for, 19–20, 47. *See also* Pepusch, John Christopher

Hendel. *See* Handel, George Frideric

Heyams. *See* Haym, Nicolino Francesco

Higgons, Mr (Dutch contortionist), 125

Highfill, Philip H., Jr., xiii

Hill, Aaron (manager), to Collier about actors' riot, 142–46; manages Drury Lane, xix–xx, 124; manages the Haymarket, xx, 147, 156, 159, 165, 175–76, 183

Hill, Gilbert (assistant manager), 143–44

"Historical Remarks Respecting the Introduction of Operas in England" (anon.), xxx

Holcomb, Henry (singer; *also* "The Boy"?), 2
Hollinsworth, Mr (house servant), 87
Hook, Lucyle, xxvii
Hotson, Leslie, xiv, 53, 76
Howard, Henry. *See* Suffolk, sixth Earl of
Hughes, Francis (singer): alternates with Valentini, 20; salary, 38
Hume, Robert D., xxi, xxiv, 118
Husband, Benjamin (actor): salary, 133
Huseboe, Arthur R., 74
Hydaspes. See Mancini, Francesco
Hyde, Mary, xxxii, xxxvii, xxxviii

Idaspe. See Mancini, Francesco
Igl. *See* Eccles, Henry
Indian Kings, The Four, 125
Island Princess, The. See Motteux, Peter Anthony
Iuens, Mlle. *See* Evans, Mrs

James, Mr (tradesman), 93
Jennens, Robert: letter to Coke, xxvii
Johnson, Benjamin (actor), 117; salary, 132
Jones, Ed: witnesses document, 214
Jouberti, Signore (Venetian Ambassador's Secretary? *also* Berti), 61–63, 71–72, 109–11

Kaite. *See* Kytch, Jean Christian
Keally, Joseph: letters from Congreve to, 5, 9
Keene, Theophilus (actor), 12; riots at Drury Lane, 143–44
Keitch *or* Keitsh. *See* Kytch, Jean Christian
Kenny, Shirley Strum, xxi
Kent, Henry Grey, twelfth Earl, later Duke of (Lord Chamberlain), xxviii–xxix, xxxiii, 29, 53, 121, 136; approves plans for private concert, 239; approves Swiney-Vanbrugh contract, 7; approves transfers of actors, 5, 12, 13; to Coke about the Union of 1708, 43–43; conspires against Rich, 117, 126; delegates operatic matters to Coke, xxix, 106; and Farquhar benefits, 104–5; insecurity of position, 113; letter from Estcourt, 44–45; licenses William Collier, 136; notified of contract disputes with performers, 29, 46–48, 56–57, 59, 61–62, 65, 66, 79; orders Swiney to receive "sworn Comedians," 128, 129,

130–31; orders Union of 1708, xviii, 31, 49–50, 58; petitioned by renegade actors, 51–52; and proposed royal subsidy of opera, 83–85; regulations for Haymarket proposed to, 132–35; silences Drury Lane, xix, 122, 123–25, 126, 136; stops concert competing with the Haymarket, 73–74; Swiney-Tunbridge quarrel referred to, 21–22. *See also* Genre separation in the London theatres
Kern, Ronald C., xxxiii, 59, 74
Killigrew, Charles (Master of the Revels), 135–36; protests silencing of Drury Lane, 124; theatre shareholder, 75
King Arthur. See Dryden, John
King's Company, xvii
Kinnaston, Mr (theatre shareholder), 75
Knapp, J. Merrill, xxiii
Kytch, Jean Christian (musician; *also* Creitch, Kaite, Keitch, Keitsh, Kyber, Kytes, Kytsch), 128; in Haymarket orchestra, 151, 158, 159; petitions to join Haymarket orchestra, 31; plays in private concerts, 191–92; salary, 119, 133, 135, 179; signs receipt, 187

L'Abbé's Scholar (dancer; brother of Anthony?), 68, 70
La Borde, Mr (musician): salary at the Haymarket, 39
Lacy, Margaret (theatre shareholder), 75
Lady's Last Stake, The. See Cibber, Colley
Lagarde. *See* Delagarde, Charles
Lamb family: Coke's connection with, xxv; descent of Coke papers in, xxv, xxix–xxx; Hon. George Lamb separates and loans Coke papers, xxx, xxxi, xxxviii–xxxix, 196, 205
Langhans, Edward A., xiii
Lansdowne, Lord. *See* Granville, George, first Baron Lansdowne
Laroon, John (musician): salary at the Haymarket, 33, 38, 69, 79
La Sere, Mr (musician): salary at the Haymarket, 39
Lasocki, David, 31, 32, 180
La Tour, Peter (musician), 31; complaint against Rich, 47; in Haymarket orchestra roster, 133, 151, 158, 159; petitions to

Oldfield, Anne (actress; *also* Olfield): considered for partnership at the Haymarket, 131; joins Haymarket, 5, 12; protests against Rich, 117; salary, 132
Olleson, Philip, 28
Orchestra rosters, 30–31, 32–33, 38–39, 68–69, 78–79, 118–19, 127–28, 133, 151–52, 158–59, 159–60, 179–80
Orlando Furioso. See Purcell, Daniel
Orm, Mrs (singer), 172, 173–74
Ormonde, James Butler, second Duke of, 80, 114, 164, 165
Opera: account of subscription money in 1715, 237; box office reports, 156–57, 160–61, 162–63, 164, 165–66; daily charges, 67–70, 88–90; daily receipts in 1708, 90–91; discussed in *Muses Mercury*, 30, 81–82; "English," xxi; financial estimates for 1708–9, 103–4; Haymarket finances in 1711, 172–73; Haymarket salaries in 1708, 78–79; Haymarket salaries in 1710–11, 164; Italian, xxi–xxiv; musicians' salaries, 30–31, 32–33, 38–39, 68–69, 78–79, 118–19, 127–28, 179–80; orders for disbursing subscription money, 175–76, 183–84; payments to performers in 1713, 199–201; performers in 1708, 38–39, 67–70, 76–77, 78–79; salaries of house servants, 86–88; semiopera, xxi, xxii, xxiv; subscription arrangements for *Antiochus*, 180–81, 182, 182–83; Vanbrugh's financial estimates for, 40–41, 67–70, 75–76; Vanbrugh's statement of opera account, 97–98
Otway, Charles, Capt. (*also* Ottway): witnesses Swiney-Tunbridge quarrel, 25–26

Pack, George (actor): made rehearsal manager, 143; petitions for reinstatement, 51–52
Paisible, James (musician; *also* Passible, Paysible, Presible), 31; complaint against Rich, 47; listed in Haymarket orchestra roster, 133, 151, 158, 159; performs in private concert, 192; petitions to join Haymarket orchestra, 30; salary, 31, 33, 38, 69, 78, 119, 127, 179
Papuch *or* Papusch. *See* Pepusch, John Christopher

Peer, William (house servant), 87
Pellegrini, Cavaliero Valeriano (singer; *also* Signor Valerian), 199, 200–201
Pendry, Mrs (house servant), 87
Penkethman, William (actor; *also* Pinkethman): salary, 133; summer theatre at Greenwich, 143, 145; transfers to Haymarket, 5, 117
Peplo, Mr (house servant; Jonathan Peploe?), 87
Pepusch, John Christopher (musician and composer; *also* Papuch, Papusch, Pepush), 3, 4, 121, 217; listed in Haymarket roster, 33, 34, 134, 151, 158, 159; performs in private concerts, 191–92; salary, 30, 68, 77, 78, 118, 127; Vanbrugh plans to make a sharer, 99
—*Thomyris: or, The Royal Amazon* (English libretto by Motteux, music by Bononcini and Scarlatti), xxii, 18, 98. *See also* Heidegger, John Jacob
Perkins, John: bills payable to, 106
Peryn, Mrs (house servant), 86
Phillips, Griffantius (Queen's Messenger), 221–22, 222–23
Pietrino. *See* Chaboud, Pietro
Pietro. *See* Chaboud, Pietro
Pilotta. *See* Schiavonetti, Elizabetta Pilotta
Pilotti. *See* Schiavonetti, Giovanni
Pinkethman. *See* Penkethman, William
Pitchford, Mr (musician; *also* Pitshford, Pitzford): listed in Haymarket orchestra roster, 151, 158, 159; salary, 30
Pix, Mary
—*Spanish Wives, The*, 52
Plank, Mr (musician): listed in Haymarket orchestra roster, 127
Plumner, Mr (house servant), 87
Pope, Alexander: on Mrs Tofts, 110
Popeley, William (musician; *also* Poptry): listed in Haymarket orchestra roster, 133, 135
Porter, Mary (actress): petitions for reinstatement, 51–52; salary, 132
Porter, Mr (house servant), 88
Portland, Henry Bentinck, second Earl of, later Duke of, 139, 141, 142
Post-Boy Robb'd of His Mail, The. See Gildon, Charles